Understanding Operating Systems

Understanding Operating Systems

Reid Barnes

CLANRYE
INTERNATIONAL
www.clanryeinternational.com

Clanrye International,
750 Third Avenue, 9th Floor,
New York, NY 10017, USA

ISBN: 978-1-64726-107-8

Cataloging-in-Publication Data

Understanding operating systems / Reid Barnes.
   p. cm.
Includes bibliographical references and index.
ISBN 978-1-64726-107-8
1. Operating systems (Computers). 2. Systems software. I. Barnes, Reid.
QA76.77 .U53 2022
005.43--dc23

For information on all Clanrye International publications
visit our website at www.clanryeinternational.com

Contents

Preface

The system software which manages the hardware and software resources of a computer is known as operating software. It acts as an intermediary between programs and computer hardware, particularly for hardware functions such as input and output, and memory allocation. Some of the different components of an operating system are kernel, user interface and computer network. Kernel, also called the core of the operating system, provides the most basic level of control over all the hardware resources in the computer. User interface, also known as a shell, is the component of the operating system which is integral for a human to interact with the computer. Command line interface and graphical user interface are the two major types of user interface. This book provides significant information of this discipline to help develop a good understanding of operating systems and related fields. It presents this complex subject in the most comprehensible and easy to understand language. Those in search of information to further their knowledge will be greatly assisted by this book.

To facilitate a deeper understanding of the contents of this book a short introduction of every chapter is written below:

Chapter 1- The computer hardware, software and other computer services are managed by a system software known as operating system. A few of such operating systems are Unix, Linux, Mac OS, Chrome OS, Microsoft Windows, etc. This is an introductory chapter which will briefly introduce all these different operating systems.

Chapter 2- Memory management component of an operating system is concerned with the allocation of memory processes to maximize efficiency. The communication between the processing system with another processing system or human is referred to as input output system. All these operating system components have been carefully analyzed in this chapter.

Chapter 3- There are various types of operating systems which can be categorized as serial processing operating system, batch processing operating system, network operating system, distributed operating system, real time operating system, embedded operating system, etc. This chapter has been carefully written to provide an easy understanding of these types of operating systems.

Chapter 4- The system which runs distributed applications on multiple computers linked by communications is termed as distributed operating system. It has five different architectural styles namely layered architecture, object based architecture, data-centered architecture, event based architecture and hybrid architecture. This chapter discusses in detail these different styles of distributed operating system.

Chapter 5- A thread refers to a single sequence stream within a process that allows multiple executions of streams. Thread libraries are used by programmers for the creation and management of threads. The topics elaborated in this chapter will help in gaining a better perspective about threads used in operating systems.

Chapter 6- The process that is concerned with the protection of operating system from threats, viruses, trojans, malware, etc. is known as operation system security. Some of its policies and procedures are acceptable use policy, access control policy, information security policy, incident response policy, etc. The topics elaborated in this chapter will help in gaining a better perspective about operating system security.

Chapter 7- Deadlock is referred to as a condition where a computer process waits for a resource which is being used by another process. Deadlock handling has three main methods which are deadlock detection, deadlock prevention and deadlock avoidance. This chapter closely examines the varied aspects of deadlock to provide an extensive understanding of the subject.

Finally, I would like to thank the entire team involved in the inception of this book for their valuable time and contribution. This book would not have been possible without their efforts. I would also like to thank my friends and family for their constant support.

Reid Barnes

Introduction to Operation System

The computer hardware, software and other computer services are managed by a system software known as operating system. A few of such operating systems are Unix, Linux, Mac OS, Chrome OS, Microsoft Windows, etc. This is an introductory chapter which will briefly introduce all these different operating systems.

An operating system (OS) is a set of programs that control the execution of application programs and act as an intermediary between a user of a computer and the computer hardware. OS is software that manages the computer hardware as well as providing an environment for application programs to run.

Operating System Objectives

The objectives of OS are:

- To make the computer system convenient and easy to use for the user.

- To use the computer hardware in an efficient way.

- To execute user programs and make solving user problems easier.

Computer System

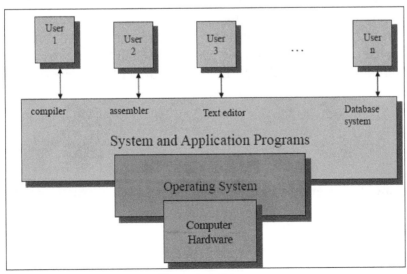

Computer system.

A computer system can be divided into four components: the hardware, the operating system, the application programs and the users. The abstract view of system components is shown in figure above.

- Hardware: Such as CPU, memory and I/O devices.

- Operating system: Provides the means of proper use of the hardware in the operations of the computer system, it is similar to government.

- Application programs: Solve the computing problems of the user, such as: compilers, database systems and web browsers.

- Users: Peoples, machine, or other computer.

I/O Structure

A computer system consists of CPUs and multiple device controllers that are connected through a common bus. The device controller is responsible for moving the data between the peripheral devices that it controls and its local buffer storage. Typically, operating systems have a device driver for each device controller.

To start an I/O operation, the device driver loads the appropriate registers within the device controller. The device controller examines the contents of these registers to determine what action to take. The controller starts the transfer of data from the device to its local buffer. Once the transfer of data is complete, the device controller informs the device driver via an interrupt that it has finished its operation. The device driver then returns control to the operating system. For other operations, the device driver returns status information.

For moving bulk data, direct memory access (DMA) is used. After setting up buffers, pointers, and counters for the I/O device, the device controller transfers an entire block of data directly to or from its own buffer storage to memory, with no intervention by the CPU. Only one interrupt is generated per block, to tell the device driver that the operation has completed, rather than the one interrupt per byte generated for low-speed devices.

Operating System Functions

OS performs many functions such as:

- Implementing user interface.

- Sharing HW among users.

- Allowing users to share data among themselves.

- Preventing users from interfering with one another.

- Scheduling resource among users.

- Facilitating I/O operations.

- Recovering from errors.

- Accounting for resource storage.

- Facilitating parallel operations.

- Organizing data for secure and rapid access.

- Handling network communications.

Operating System Categories

The main categories of modern OS may be classified into three groups which are distinguished by the nature of interaction that takes place between the computer and the user:

Batch System

In this type of OS, users submit jobs on regular schedule (e.g. daily, weekly, monthly) to a central place where the user of such system did not interact directly with computer system. To speed up the processing, jobs with similar needs were batched together and were run through the computer as a group. Thus, the programmer would leave the programs with the operator. The output from each job would send to the appropriate programmer. The major task of this type was to transfer control automatically from one job to the next.

Disadvantages of Batch System

- Turnaround time can be large from user standpoint.

- Difficult to debug program.

Time-Sharing System

This type of OS provides on-line communication between the user and the system, the user gives his instructions directly and receives intermediate response, and therefore it called interactive system.

The time sharing system allows many users simultaneously share the computer system. The CPU is multiplexed rapidly among several programs, which are kept in memory and on disk. A program swapped in and out of memory to the disk.

Time sharing system reduces the CPU ideal time. The disadvantage is more complex.

Real Time Operating System

Real Time System is characterized by supplying immediate response. It guarantees that critical tasks complete on time. This type must have a pre-known maximum time limit for each of the functions to be performed on the computer. Real-time systems are used when there are rigid time requirements on the operation of a processor or the flow of data and real-time systems can be used as a control device in a dedicated application.

The airline reservation system is an example of this type.

Performance Development of OS

On-line and Off-line Operation

A special subroutine was written for each I/O device called a device controller. Some I/O devices has been equipped for either on-line operation (they are connected to the processor), or off-line operations (they are run by control unit).

Buffering

A buffer is an area of primary storage for holding data during I/O transfer. On input, the data are placed in the buffer by an I/O channel, when the transfer is complete the data may be accessed the processor. The buffing may be single or double.

Spooling (Simultaneously Peripheral Operation On-line)

Spooling uses the disk as a very large buffer. Spooling is useful because device access data that different rates. The buffer provides a waiting station where data can rest while the slower device catches up. Spooling allows overlapping between the computation of one job and I/O of another job.

Multiprogramming

In multiprogramming, several programs are kept in main memory at the same time, and the CPU is switching between them, thus the CPU always has a program to be executed. The OS begins to execute one program from memory, if this program need wait such as an I/O operation, the OS switches to another program. Multiprogramming increases CPU utilization. Multiprogramming system provide an environment in which the various system resources are utilized effectively, but they do not provide for user interaction with the computer system.

Advantages

- High CPU utilization.

- It appears that many programs are allotted CPU almost simultaneously.

Disadvantages

- CPU scheduling is requires.

- To accommodate many jobs in memory, memory management is required.

Parallel System

There is more than one processor in the system. These processors share the computer bus, clock, memory and I/O devices.

The advantage is to increase throughput (the number of programs completed in time unit).

Distributed System

Distribute the computation among several physical processors. It involves connecting 2 or more independent computer systems via communication link. So, each processor has its own O.S. and local memory; processors communicate with one another through various communications lines, such as high-speed buses or telephone lines.

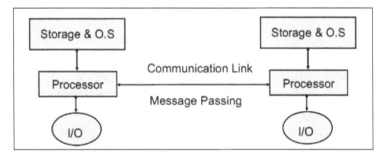

Advantages of Distributed Systems

- Resources Sharing: You can share files and printers.

- Computation speed up: A job can be partitioned so that each processor can do a portion concurrently (load sharing).

- Reliability: If one processor failed the rest still can function with no problem.

- Communications: Such as electronic mail, ftp.

Personal Computer

Personal computers: computer system dedicated to a single user. PC operating systems were neither multi-user nor multi-tasking. The goals of PC operating systems were to maximize user convenience and responsiveness instead of maximizing CPU and I/O utilization. Examples: Microsoft Windows and Apple Macintosh.

Operating System Operations

Modern operating systems are interrupt driven. If there are no processes to execute, no I/O devices to service, and no users to whom to respond, an operating system will sit quietly, waiting for something to happen. Events are almost always signaled by the occurrence of an interrupt or a trap. A trap is a software-generated interrupt caused either by an error (for example, division by zero or invalid memory access) or by a specific request from a user program that an operating-system service be performed. For each type of interrupt, separate segments of code in the operating system determine what action should be taken. An interrupt service routine is provided that is responsible for dealing with the interrupt.

Since, the operating system and the users share the hardware and software resources of the computer system, we need to make sure that an error in a user program could cause problems only for the one program that was running. With sharing, many processes could be adversely affected by a bug in one program. A properly designed operating system must ensure that an incorrect (or malicious) program cannot cause other programs to execute incorrectly.

Dual-Mode Operation

We must be able to distinguish between the execution of operating-system code and user defined code. The approach is to separate the two modes of operation: user mode and kernel mode (also called supervisor mode, system mode, or privileged mode). A bit, called the mode bit is added to the hardware of the computer to indicate the current mode: kernel (0) or user (1). The dual mode of operation provides us with the means for protecting the operating system from errant users and errant users from one another.

System calls provide the means for a user program to ask the operating system to perform tasks reserved for the operating system on the user program's behalf.

Protection CPU

To ensure that the operating system maintains must control over the CPU. We must prevent a user program from getting stuck in an infinite loop or not calling system services and never returning control to the operating system. To accomplish this goal, we can use a timer. A timer can be set to interrupt the computer after a specified fixed or variable period.

Operating System Kernel

The kernel is the central module of an operating system (OS). It is the part of the operating system that loads first, and it remains in main memory. Because it stays in memory, it is important for the kernel to be as small as possible while still providing all the essential services required by other parts of the operating system and applications. The kernel code is usually loaded into a protected area of memory to prevent it from being overwritten by programs or other parts of the operating system.

Typically, the kernel is responsible for memory management, process and task management, and disk management. The kernel connects the system hardware to the application software. Every operating system has a kernel. For example the Linux kernel is used numerous operating systems including Linux, FreeBSD, Android and others.

The Microkernel

The design of a microkernel determines that it has only functions for a simple inter-process communication, memory management and scheduling. All these functions are operation in the kernel mode but the rest runs in the user mode. The microkernel is not implemented as one huge process. The functionality of the Microkernel is divided in several processes the so called Servers. In best case only these Servers get more privileges which need them to do their tasks. All servers are separated from the system and each process has its own address space. The result is that the microkernel cannot start functions directly. It has to communicate via "Message Passing" which is an inter-process communication mechanism which allows Servers to communicate to other Servers. Because of this implementation errors affect only the process in which it occurs. This modularization allows exchanging servers without jamming the whole system. The communication via inter-process communication produce more overhead then a function call and more contexts switches the monolithic kernel. The result of the context switches is a major latency, which results in a negative performance.

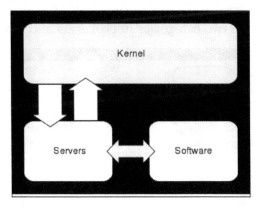

The Monolithic Kernel

In contrast to the microkernel the monolithic kernel includes more functions, so there are more services that run in kernel-mode like all device drivers, dispatcher, scheduling, virtual memory, all inter-process communication (not only the simple IPC as in a microkernel), the (virtual) file system and the system calls, so only applications run in user-mode. The monolithic kernel is implemented as one process, which runs in one single address space. All kernel services are running in one kernel address space, so the communication between these services is simpler, because the kernel processes the ability to call all functions directly like a program in user-space. The ability to perform system calls results in better performance and simpler implementation of the kernel. The crash or bug in one module which is running in kernel-mode can crash the whole system.

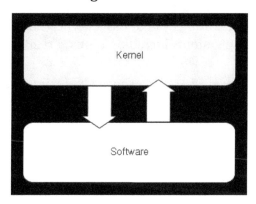

The Hybrid Kernel

The hybrid kernel design is something between the microkernel and the monolithic kernel (that is the reason for the name). The hybrid kernel runs the same processes in kernel-mode microkernel. Additional the hybrid kernel runs the application IPC and the device drivers in kernel mode. In the user-mode is used for UNIX-Server, File-Server and applications. The goal of this architecture is to get the performance benefits of a monolithic kernel, with the stability of a microkernel. The result is a microkernel-like structure in monolithic kernel and a controversy about the need of an extra category for this kernel or only have the two categories microkernel and monolithic kernel.

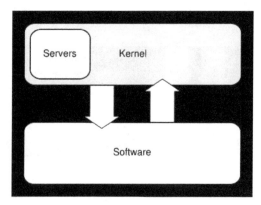

Kernel Subsystems

Here, we get an overview of the Windows Vista, Linux 2.6.28 and FreeBSD 7.0 kernel subsystems. The overview begins with all Linux kernel subsystem, following by the

FreeBSD and Vista kernel subsystem. At last there is a short look into the network protocol stack.

The Linux Kernel Architecture

The Linux kernel is a monolithic kernel, but it also a modular kernel. The Linux kernel possesses the ability to load and unload kernel-code. So, the Linux kernel can load drivers for new devices on demand.

Linux Process Management

Linux kernel saves all pieces of information in a data structure. These data structure contains information like open files, the address space of the process, status of the process. To identify a process each process contains a process identifier called PID. The PID is a number of the type (in most cases) int but uses only the length of short int (32768) to be compatible with older UNIX or Linux versions. Linux, FreeBSD and Windows Vista using a five-state process management model.

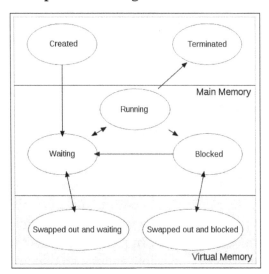

Each process is in one of the following five states: Running the task is running or in run queue and awaits to run, Interruptible the process sleeps (blocked) and waits on a condition or a wake up signal to switch in the Running state, Uninterruptible – like Interruptible but the process cannot wake up via signal to switch in the Running state, Zombie the task has finished but the parent has made the wait4() system call to free the process descriptor, Stopped the execution of the process was stopped and the process has no possibility to switch back to Running state.

One important aspect of the process is the executed code which is read from an executable file and runs in within the address space. In general, the execution of the program is placed in user-space till a system call or exception switches it to the kernel-space. The kernel is now in the process context which means that the kernel precedes a job in the name of this task. Then this process switched back to user-space if not the scheduler starts a process with a higher priority. All processes are organized in a hierarchy and each process is a descendant of the init-process, which has the PID of 1 and start as the last step of the booting system. Each process has no or several child-processes, so each process has exact on parent-process. To create a new process Linux uses the functions fork() and exec(). The function fork () creates a copy of the actual task that PID and PPID (parent-PID) differs from the original task. The copy of all resources would be too costly. So there are only the the resources duplicated which are used by both processes (called copy-on-write). The exec() function loads code in the address space and execute it. (Often a fork() is used before exec()). In Linux threads are only processes that are both share some resources and address space. For a computation in the background the kernel can spawn kernel-threads that are only working in the kernel-space and have no address space. To end a process the system call exit() is used or when a process must end because of an exception or a signal. When a process ends the parent gets a signal, free resources and calls schedule() to switch to another process. At last the process descriptor is freed. If parent process ends before the child process the child process must bound to another process, because of the process hierarchy.

Linux Process Scheduling

Since the 2.6.23 kernel Linux uses a Completely Fair Scheduler (CFS). On real hardware only one single task can run at once. Most fair would be running each process with 1/n of the processors physical power. So while one task runs, the other tasks that are waiting for the CPU are at a disadvantage, because the current task gets an unfair amount of CPU time. In CFS this fairness imbalance is expressed and tracked via the per-task p->wait_runtime (nanosec-unit) value. wait_runtimeïs the amount of time the task should now run on the CPU for it to become completely fair and balanced. CFS's task picking logic is based on this p- >wait_runtime value. It always tries to run the task with the largest p->wait_runtime value. In other words, CFS tries to run the task with most need for more CPU time. In practice the task runs only the amount of time until the p->wait_runtime value is low enough so that another task needs to run. To decide which task should run they are sorted in a time ordered red-black-tree. The CFS has additionally classes with variable priorities. When they are no more runnable task in one class the CFS runs tasks from the next class.

The Linux System Calls

System calls are function calls (most times) with the return value long to indicate of a success or failure. If a failure accrues an error code number is written in errno which is a global variable. Each system call has its own unique number. When an application makes a system call it transmitted a number to the kernel, which has a table with all system calls (dependent on the architecture). To perform a system call Linux uses a software-interrupt. The exception arranges that the system switches in the kernel mode. As a new feature the sysenter for x86- processors allows a faster system call. When the system call finishes the process switched back in user-space and continues the process.

Linux Interrupt Handling

All devices that can make an interrupts have an interrupt-handler, which is part of the driver and are C-functions. The interrupt-handler is also called interrupt-service-routine (ISR). First the action of ISR is that it affirms the interrupt so the device can continue to work. Interrupts are complex and are divided in the top-halves and the bottom-halves. The top-halves are for time critical work and are started when an interrupt accrues. All rest work which is not time critical is done in the bottom-halves. The Linux provides the possibility activate or deactivate interrupts (all or individual). For the bottom-halves work Linux provides actually three different mechanisms Softirqs, Tasklets and Work-Queues.

Linux Kernel Synchronization

Shared-Memory-Applications are applications using the same resources. These resources must be protected against race conditions. Race conditions occur when the output and/or result of the process is unexpectedly and critically dependent on the sequence or timing of other events (two signals racing each other to influence the output first). Race conditions lead to errors which are difficult to localize. One protection mechanism is locking. Each resource is locked by one process, so other processes cannot use them as long as it is locked by this process. Locking resources can lead to deadlocks. Deadlocks occur when process 1 sets a lock for a resource A and process 2 on the resource B. Process 1 wants to lock resource B but cannot and waits. Process 2 wants to lock resource A but cannot and waits too. Each process cannot continue because the resource it needs is never be freed. Linux possesses mechanisms against race conditions and dead locking. Atomic operations are a collection of instructions which cannot be interrupted. Spinlocks are locks and processes which want the lock are in a busy-loop to get that lock. A modification is the Reader-Writer-Spinlock that allows multiple processes to read but not to write on the same resource. Another mechanism is the semaphore it is also called sleeping lock. The first process sets a lock on resource. If a second process needs that resource this process is sent to sleep and awakes when the resource is freed. There is also Read-Write-Semaphore as is the case with spinlocks. One similar method is the completion-variable. The completion-variable is used after a task has finished waking other tasks. New in the 2.6 kernel is the seq-lock, which is lock and a sequence counter. It favours write processes and solves the problem of writer starvation.

Linux Timer and Time-Management

For events like refreshing the system-uptime, the time of the day, rescheduling the time and timer-interrupt are of great importance. Since the 2.5 kernel the timer interrupt uses a frequency of 1000Hz. This time period is also called "tick". An architecture independent mechanism to trigger and program timer-interrupts is the system timer. To execute Kernel-Code to a specific time the kernel can set, the so called Dynamic Timers or Kernel Timer. To delay the execution of code uses the Busy Loop, which could have an accuracy of micro seconds. For longer delays the task should be send to sleep and wake up in a defined time of seconds.

Linux Memory Management

To organize memory, it is divided into blocks, called pages. Pages are depending on the architecture and can support different page sizes, (usually 4 kByte on 32Bit-Architecture and 8 kByte on 64Bit-Architecture). Hardware limitation does not allow treating all pages equal due to the physical address. Linux uses three different zones. The ZONE_DMA for DMA-enabled Pages, the ZONE_NORMAL for regular Pages and ZONE_HIGHMEM for pages that are not permanently mapped in the address space of the kernel. Allocating and freeing data structures is one of the most common operations inside a kernel. Instead of allocating memory for every single data structure it exists a Free-List (Slablayer). Whenever space for a data structure is needed it picks instead the allocated space of one objects of the Free-List. The user-space uses instead stacks which have a large and dynamic space. The page-cache is a cache consisting of pages. To analyse if a page is already cashed Linux uses a Radix-Tree. The Radix-Tree is a binary tree which allows a fast search for the desired page. The buffer-cache is not separated from the page cache. These two caches are not separated because the synchronization of these is complicate. The memory of the cash is limited and pages must be written back. Pages are written back when pages are too old or the memory is nearly fueled.

The BSD Kernel Architecture

The free BSD kernel is a monolithic kernel, which can load and unload kernel modules as does a Linux kernel.

The BSD Process Management

Each thread of execution is a process. For each process there is a struct called proc, which has all relevant pieces of information like the PID PPID, the priority of the process and the state of the process. There are five different stats: SIDL, SRUN, SSLEEP, SSTOP and SZOMB. The function fork() creates a copy of the actual task that PID and PPID (parent-PID) differs from the original task. The copy of all resources would be too costly so there are only the the resources duplicated which are used by both processes (called copy-onwrite). The parent-child relationship induces a hierarchical structure on the set of processes in the system. A process can overlay itself with the memory image of another program, passing to the newly created image a set of parameters, using the system call execve. Usually a process terminated via the exit system call, sending 8 bits of exit status to its parent. When the parent process terminated before the child process, the child process must bind to another process because of the hierarchical process structure.

The BSD Process Scheduling

FreeBSD uses a time-share scheduler, the process priority is periodically recalculated based on various parameters, like the amount of CPU time it has used, the amount of memory resources it holds or requires for execution. The scheduler a multilevel feed-back queue which prefers short jobs and I/O-bound processes. At the base level queue the processes circulate in round robin fashion until they complete and leave the system. Each process starts with a value, the nice value. It is a number between -20 and 20. The second value is the realtime-priority which is a number between 0 and 99. The timeslice a value that decided how long a process runs before it gets preempted. A process must not spend all its timeslice in one turn it can reschedule. A process without timeslice cannot run and gets a new timeslice when all other process spends their timeslice. The result is that most I/O-bound process can preempt a processor-bound process, but processor-bound processes have a greater timeslice. Some tasks require more precise control over process execution called realtime scheduling, which must ensure that processes finish computing their results by a specified deadline or in a particular order. The FreeBSD kernel implements realtime scheduling with a separate queue from the queue used for regular time-shared processes. A process with a real-time priority is not subject to priority degradation and will only be preempted by another process of equal or higher real-time priority. The FreeBSD kernel also implements a queue of processes running at idle priority. A process with an idle priority will run only when no other process in either the real-time or time-shares scheduled queues is runnable and then only if it's idle priority is equal or greater than all other runnable idle priority processes.

BSD System Calls

System calls are function calls with the return value long to indicate of a success or failure. If a failure accrues an error code number is written in errno which is a global variable. Each system call has its own unique number. When an application makes a system call it transmitted a number to the kernel, which hast table with all system call (dependent on the architecture). The exception arranges that the system switches in the kernel mode. When the system call finishes the process switched back in user-space and continues the process. BSD can also emulate Linux system calls.

BSD Interrupt Handling

In freeBSD interrupt handlers are high-priority threads which run with interrupts enabled and may block on mutex. These schemes are called interrupt threads. Interrupt threads simplifies the locking in the kernel. The freeBSD kernel is preemptive and allows to preempt a interrupt thread by a higher-priority interrupt thread. Interrupt threads run real-time kernel priority.

BSD Kernel Synchronization

The OS must assure that not two (or more) processes use the same resources at the same time, FreeBSD uses look mechanisms and atomic operations. To short a resource for a short amount of time, freeBSD uses mutexes, which are spinlocks. A mutex is a lock and is owned by the process, who first claims the resource. No other process can get the mutex until it is released by the other process. These locks can acquired recursively, but should not send to sleep. Shared/Exclusive locks are reader/writer locks that allow multiple processes to read but only one process to write. These locks can also send to sleep. Some variables are protected via atomic operations. Because these variables can only access by these operations they do not need to be locked.

BSD Timer and Time-Management

Clock-Interrupts are interrupting occurring in fixed intervals. The amount of time between two clock interrupts is a tick. The tick most BSD system is 10ms (100Hz). FreeBSD provides two levels that coherent with all time-related work. The hardclock level does jobs like the incrementation of time of day. It runs the current process's virtual and profile time (decrease the corresponding timers) and Schedule softclock interrupts if any callouts should be triggered. The other level is the clock software interrupt level which is the real-time timer in processes. It liable for retransmitting dropped network packets. It is responsible for the watchdog timers on peripherals that require monitoring and used when the process-rescheduling event occurs.

BSD Memory Management

To organize memory FreeBSD uses pages, too. As in Linux the address space is divided in different zones. The using of free-list for data structures (slablayer) have is origins in BSD (Linux adopted it). In user-space freeBSD also provides stacks as a large and dynamic memory. FreeBSD uses a LRU replacement system for the decide which pages are swapped. If more memory is needed freeBSD can swap a whole process. freeBSD uses a page hash table instead of a radix-tree. So freeBSD has to look in a double linked list to decide if a page is already in the cache.

The Windows Vista Kernel Architecture

Windows Vista differs in the kernel architecture from Linux and FreeBSD. Instead of a monolithic kernel, Windows Vista uses a so called hybrid kernel.

Windows Vista Process Management

The unit for a process in Vista is a thread. Vista has a container which contains at least one thread. Each process has a virtual address space executable code, open handles to system objects, a security context, a unique process identifier, environment variables, a priority class, minimum and maximum working set sizes, and at least one thread of execution. The process started with a single thread (primary thread) but can create additional threads from any of its threads. All threads of a process share its virtual address space and system resources. In addition, each thread maintains exception handlers, a scheduling priority, thread local storage, a unique thread identifier, and a set of structures the system will use to save the thread context until it is scheduled. The thread context includes the thread's set of machine registers, the kernel stack, a thread environment block, and a user stack in the address space of the thread's process. Threads can also have their own security context, which can be used for impersonating clients.

Windows Vista Process Scheduling

Because a process contains one or more threads, Windows Vista has to schedule these threads. Microsoft Windows supports preemptive multitasking. On a multiprocessor computer, the system can simultaneously execute as many threads as there are processors on the computer. A job object allows groups of processes to be managed as a unit. Job objects are nameable, securable, sharable objects that control attributes of the processes associated with them. Operations performed on the job object affect all processes associated with the job object. Because Windows Vista is multitasking system each process runs for short time and not until it is finished. Each process gets a time slice. A time slice is the amount of time in which a process can run. To decide which thread should run first each thread has a priority level.

The priority levels range from zero (lowest priority) to 31 (highest priority). Only the zero-page thread can have a priority of zero. (The zero-page thread is a system thread responsible for zeroing any free pages when there are no other threads that need to run.) The system treats all threads with the same priority as equal. The system assigns time slices in a round-robin fashion to all threads with the highest priority. If none of these threads are ready to run, the system assigns time slices in a round-robin fashion to all threads with the next highest priority. If a higher-priority thread becomes available to run, the system ceases to execute the lower-priority thread (without allowing it to finish using its time slice), and assigns a full time slice to the higher-priority thread. The priority of each thread is determined by the priority class of its process and the priority level of the thread within the priority class of its process. Windows Vista has a function which can temporarily increase the priority level of a thread, which hast a priority between 0 and 15. This is called Priority Boost and ensures that threads do not starve (wait forever to get processor time). After raising a thread's dynamic priority, the scheduler reduces that priority by one level each time the thread completes a time slice, until the thread drops back to its base priority.

Windows Vista System Calls

A system call in Windows Vista is function in the Windows API. The system locks the EAX-register, places a number into the register. Then the sysenter instructions are called to switch to the kernel mode. Because of the number in the EAX-register the kernel can perform the needed task and switch back the user mode.

Windows Vista Interrupts

Hardware and software interrupts differ on each computer. The kernel treats interrupts on all machines in a similar way by virtualizing the interrupt processing mechanism. The hardware abstraction layer (HAL) is responsible for providing a virtual interrupt mechanism to the kernel. Interrupts have a priority the interrupt request level (IRQL). Windows provides interrupt masking. Interrupt masking is a mechanism that masks all interrupts with the same or lower IRQL that the actually interrupt has. If an interrupt occurs at a higher IRQL, then the higher priority interrupt is serviced immediately. When an interrupt occurs, it is handled by a function called an interrupt service routine (ISR). Data structures called an interrupt dispatch tables (IDT) track which interrupts service routine(s) will handle the interrupts occurring at each IRQL. A separate interrupt dispatch table is associated with each processor. So each processor can potentially associate different interrupt service routines with the same IRQL, or one processor can to handle all interrupts. The kernel supplies the interrupt service routines for many system interrupts such clock ticks, power failure, and thread dispatching. Other interrupt service routines are provided by the device drivers that manage peripheral hardware devices such as network adapters, keyboards, pens, and disk drives. A device driver associates its interrupt service routine with an IRQL by constructing an interrupt object and passing it to the kernel. The kernel then connects the interrupt object to the appropriate interrupt dispatch table entry. When an interrupt occurs at the device's IRQL, the kernel locates the device driver's interrupt service routine using the interrupt object. More than one interrupt object can be associated with each IRQL, so multiple devices could potentially share the same IRQL. When a device driver is unloaded, it simply asks the kernel to disconnect its interrupt objects from the interrupt dispatch table. Interrupt objects increase device driver portability by providing a way to connect and disconnect interrupt.

Windows Vista Kernel Synchronization

Because Windows Vista is multitasking OS, it needs synchronization objects in order to access shared data. The kernel is responsible for creating, maintaining, and signaling synchronization objects. Although the Executive creates a number of complex synchronization objects, each of these contains at least one kernel synchronization object. When a process waits on a synchronization object, the kernel changes its dispatcher state from running to waiting. When the object finally becomes unlocked, the kernel changes the dispatcher state of the process that was waiting from waiting to ready.

Usually processor spent no time in polling the object in a loop. The process that is waiting does not execute at all until the object is unlocked. The kernel also has a type of lock called a spin lock which does loop until it becomes unlocked. Spin locks are only used in very special cases in the kernel and in device drivers. Similar to the Linux atomic operations, Windows Vista has the kernel transaction manger (KTM). The KTM enables applications to use atomic transactions on resources by making them available as kernel objects.

Windows Vista Timer and Time-Management

Windows Vista uses a timer interrupt frequency of 100 Hz (66.6 on multiprocessors). For a better timer interrupt resolution Windows uses a high precision event timer (HPET). The HPET is hardware timer and has a higher precision then the real time clock.

Windows Vista Memory Management

The virtual address space of each process can be smaller or larger than the total physical memory available on the computer. The subset of the virtual address space of a process that resides in physical memory is known as the working set. If the threads of a process attempt to use more physical memory than is currently available, the system pages some the memory contents to disk. The total amount of virtual address space available to a process is limited by physical memory and the free space on disk available for the paging file. To maximize its flexibility in managing memory, the system can move pages of physical memory to and from a paging file on disk. When a page is moved in physical memory, the system updates the page maps of the affected processes. When the system needs space in physical memory, it moves the least recently used pages of physical memory to the paging file. Manipulation of physical memory by the system is completely transparent to applications, which operate only in their virtual address spaces. Because the RAM is limited Windows Vista more processes can share the same page until one process wants to write to this shared page. (This is called Copy-on-Write Protection).

The Network Protocol Stack

A protocol stack is a software implementation of a computer networking protocol suite. The suite is the definition of the protocols, and the stack is the software implementation of them. Most protocols are used for one purpose. The modularization makes design 8 and evaluation easier. Because each protocol module usually communicates with two others, they are commonly imagined as layers in a stack of protocols. The lowest protocol is designed to realize physical interaction of the hardware. Higher layer adds more features. User applications are the topmost layers. The OSI (open system interconnection) model is the best known. In practical implementation, protocol stacks are often divided into three major sections: media, transport, and applications. A particular operating system or platform will often have two well-defined software interfaces: one between the media and transport layers, and one between the transport layers and applications. The media-to-transport interface defines how transport protocol software makes use of particular media and hardware types ("card drivers"). For example, this interface level would define how TCP/IP transport software would talk to Ethernet hardware. Examples of these interfaces include ODI and NDIS in the Microsoft Windows and DOS environment (NdisWrapper in Linux and Project Evil for FreeBSD). The application-to-transport interface defines how application programs make use of the transport layers. For example, this interface level would define how a web browser program would talk to TCP/IP transport software. Examples of these interfaces include Berkeley sockets and System V streams in the Unix-like OS, and Winsock in Microsoft Windows.

Alternatives for a Kernel-based OS

A kernel provides many practical features, but is not required to run a computer. Historical the first operating systems do not contain a kernel. The OS was implemented for only one type of machine (all with the same hardware specification). The OS do not support any hardware abstraction. Today this sort of implementation is used in embedded systems and some game consoles. There is another reason for using a kernel-less architecture. KLOS (kernel-less operating system) uses architecture because each service call results in a larger overhead because of the context switch. The heart of KLOS is the Event Core. It contains the only part which runs in the privileged mode (Ring 0) the rest of the Event Runs in the unprivileged mode (Ring 3). The Ring-0 Event Stubs running in privileged mode. There is one event stub for every hardware interrupt and exception that the underlying processor supports. KLOS implemented new protections to secure the stability of the OS. The service calls do not need to access the Ring 0 and produce so less overhead. Test results confirm the better performance of the service call mechanism of KLOS with an amount of protection that is nearly as good as other current operating systems.

The Kernel Subsystem Comparison

At first it is useful to compare the Linux kernel and the FreeBSD kernel. Because both are UNIX-like OS, they share some similarities. The structure of a process and his creation are nearly identical. The differences in the scheduling are significant. The new CFS of Linux is not automatically better as the scheduler in FreeBSD. The FreeBSD 7.0 was about 15% better in MySQL the Linux 2.6.23 kernel. The interrupts in FreeBSD 7.0 and Linux differs. Interrupt threads greatly simplifies locking in the kernel and can easily pre-empted by higher priority threads. FreeBSD and Linux use similar techniques for kernel synchronization and memory management. Windows Vista has more differences. It begins with another understanding of processes which results in other scheduling. Windows Vista uses more objects to handle things like the interrupt object or the kernel object by atomic transmissions.

Difference Between Monolithic Kernel and Microkernel

Inter Process Communication

A process means the representation of a program in memory. It may consist of smaller, programmer defined parts called "threads". Threads allow virtually parallel execution of different sections of a program. A thread is the smallest unit of executable code. A process can consist of several threads. In the next sections a thread and a process are meant to be equal, if not otherwise stated.

The earliest concept of inter-process communication (IPC) is called signals. It is widely used in Unix systems. Signals are predefined numerical constants, e.g. KILL, STOP, etc., which are sent to a process by a user, the operating system or another process. The signals are received by so called signal handlers, simple procedures, which belong to each process. This system is fast, but the problem is, that the signals have to be pre-defined numbers. Existing signals cannot be changed, because then, processes would react a different way than expected. New signals have to be standardized, which is too tedious for implementing just a single application.

Another solution for communication is the so called sockets. A process binds itself to one socket (or more), and "listens" to it, i.e. from then on, it can receive messages from other processes. Most of the sockets are full duplex. The owner of a socket, i.e. the process which is bind to a socket, is also called server, while the other processes are called clients. Because messages sent through sockets are not limited to numerical values, the information could be more than just control signals. There is no limitation upon extensibility, as long as the server knows what the received messages mean.

A system more powerful than sockets are message queues. Built as a fifo queue, a message queue stores all incoming messages, sent by other processes and sorts them, based on their priority. One process can have more than one message queue, with every message queue being responsible for different kinds of messages.

While monolithic kernels use signals and sockets to ensure inter process communication, the μ-kernel approach uses message queues. It grants, that all parts of the system are exchangeable.

System components of the monolithic kernels are somewhat "hardwired". This prevents extensibility. The first μ-kernels poorly implemented the IPC and were slow on context switches.

Memory Management

Monolithic kernels implement everything needed for memory management in kernel space. This includes allocation strategies, virtual memory management, and page replacement algorithms.

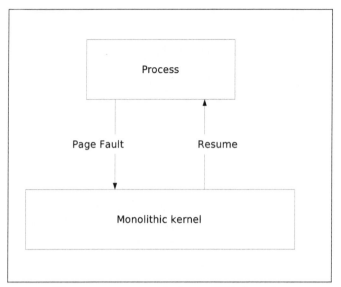

Memory management of monolithic kernels.

First generation µ-kernels delegate the memory management to user space, controlling just the basic access rights. One of the servers is responsible for managing page faults and reserving new memory. Every time a page fault occurs, the request has to take the way through the kernel to the pager. The pager must enter privileged mode to get access to memory and get back to user mode. Then it sends the result back to the triggering process (again through the kernel). The whole procedure to handle page faults or reserve new memory pages is tedious and time consuming.

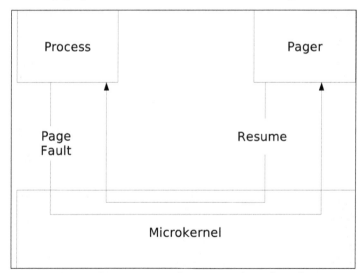

Memory Management of 1st-generation µ-kernels.

To solve the performance loss, second generation µ-kernels have more refined strategies of memory management, e.g. L4. With L4 every process has got three memory management primitives: map, grant and flush. A process maps memory pages to another process if he wants to share these pages. When a process grants pages to another process, he cannot access them anymore, and they are under the other process' control, as long as the granting process does not flushes them. Flushing regains granted and mapped memory pages. This system now works as follows: The μ-kernel reserves the whole system memory at start up to one process, the base system process, which resides (like all other processes) in user space. If a process needs memory, he doesn't have to take the way through the kernel anymore, but directly asks the base system process. Because every process can only grant/map/flush the memory pages it owned before, memory protection still exists. That way the overhead of context switches is reduced to a minimum and performance is increased.

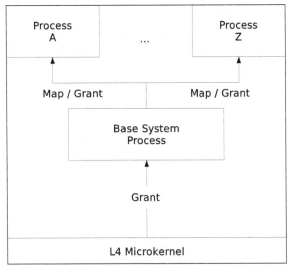

Memory management of the L4.

Security and Stability

The protection of system processes from being modified by the user or other processes is an important feature of the kernel. With an introduction of multitasking (and multithreading) new problems arise, concerning isolation of memory and processes. These problems include issues like race conditions, memory protection and system security itself. The kernel must be able to grant that in case a process cracks down, the system's performance will not be influenced. This is a more or less simple task if we talk about processes, which run in user space. But what happens, if a process crashes inside the kernel? Because of the "hardwiring" of system processes and the resulting dependency of the monolithic approach, it is assumable that other processes will also crash, resulting in a system-wide halt.

I/O Communication

I/O communication works through interrupts, issued by or sent to the hardware. Monolithic kernels (and most of the first generation μ-kernels) run device drivers inside the kernel space. Hardware interrupts are directly handled by kernel processes. To add or change features provided by the hardware, all layers above the changed layer in the monolithic kernel also have to be changed in the worst case.

The concept of so called modules was introduced to achieve more independence and separation from the kernel. One module represents parts of a driver and is un loadable during runtime. That way, drivers which are not needed by the system are not loaded and memory is preserved. But kernel modules are still binary kernel-dependent. This means, modules working with monolithic kernel of generation A (e.g.: Linux 2.4.0) are not granted to cooperate with its successor (e.g.: Linux 2.4.2). Source compatibility is often assured, but not always. If concepts change too much inside the monolithic kernel, modules need not just a recompilation, but a complete code adaption.

The μ-kernel approach doesn't handle I/O communication directly. It only ensures the communication. Requests from or to the hardware are redirected as messages by the μ-kernel to the servers in user space. If the hardware triggers an interrupt, the μ-kernel sends a message to the device driver server, and has nothing more to do about it. The device driver server takes the message and sends it to the right device driver. That way it is possible to add new drivers, exchange the driver manager without exchanging drivers or even exchange the whole driver management system without changing any other part of the system. It is not desirable to put the drivers into kernel space, as it was done by the first generation of μ-kernels, to get acceptable performance. That way the size grows and the kernel cannot be fully held in the processor's cache memory.

Extensibility and Portability

Extensibility is the most prominent fact for μ-kernels. It is, beside its size, one of the biggest differences to monolithic kernels.

Adding new features to a monolithic system means recompilation of the whole kernel, often including the whole driver infrastructure. If you have a new memory management routine and want to implement it into a monolithic architecture, modification of other parts of the system could be needed. In case of a μ-kernel the services are isolated from each other through the message system. It is enough to implement the new memory manager. The processes which formerly used the other manager, do not notice the change. μ-kernels also show their flexibility in removing features. That way a μ-kernel can be the base of a desktop operating system, as well as of real-time appliances in single chip systems. On the other hand μ-kernels it must be highly optimized for the processor they are intended to run on. It was shown, that it is not sufficient to just introduce a "compatibility layer" between kernel and processor as it was done with first generation μ-kernels. That way, μ-kernels are kept machine independent and could be easily be ported. Unfortunately, this approach prevented those μ-kernels from achieving the necessary performance and thus flexibility. The introduction of such a layer between the kernel and processor has several implications:

- Such a μ-kernel cannot take advantage of specific hardware.

- It cannot take precautions to circumvent or avoid performance problems of specific hardware.

- μ-kernels form the lowest layer of operating system. Therefore even the algorithms used inside the μ-kernel and its internal concepts are extremely processor dependent.

Implementations

This is just a short overview presenting implementations of monolithic kernels, μ-kernels and hybrids.

Monolithic Kernel

GNU/Linux

GNU/Linux is a free available, open source implementation of Unix, developed by thousands of individuals. It is a typical representing of a monolithic kernel. Continuously enhanced, it often changes its structure. Changing parts of the kernel means complete recompilation.

All system functions, including the whole process and memory management, process and thread scheduling, I/O functionality and drivers are implemented in kernel space. The I/O communication, provided by so called modules, which can be inserted and removed during runtime, are built against the kernel, i.e.: If the kernel changes, the set of modules changes too. The estimated size of an average monolithic kernel is about twenty to thirty megabytes resulting in a tedious maintenance process.

Hybrid Kernel

Mach

Mach is a μ-kernel of the first generation, designed and developed at the Carnegie Mellon University. It represents the base, among others, of Next, Mac OS X, and built the foundation for a lot of other μ-kernels designs. It was thought as a small-sized highly portable kernel which includes just a minimum set of kernel functions. The poor performance Mach showed in comparison to monolithic kernels led to the assumption, that μ-kernels cannot be fast. But second generation μ-kernels proved, that the lack of performance came due implementation issues, not due the μ-kernel design itself. Several mistakes of the first generation μ-kernels (e.g. Mach) can be pointed out:

- To ease portability, the designers introduced an additional layer between the kernel and the CPU. That way, only the layer should be optimized for a given processor, but this approach turned out to be wrong.

- Because of poor performance, device drivers were put back into kernel space. This resulted in a bloated kernel, which couldn't reside in processor cache anymore.

- Mach's Inter-process communication is too tedious and time-consuming.

Windows NT

Microsoft introduced the kernel for their Windows NT at the beginning of the 1990s. It was planned to be a µ-kernel, but due lack of performance, Microsoft decided to put a lot of system services back into kernel space, including, among others, device drivers and communication stacks. This bloated the kernel and it became bigger than most monolithic kernels were that time.

NT (including the kernel) is designed as an object-oriented operating system. Therefore, all basic structures, like processes, threads, device drivers, and others are implemented as objects, handled by an object manager. The kernel talks to the hardware through a so called Hardware Abstraction Layer (HAL), which favours porting to other system architectures.

Microkernel

QNX

QNX ("Quick Unix") is the most popular pure µ-kernel based operating system for re-altime applications. Realtime applications emphasize on predictability and stability. Examples of realtime appliances are embedded systems like microwaves, dishwashers, car safety systems, cell phones, etc. Primary targeted to the embedded market, it is also available as desktop version.

Only the most fundamental primitives like signals, timers and scheduling reside inside kernel space resulting in a just 64 kilobyte-sized kernel. All other components, e.g.: protocol stacks, drivers and file systems, run outside the kernel. All processes communicate via a single virtual messaging bus that lets you plug in or plug out any component on the fly. The kernel of QNX (called neutrino) is posix compliant, implemented in C and can be therefore easily tailored to different platforms and operating systems.

Developers can easily strip down the QNX kernel and remove unwanted functionality, e.g.: memory protection, which is implemented as a module. If the target applications don't need the property, it can be easily removed, without editing any source code. QNX allows running, testing and debugging drivers during runtime, due their kernel space independency.

L4

The L4 μ-kernel was implemented at the TU Dresden by the Systems Architecture Group in cooperation with the IBM Watson research centre. It belongs to the second generation of μ-kernels. It proved together with the QNX neutrino kernel, that μ-kernels can be as fast as their monolithic counterparts allowing easy extensibility.

Multiple operating systems running simultaneously on top of a μ-kernel.

Multiple operating systems on top of the same base services.

The performance is reached by the small size (12 kilobytes of code) and optimized inter-process communication (IPC). Due just three basic abstractions and seven system calls, on top of these abstractions, which are implemented in kernel space, allowing the L4 to completely residing in the processor's first-level cache. All other functions, like memory management, device drivers, interrupt handling; protocol stacks, etc. reside in user space. That way, the L4 just controls access to the hardware and does basic thread management. Hardware interrupts are forwarded to the user space as messages. The kernel is not involved in processing them. Memory management is completely done in user space and fast address space switches are assured through processor optimized code.

Applications 1		Applications n
Libraries 1		Libraries n
OS 1	...	OS n

Drivers	Stacks	...
CPU including Microkernel		
Hardware		

The μ-kernel is integrated into the processor's architecture.

System Call

In computing, a system call is the programmatic way in which a computer program requests a service from the kernel of the operating system it is executed on. A system call is a way for programs to interact with the operating system. A computer program makes a system call when it makes a request to the operating system's kernel. System call provides the services of the operating system to the user programs via Application Program Interface(API). It provides an interface between a process and operating system to allow user-level processes to request services of the operating system. System calls are the only entry points into the kernel system. All programs needing resources must use system calls.

Services Provided by System Calls

- Process creation and management,

- Main memory management,

- File Access, Directory and File system management,

- Device handling(I/O),

- Protection,

- Networking, etc.

Types of System Calls

There are mainly five types of system calls. These are explained in detail as follows:

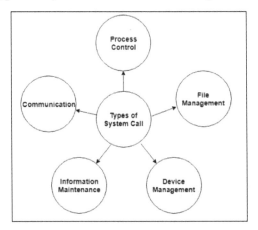

Here are the types of system calls:

- Process Control: These system calls deal with processes such as process creation, process termination etc.

- File Management: These system calls are responsible for file manipulation such as creating a file, reading a file, writing into a file etc.

- Device Management: These system calls are responsible for device manipulation such as reading from device buffers, writing into device buffers etc.

- Information Maintenance: These system calls handle information and its transfer between the operating system and the user program.

- Communication: These system calls are useful for interprocess communication. They also deal with creating and deleting a communication connection.

Some of the examples of all the above types of system calls in Windows and Unix are given as follows:

Types of System Calls	Windows	Linux
Process Control	CreateProcess()	fork()
	ExitProcess()	exit()
	WaitForSingleObject()	wait()
File Management	CreateFile()	open()
	ReadFile()	read()
	WriteFile()	write()
	CloseHandle()	close()

Device Management	SetConsoleMode()	ioctl()
	ReadConsole()	read()
	WriteConsole()	write()
Information Maintenance	GetCurrentProcessID()	getpid()
	SetTimer()	alarm()
	Sleep()	sleep()
Communication	CreatePipe()	pipe()
	CreateFileMapping()	shmget()
	MapViewOfFile()	mmap()

There are many different system calls as shown above. Details of some of those system calls are as follows:

- wait(): In some systems, a process may wait for another process to complete its execution. This happens when a parent process creates a child process and the execution of the parent process is suspended until the child process executes. The suspending of the parent process occurs with a wait() system call. When the child process completes execution, the control is returned back to the parent process.

- exec(): This system call runs an executable file in the context of an already running process. It replaces the previous executable file. This is known as an overlay. The original process identifier remains since a new process is not created but data, heap, stack etc. of the process are replaced by the new process.

- fork(): Processes use the fork() system call to create processes that are a copy of themselves. This is one of the major methods of process creation in operating systems. When a parent process creates a child process and the execution of the parent process is suspended until the child process executes. When the child process completes execution, the control is returned back to the parent process.

- exit(): The exit() system call is used by a program to terminate its execution. In a multithreaded environment, this means that the thread execution is complete. The operating system reclaims resources that were used by the process after the exit() system call.

- kill(): The kill() system call is used by the operating system to send a termination signal to a process that urges the process to exit. However, kill system call does not necessary mean killing the process and can have various meanings.

Examples of Operating System

UNIX

Unix and Unix-like operating systems are a family of computer operating systems that are derived from the original Unix System from Bell Labs.

Initial proprietary derivatives included the HP-UX and the SunOS systems. However, growing incompatibility between these systems led to the creation of interoperability standards like POSIX. Modern POSIX systems include Linux, its variants, and Mac OS.

Unix is the most powerful and popular multi-user and multi-tasking Operating System. The basic concepts of Unix were originated in the Multics project of 1969. The Multics system was intended as a time-sharing system that would allow multiple users to simultaneously access a mainframe computer.

Ken Thompson, Dennis Ritchie, and others developed the basic building blocks of Unix including a hierarchical file system, i.e, the concepts of processes and a command line interpreter for the PDP-7. From there, multiple generations of Unix were developed for various machines.

Growing incompatibility between these systems led to the creation of interoperability standards like POSIX and Single Unix Specification.

Unix programs are designed around some core philosophies that include requirements like single purpose, interoperable, and working with a standardized text interface. Unix systems are built around a core kernel that manages the system and the other processes.

Kernel subsystems may include process management, file management, memory management, network management and others.

Salient Features of UNIX

There are several prominent features of Unix, and few among them are stated below:

- It is a multi-user system where the same resources can be shared by different users.

- It provides multi-tasking, wherein each user can execute many processes at the same time.

- It was the first operating system that was written in a high-level language (C Language). This made it easy to port to other machines with minimum adaptations.

- It provides a hierarchical file structure which allows easier access and maintenance of data.

- Unix has built-in networking functions so that different users can easily exchange information.

- Unix functionality can be extended through user programs built on a standard programming interface.

UNIX Architecture

There are two important divisions in UNIX operating system architecture.

- Kernel,

- Shell.

In simple words you can say:

- Kernal: Interacts with the machine's hardware.

- Shell: Interacts with the user.

The Kernel

The kernel of UNIX is the hub (or core) of the UNIX operating system. Kernel is a set of routines mostly written in C language.

User programs that need to access the hardware (like hard disk or terminal) use the services of the Kernel, which performs the job on the user's behalf.

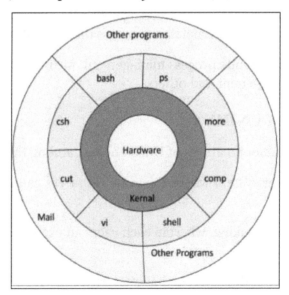

User interacts with the Kernal by using System calls. Kernel allocates memory and time to programs and handles the file store and communications in response to system calls.

As an illustration of the way that the unix shell and the kernel work together, suppose a user types mv myfile myfile1 (which has the effect of renaming the file myfile). The unix shell searches the file store for the file containing the program mv, and then requests the kernel, through system calls, to execute the program mv on myfile. When the process mv myfile has finished running, the unix shell then returns the UNIX prompt to the user, indicating that it is waiting for further commands. Some other functions performed by the kernel in Unix system are:

- Managing the machine's memory and allocating it to each process and decides their priorities.
- Scheduling the work done by the CPU so that the work of each user is carried out as efficiently as is possible.
- Organizing the transfer of data from one part of the machine to another.
- Accepting instructions from the Unix shell and carrying them out.
- Enforcing the access permissions that are in force on the file system.

The kernel has to do a lot of this work even if no user program is running. It is often called the operating system – a program's gateway to the computer's resources.

The Shell

UNIX Shell acts as a medium between the user and the kernel in Unix system. When a user logs in, the login program checks the username and password and then starts another program called the shell.

Computers don't have any inherent capability of translating commands into action. This requires a command line interpreter (CLI) and this is handled by the "Outer Part" of the operating system i.e. Shell. It interprets the commands the user types in and arranges for them to be carried out.

The commands are themselves programs: when they terminate, the shell gives the user another prompt (% on our systems).

Even though there is only one kernel running on the Unix system, there could be several shells in action – for each user who is logged in.

In every Unix system, the user can customize his own shell, and users can use different shells on the same machine. The shell keeps a list of the commands you have typed in. If you need to repeat a command, use the cursor keys to scroll up and down the list or type history for a list of previous commands.

You can use any one of these Unix shells if they are available on your system. And you can switch between the different Unix shells once you have found out if they are available.

- TC shell (tcsh),

- Korn shell (ksh),

- Bourne Again SHell (bash),

- Bourne shell (sh),

- C shell (csh).

Linux

Linux is an operating system. In fact, one of the most popular platforms on the planet, Android, is powered by the Linux operating system. An operating system is software that manages all of the hardware resources associated with your desktop or laptop. To put it simply, the operating system manages the communication between your software and your hardware. Without the operating system (OS), the software wouldn't function.

The Linux operating system comprises several different pieces:

- Bootloader: The software that manages the boot process of your computer. For most users, this will simply be a splash screen that pops up and eventually goes away to boot into the operating system.

- Kernel: This is the one piece of the whole that is actually called Linux. The kernel is the core of the system and manages the CPU, memory, and peripheral devices. The kernel is the lowest level of the OS.

- Init system: This is a sub-system that bootstraps the user space and is charged with controlling daemons. One of the most widely used init systems is system which also happens to be one of the most controversial. It is the init system that manages the boot process, once the initial booting is handed over from the bootloader (i.e., GRUB or GRand Unified Bootloader).

- Daemons: These are background services (printing, sound, scheduling, etc.) that either starts up during boot or after you log into the desktop.

- Graphical server: This is the sub-system that displays the graphics on your monitor. It is commonly referred to as the X server or just X.

- Desktop environment: This is the piece that the users actually interact with. There are many desktop environments to choose from (GNOME, Cinnamon, Mate, Pantheon, Enlightenment, KDE, Xfce, etc). Each desktop environment includes built-in applications (such as file managers, configuration tools, web browsers, and games).

- Applications: Desktop environments do not offer the full array of apps. Just like Windows and macOS, Linux offers thousands upon thousands of high-quality software titles that can be easily found and installed. Most modern Linux distributions include App Store-like tools that centralize and simplify application installation. For example, Ubuntu Linux has the Ubuntu Software Center which allows you to quickly search among the thousands of apps and install them from one centralized location.

Characteristics and Architecture of Linux Operating System

Linux has several silent features, some of the important ones are:

- Multiuser Capability: This is a capability of Linux OS where, the same computer resources – hard disk, memory, etc. are accessible to multiple users. Of course, not on a single terminal, they are given different terminals to operate from. A terminal will consist of at least a Monitor/VDU, keyboard and mouse as input devices. All the terminals are then connected to the main Linux Server or Host Machine, whose resources and connected peripheral devices such as printer, can be used.

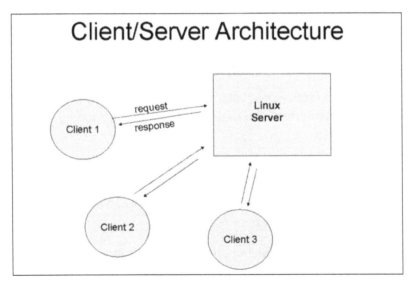

- Client/Server Architecture is an example of multiuser capability of Linux, where different clients are connected to a Linux server. The client sends request to the server with a particular data and server requests with the processed data or the file requested, client terminal is also known as a Dumb Terminal.

- Multitasking: Linux has the ability to handle more than one job at a time, say for example you have executed a command for sorting for a huge list and simultaneously typing in a notepad. This is managed by dividing the CPU time intelligently by the implementation of scheduling policies and the concept of context switching.

- Portability: Portability was the one of the main features that made Linux so popular among the users, but portability doesn't mean that it is smaller in file size and can be carried on pen drive, CDs and memory cards. Instead, here portability means that Linux OS and its application can work on different types of hardware's in the same way. Linux kernel and application programs support their installation even on very least hardware configuration.

- Security: Security is a very important part of any OS, for the organizations/user who is using the system for their confidential works; Linux does provide several security concepts for protecting their users from unauthorized access of their data and system.

Linux provide three main security concepts are:

- Authentication: This simply implies claiming the person whom you are by assigning passwords and login names to individual users, ensuring that nobody can gain access to their work.

- Authorization: At the file level Linux has authorization limits to users, there are read, write and execute permissions for each files which decide who can access a particular file, who can modify it and who can execute it.

- Encryption: This feature encodes your files into an unreadable format that is also known as 'cyphertext', so that even if someone succeeds in opening it your secrets will be safe.

- Communication: Linux has an excellent feature for communicating with the fellow users; it can be within the network of a single main computer, or between two or more such computer networks. The users can easily exchange mail, data, and program through such networks.

Linux System Architecture is consists of following layers:

- Hardware layer: Hardware consists of all peripheral devices (RAM/ HDD/ CPU etc).

- Kernel: Core component of Operating System, interacts directly with hardware, and provides low level services to upper layer components.

- Shell: An interface to kernel, hiding complexity of kernel's functions from users. Takes commands from user and executes kernel's functions.

- Utilities: Utility programs giving user most of the functionalities of an operating systems.

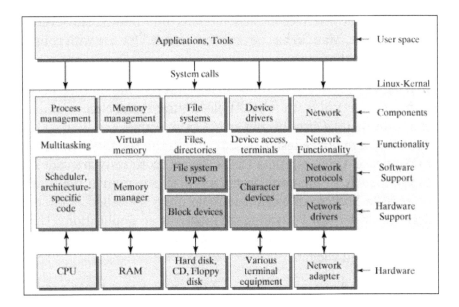

Working of Linux

Linux was designed to be similar to UNIX, but has evolved to run on a wide variety of hardware from phones to supercomputers. Every Linux-based OS involves the Linux kernel—which manages hardware resources—and a set of software packages that make up the rest of the operating system.

The OS includes some common core components, like the GNU tools, among others. These tools give the user a way to manage the resources provided by the kernel, install additional software, configure performance and security settings, and more. All of these tools bundled together make up the functional operating system. Because Linux is an open source OS, combinations of software can vary between Linux distributions.

Mac OS

Mac OS is an, operating system (OS) developed by the American computer company Apple Inc. The OS was introduced in 1984 to run the company's Macintosh line of personal computers (PCs). The Macintosh heralded the era of graphical user interface (GUI) systems, and it inspired Microsoft Corporation to develop its own GUI, the Windows OS.

Apple's marketing for the introduction of the Macintosh focused heavily on its operating system's intuitive ease of use. Unlike virtually all other contemporary PCs, the Mac OS (initially designated simply System Software, with a version number appended) was graphically based. Rather than typing commands and directory paths at text prompts, users moved a mouse pointer to visually navigate the Finder—a series of virtual folders and files, represented by icons. Most computer operating systems eventually adopted the GUI model. In the 1980s Apple made an agreement allowing Microsoft to use certain aspects of the Mac interface in early versions of Windows. However, except for a brief period in the 1990s, Mac OS has never been licensed for use with computers made by manufacturers other than Apple.

Later Mac OS releases introduced features such as Internet file sharing, network browsing, and multiple user accounts. In 1996, Apple acquired rival NeXT Computers, which was founded by Steven Jobs after his departure from Apple, and in 2001 the company rolled out Mac OS X, a major redesign based on both the NextStep system and Apple's most recent OS release. OS X ran on a UNIX kernel (core software code) and offered technical advances such as memory protection and preemptive multitasking, along with a more versatile Finder, an elegant-looking interface called Aqua, and a convenient graphical "Dock" bar for launching frequently used applications. Updates to OS X added features such as automated backups and a "Dashboard" manager for small, handy applications called widgets.

From 2007, Apple unveiled a number of mobile devices that could access the Internet, including the iPhone smartphone and the iPad tablet computer. Apple soon emphasized the ability of OS X to connect with these devices. In 2011, Apple introduced iCloud, a cloud computing service that allowed users to share data among all of their Apple devices, for both OS X and the mobile operating system iOS. Apple added more features allowing connectivity between devices to successive updates of OS X, iOS, and later watchOS (the operating system for the Apple Watch smartwatch). These features included the ability to receive phone calls (made to the iPhone) and the means of quickly sharing data (such as photos and text) among devices.

iOS

iOS is a mobile operating system developed by Apple. It was originally named the iPhone OS, but was renamed to the iOS in June, 2009. The iOS currently runs on the iPhone, iPodtouch, and iPad.

Like modern desktop operating systems, iOS uses a graphical user interface, or GUI. However, since it is a mobile operating system, iOS is designed around touchscreen input, rather than a keyboard and mouse. For example, applications, or "apps," can be opened by a single tap, rather than a double-click. Different screens can be viewed by swiping your finger across the screen, rather than clicking on open windows.

Since, iOS is designed to be simple and easy to use, it does not include several features found in a traditional operating system. For example, you cannot manage files and folders like you can in Mac OS X or Windows. You also have limited access to iOS system settings. Instead of modifying application preferences from within each program, most settings need to be adjusted within the Settings app. Additionally, while you can run multiple programs at once, you can only view one open program at a time.

While Apple's iOS provides a more basic user interface than Mac OS X, each new version adds more features. For example, iOS 2 provided access to the App Store, which allowed users to download and install third-party apps on their iPhones. iOS 3 added copy and paste functionality and iPad support. iOS 4 was the first version to support multitasking and added the GameCenter feature. iOS 5 introduced the Siri voice assistant (only available on the iPhone 4S), and provided new cloud connectivity features.

Chrome OS

Google Chrome OS is an open source lightweight operating system (OS). It uses one-sixtieth as much hard drive space as Windows 7 and is intended for netbooks or tablet PCs that access Web-based applications and stored data from remote servers.

The Chrome OS is so lean that boot time is about seven seconds. Google released the source code for Chrome OS in July 2009 under the BSD license as part of a larger project called Chromium. The operating system is built on top of a Linux kernel and runs on Intel x86 and ARMchips.

The only software application Google Chrome OS runs locally is Google's browser, which is also called Chrome. Both the Chrome OS and browser share an auto-update feature that allows Google to push updates by using secure sockets layer (SSL). The end user is not able to refuse a security update or change back to a previous version.

Chrome OS is not available for download. Instead, Google is partnering with original equipment manufacturers (OEMs) including Samsung, Hewlett-Packard, Lenovo and Intel to manufacture hardware devices capable of using the OS. Although Chrome OS will support hard disk drives, Google is encouraging its partners to use solid-state drives, which have no moving parts.

Android (Operating System)

Android is a mobile operating system developed by Google. It is used by several smartphones and tablets. Examples include the Sony Xperia, the Samsung Galaxy, and the Google Nexus One.

The Android operating system (OS) is based on the Linux kernel. Unlike Apple's iOS, Android is open source, meaning developers can modify and customize the OS for each phone. Therefore, different Android-based phones often have different graphical user interfaces GUIs even though they use the same OS.

Android phones typically come with several built-in applications and also support third-party programs. Developers can create programs for Android using the free Android software developer kit (SDK). Android programs are written in Java and run through a Java virtual machine JVM that is optimized for mobile devices. The "Dalvik" JVM was used through Android 4.4 and was replaced by Android Runtime or "ART" in

Android 5.0. Users can download and install Android apps from Google Play and other locations.

If you are unsure what operating system your phone or tablet uses, you can view the system information by selecting "About" in the Settings menu. This is also a good way to check if your device meets an app's system requirements. The name "Android" comes from the term android, which is robot designed to look and act like a human.

Microsoft Windows

Windows is a series of operating systems developed by Microsoft. Each version of Windows includes a graphical user interface, with a desktop that allows users to view files and folders in windows. For the past two decades, Windows has been the most widely used operating system for personal computers PCs.

Microsoft Windows is designed for both home computing and professional purposes. Past versions of Windows home editions include Windows 3.0, Windows 3.1, Windows 95, Windows 98, Windows Me, Windows XP, and Windows Vista. The current version, Windows 7, was released in 2009.

The first business-oriented version of Windows, called Windows NT 3.1, was in 1993. This was followed by Windows 3.5, 4.0, and Windows 2000. When Microsoft released Windows XP in 2001, the company simply created different editions of the operating system for personal and business purposes. Windows Vista and Windows 7 have followed the same release strategy.

Windows is designed to run on standard x86 hardware, such as Intel and AMD processors. Therefore, it can be installed on multiple brands of hardware, such as Dell, HP, and Sony computers, as well as home-built PCs. Windows 7 also includes several touchscreen features, that allow the operating system to run on certain tablets and computers with touchscreen displays. Microsoft's mobile operating system, Windows Phone, is designed specifically for smartphones and runs on several brands of phones, including HTC, Nokia, and Samsung.

Types of Operating System Services

Following are the services provided by an operating system for the convenience of users:

Program Execution

The purpose of computer system is to allow the users to execute programs in an efficient manner. The operating system provides an environment where the user can conveniently run these programs. The user does not have to worry about the memory allocation or de-allocation or any other thing because these things are taken care of by the operating system.

To run a program, the program is required to be loaded into the RAM first and then to assign CPU time for its execution. Operating system performs this function for the convenience of the user. It also performs other important tasks like allocation and de-allocation of memory, CPU scheduling etc.

I/O Operations

Each program requires an input and after processing the input submitted by user it produces output. This involves the use of I/O devices. The operating system hides the user from all these details of underlying hardware for the I/O. So the operating system makes the users convenient to run programs by providing I/O functions. The I/O service cannot be provided by user-level programs and it must be provided by the operating system.

File System Manipulation

While working on the computer, generally a user is required to manipulate various types of files like as opening a file, saving a file and deleting a file from the storage disk. This is an important task that is also performed by the operating system.

Thus operating system makes it easier for the user programs to accomplish their task by providing the file system manipulation service. This service is performed by the 'Secondary Storage Management' a part of the operating system.

Communication

Operating system performs the communication among various types of processes in the form of shared memory. In multitasking environment, the processes need to communicate with each other and to exchange their information. These processes are created under a hierarchical structure where the main process is known as parent process and the sub processes are known as child processes.

Error Detection

Operating system also deals with hardware problems. To avoid hardware problems the operating system constantly monitors the system for detecting the errors and fixing these errors (if found). The main function of operating system is to detect the errors like bad sectors on hard disk, memory overflow and errors related to I/O devices. After detecting the errors, operating system takes an appropriate action for consistent computing.

This service of error detection and error correction cannot be handled by user programs because it involves monitoring the entire computing process. These tasks are too critical to be handed over to the user programs. A user program, if given these privileges; can interfere with the corresponding operation of the operating systems.

Resource Allocation

In the multitasking environment, when multiple jobs are running at a time, it is the responsibility of an operating system to allocate the required resources (like as CPU, main memory, tape drive or secondary storage etc.) to each process for its better utilization. For this purpose various types of algorithms are implemented such as process scheduling, CPU scheduling, disk scheduling etc.

Accounting

Operating system keeps an account of all the resources accessed by each process or user. In multitasking, accounting enhances the system performance with the allocation of resources to each process ensuring the satisfaction to each process.

Protection System

If a computer system has multiple users and allows the concurrent execution of multiple processes, then the various processes must be protected from one another's activities.

Operating System Services as Resource Manager

Operating system works as a resource manager to manage the resources efficiently in a computer such as processor, memory, input/output devices etc. To decide about which resources are used by which running programs and how to administer them, is known as the resource management. Operating system assigns the computer resources to processes for an efficient use; therefore, it plays an important role as a resource manager while ensuring the user satisfaction.

To manage the computer resources most effectively the OS decides which program should run at what time, how much memory should be allocated for an execution of a program, where to save the file so that disk space can be optimally utilized etc. Below given are some of the important services performed by operating system as a resource manager:

Process Management

In multiprocessing environment, operating system allows more than one application (or process) to run simultaneously. Process management is a part of an operating system which manages the processes in such a way that system performance can be enhanced. The operating system deals with other types of activities also that includes user programs and system programs like as printer spooling virtual memory, swapping etc.

A process is an activity that needs certain resources to complete its task. Various computer resources are CPU time, main memory, and I/O devices. These resources are allocated to the processes and based on decision that which process should be assigned for the allocation of resource and this decision is taken by process management implementing the process scheduling algorithms.

It is important to note that a process is not a program. A process is only one instant of a program in execution. There are many processes running the same program.

The five major activities of an operating system in regard to process management are:

- Creation and deletion of user and system processes.

- Suspension and re-activation of processes.

- A mechanism for process synchronization.

- A mechanism for process communication.

- A mechanism for deadlock handling.

Main-Memory Management

Memory management is the most important part of an operating system that deals directly with both the primary (known as main memory) memory and secondary memory. The main memory is a large array of bytes and each byte has its own address. Main memory provides the storage for a program that can be accessed directly by the CPU for its exertion. So, for a program to be executed, the primary task of memory management is to load the program into main memory.

Memory management performs mainly two functions, these are:

- Each process must have enough memory in which it has to execute.

- The different locations of memory in the system must be used properly so that each and every process can run most effectively.

Operating system loads the instructions into main memory then picks up these instructions and makes a queue to get CPU time for its execution. The memory manager tracks the available memory locations which one is available, which is to be allocated or de-allocated. It also takes decision regarding which pages are required to swap between the main memory and secondary memory. This activity is referred as virtual memory management that increases the amount of memory available for each process.

The major activities of an operating system in regard to memory-management are:

- Keep track of which part of memory are currently being used and by whom.

- Decide which processes should be loaded into memory when the memory space is free.

- Allocate and de-allocate memory spaces as and when required.

File Management

A file is a collection of related information defined by its creator. Computer can store files on the disk (secondary storage), which provide long term storage. Some examples of storage media are magnetic tape, magnetic disk and optical disk. Each of these media has its own properties like speed, capacity, and data transfer rate and access methods.

A file system is normally organized into directories to make ease of their use. These directories may contain files and other directories. Every file system is made up of similar directories and subdirectories. Microsoft separates its directories with a back slash and its file names aren't case sensitive whereas Unix-derived operating systems (including Linux) use the forward slash and their file names generally are case sensitive.

The main activities of an operating system in regard to file management are creation and deletion of files/folders, support of manipulating files/folders, mapping of files onto secondary storage and taking back up of files.

I/O Device Management

Input/Output device, management is a part of an operating system that provides an environment for the better interaction between system and the I/O devices (such as printers, scanners tape drives etc.). To interact with I/O devices in an effective manner, the operating system uses some special programs known as device driver. The device drivers take the data that operating system has defined as a file and then translate them into streams of bits or a series of laser pulses (in regard with laser printer).

A device driver is a specific type of computer software that is developed to allow interaction with hardware devices. Typically, this constitutes an interface for, communicating with the I/O device, through the specific computer bus or communication subsystem that the hardware is connected with. The device driver is a specialized hardware dependent computer program that enables another program, typically an operating system to interact transparently with a hardware device, and usually provides the required interrupt handling necessary for the time dependent hardware interfacing.

Secondary-Storage Management

A computer system has several levels of storage such as primary storage, secondary storage and cache storage. But primary storage and cache storage cannot be used as a permanent storage because these are volatile memories and its data are lost when power is turned off. Moreover, the main memory is too small to accommodate all data and programs. So the computer system must provide secondary storage to back up the main memory. Secondary storage consists of tapes drives, disk drives, and other media.

The secondary storage management provides an easy access to the file and folders placed on secondary storage using several disk scheduling algorithms.

The four major activities of an operating system in regard to secondary storage management are:

- Managing the free space available on the secondary-storage device.

- Allocation of storage space when new files have to be written.

- Scheduling the requests for memory access.

- Creation and deletion of files.

Network Management

An operating system works as a network resource manager when multiple computers are in a network or in a distributed architecture. A distributed system is a collection of processors that do not share memory, peripheral devices, or a clock. The processors communicate with one another through communication lines called network. The communication-network design must consider routing and network strategies, and the problems with network and security.

Most of today's networks are based on client-server configuration. A client is a program running on the local machine requesting to a server for the service, whereas a server is a program running on the remote machine providing service to the clients by responding their request.

Protection (User Authentication)

Protection (or security) is the most demanding feature of an operating system. Protection is an ability to authenticate the users for an illegal access of data as well as system.

Operating system provides various services for data and system security by the means of passwords, file permissions and data encryption. Generally computers are connected through a network or Internet link, allowing the users for sharing their files accessing web sites and transferring their files over the network. For these situations a high level security is expected.

At the operating system level there are various software firewalls. A firewall is configured to allow or deny traffic to a service running on top of the operating system. Therefore, by installing the firewall one can work with running the services, such as telnet or ftp, and not to worry about Internet threats because the firewall would deny all traffic trying to connect to the service on that port.

If a computer system has multiple users and allows the concurrent execution of multiple processes, then the various processes must be protected from one another's activities. Protection refers to mechanism for controlling the access of programs, processes, or users to the resources defined by a computer system.

Command Interpreter System

A command interpreter is an interface of the operating system with the user. The user gives commands which are executed by operating system (usually by turning them into system calls). The main function of a command interpreter is to get and execute the user specified command.

Command-Interpreter is usually not a part of the kernel, since multiple command interpreters may be supported by an operating system, and they do not really need to run in kernel mode. There are two main advantages of separating the command interpreter from the kernel.

If you want to change the way the command interpreter looks, i.e., you want to change the interface of command interpreter, then you can do that if the command interpreter is separate from the kernel. But if it is not then you cannot change the code of the kernel and will not be able to modify the interface.

If the command interpreter is a part of the kernel; it is possible for an unauthenticated process to gain access to certain part of the kernel. So it is advantageous to have the command interpreter separate from kernel.

References

- Introduction-to-operating-system: researchgate.net, Retrieved 31 March, 2019

- Kernel: webopedia.com, Retrieved 14 July, 2019

- Introduction-of-system-call: geeksforgeeks.org, Retrieved 17 May, 2019

- Different-types-of-system-calls: tutorialspoint.com, Retrieved 19 April, 2019

- Unix-introduction: softwaretestinghelp.com, Retrieved 5 February, 2019

- Architecture-of-unix-operating-system-with-an-appropriate-diagram: wingsoftechnology.com, Retrieved 26 July, 2019

- Characteristics-and-architecture-of-linux-oprating-system: linux-india.org, Retrieved 21 May, 2019

- Operating-system-services, disk-operating-system, fundamental: ecomputernotes.com, Retrieved 8 January, 2019

Operating System Components

Memory management component of an operating system is concerned with the allocation of memory processes to maximize efficiency. The communication between the processing system with another processing system or human is referred to as input output system. All these operating system components have been carefully analyzed in this chapter.

Process Management

A process is a program in execution. Process is not as same as program code but a lot more than it. A process is an 'active' entity as opposed to program which is considered to be a 'passive' entity. Attributes held by process include hardware state, memory, CPU etc.

Process memory is divided into four sections for efficient working:

- The Text section is made up of the compiled program code, read in from non-volatile storage when the program is launched.

- The Data section is made up the global and static variables, allocated and initialized prior to executing the main.

- The Heap is used for the dynamic memory allocation, and is managed via calls to new, delete, malloc, free, etc.

- The Stack is used for local variables. Space on the stack is reserved for local variables when they are declared.

Process Management is the management of processes in a software system. To manage processes, then, means managing multiple instances of programs in memory in a collaborated environment. This is typically a requirement in modern operating systems and implemented in the kernel or executive. Operating systems that support a form of process management is considered to be a multitasking operating system.

Representation

In order to manage a process, operating system designer needs to determine how to best represent a process given OS design criteria and required system resources. A process consists of the following:

- Image of the executable in memory (machine code and data).

- Memory in use by the process and its virtual address space.

- Descriptors used to represent the processes.

- Process state information (registers, stack, attributes, etc).

The operating system is required to manage the processes and allocate system resources in a fair manner to the processes that request them.

Image of Executable in Memory

Executable programs are stored as files on disk to facilitate program loading and managing. To load a program, an operating system loader loads the file into memory. The loader must also be able to understand the type of file (it must be an executable the operating system can work with) and possibly support features of these file types (like resources and debug information).

The image of the executable in memory is the current representation of the machine code and data of the image and how it appears in memory at any given time. We use the term "image" here to represent a "snapshot" of whats in memory. For example, it's like taking a camera looking at a big array of bytes and taking a photo. The array of bytes can be machine code, data, or neither. Only the program instructions know.

Some data in the program image might be useful though to other programs or even the operating system itself. This is data the program image itself does not usually use; for example, the program file can contain debugging information. A debugger can be then attached to the program and use that information.

In short, the operating system needs to be able to load the file from disk into memory somewhere in order to execute it. This can be like just loading the file into memory "as-is". The operating system or another program can then get any useful data from the program file that it may need.

Memory in use by the Process and its Virtual Address Space

Processes typically have calls to dynamically allocate memory and use stack space just like the operating system does. The operating system is required to allocate space for a process stack and heap memory for the process to use. For example, the operating system typically allocates a default stack size to all processes. The executable file for the process however can also tell the operating system to allocate a larger stack space if the process needs it.

The process heap is different. While the stack is allocated by the operating system before executing a process, the heap is not. Instead, each process has its own heap allocator in user mode. This is implemented in the C Runtime Library (CRT) using the familiar interface of malloc, free, realloc, brk, and sbrk functions. Programs that are linked with the CRT can call these functions to allocate memory. Programs that are not linked with the CRT however must implement their own heap allocator or link with another library that does.

The CRT Runtime implements a user mode heap allocator (typically a free list). The C function malloc might call brk, which calls the OS using the System API. The C function brk calls the OS in order to allocate more virtual memory to expand the heap when needed.

In short, the user mode heap works like this: The program calls malloc, which might call brk, which calls the OS using the System API to allocate virtual memory for the heap. The malloc and free family of functions implement their own user mode heap allocator. They only call the OS to allocator or free memory from the virtual address space.

In preemptive multitasking, all processes have their own virtual address space. This means every process must have their own Page Directory and associated page tables. In order to manage process specific information, we use a process control block (PCB).

Descriptors used to Represent Processes

Process Control Blocks

The process control block (PCB) maintains information that the operating system needs in order to manage a process. PCBs typically include information such as the process ID, the current state of the process (e.g. running, ready, blocked, etc.), the number of the next program instruction to be executed, and the starting address of the process in memory. The PCB also stores the contents of various processor registers (the execution context), which are saved when a process leaves the running state and which are restored to the processor when the process returns to the running state.

When a process makes the transition from one state to another, the operating system updates the information in its PCB. When the process is terminated, the operating system removes it from the process table and frees the memory and any other resources allocated to the process so that they become available to other processes. The diagram below illustrates the relationship between the process table and the various process control blocks.

The changeover from one process to the next is called a context switch. During a context switch, the processor obviously cannot perform any useful computation, and because of the frequency with which context switches occur, operating systems must minimise the context-switching time in order to reduce system overhead.

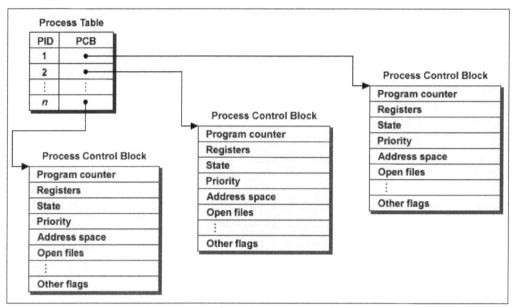

The process table and process control blocks.

Many processors contain a register that holds the address of the current PCB, and also provide special purpose instructions for saving the execution context to the PCB when the process leaves the running state, and loading it from the PCB into the processor registers when the process returns to the running state.

Process States

The simple process state diagram below shows three possible states for a process. They are shown as ready (the process is ready to execute when a processor becomes available), running (the process is currently being executed by a processor) and blocked (the process is waiting for a specific event to occur before it can proceed). The lines connecting the states represent possible transitions from one state to another.

At any instant, a process will exist in one of these three states. On a single-processor computer, only one process can be in the running state at any one time. The remaining processes will either be ready or blocked, and for each of these states there will be a queue of processes waiting for some event.

Note that certain rules apply here. Processes entering the system must initially go into the ready state. A process can only enter the running state from the ready state. A process can normally only leave the system from the running state, although a process in the ready or blocked state may be aborted by the system (in the event of an error, for example), or by the user.

Although the three-state model shown is sufficient to describe the behaviour of processes generally, the model must be extended to allow for other possibilities, such as the suspension and resumption of a process. For example, the process may be swapped out of working memory by the operating system's memory manager in order to free up memory for another process.

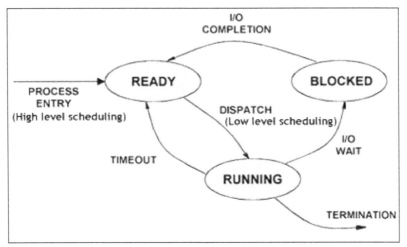

A simple three-state process state diagram.

When a process is suspended, it essentially becomes dormant until resumed by the system (or by a user). Because a process can be suspended while it is either ready or blocked, it may also exist in one of two further states - ready suspended and blocked suspended (a running process may also be suspended, in which case it becomes ready suspended).

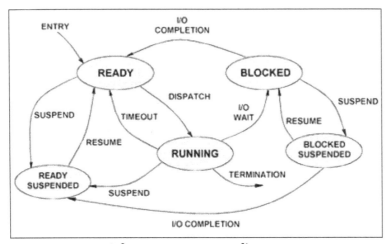

A five-state process state diagram.

The queue of ready processes is maintained in priority order, so the next process to execute will be the one at the head of the ready queue. The queue of blocked process is typically unordered, since there is no sure way to tell which of these processes will become unblocked first (although if several processes are blocked awaiting the same event, they may be prioritised within that context).

To prevent one process from monopolising the processor, a system timer is started each time a new process starts executing. The process will be allowed to run for a set period of time, after which the timer generates an interrupt that causes the operating system to regain control of the processor. The operating system sends the previously running process to the end of the ready queue, changing its status from running to ready, and assigns the first process in the ready queue to the processor, changing its status from ready to running.

Process Scheduling

The process scheduling is the activity of the process manager that handles the removal of the running process from the CPU and the selection of another process on the basis of a particular strategy.

Process scheduling is an essential part of Multiprogramming operating systems. Such operating systems allow more than one process to be loaded into the executable memory at a time and the loaded process shares the CPU using time multiplexing.

Process Scheduling Queues

The OS maintains all PCBs in Process Scheduling Queues. The OS maintains a separate queue for each of the process states and PCBs of all processes in the same execution state are placed in the same queue. When the state of a process is changed, its PCB is unlinked from its current queue and moved to its new state queue.

The Operating System maintains the following important process scheduling queues:

- Job queue: This queue keeps all the processes in the system.

- Ready queue: This queue keeps a set of all processes residing in main memory, ready and waiting to execute. A new process is always put in this queue.

- Device queues: The processes which are blocked due to unavailability of an I/O device constitute this queue.

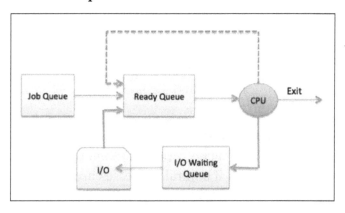

The OS can use different policies to manage each queue (FIFO, Round Robin, Priority, etc.). The OS scheduler determines how to move processes between the ready and run queues which can only have one entry per processor core on the system; in the above diagram, it has been merged with the CPU.

Two-state Process Model

Two-state process model refers to running and non-running states which are described below:

S.No.	State and Description
1	Running: When a new process is created, it enters into the system as in the running state.
2	Not Running: Processes that are not running are kept in queue, waiting for their turn to execute. Each entry in the queue is a pointer to a particular process. Queue is implemented by using linked list. Use of dispatcher is as follows. When a process is interrupted, that process is transferred in the waiting queue. If the process has completed or aborted, the process is discarded. In either case, the dispatcher then selects a process from the queue to execute.

Schedulers

Schedulers are special system software which handles process scheduling in various ways. Their main task is to select the jobs to be submitted into the system and to decide which process to run. Schedulers are of three types:

- Long-Term Scheduler.

- Short-Term Scheduler.

- Medium-Term Scheduler.

Long Term Scheduler

It is also called a job scheduler. A long-term scheduler determines which programs are admitted to the system for processing. It selects processes from the queue and loads them into memory for execution. Process loads into the memory for CPU scheduling.

The primary objective of the job scheduler is to provide a balanced mix of jobs, such as I/O bound and processor bound. It also controls the degree of multiprogramming. If the degree of multiprogramming is stable, then the average rate of process creation must be equal to the average departure rate of processes leaving the system.

On some systems, the long-term scheduler may not be available or minimal. Time-sharing operating systems have no long term scheduler. When a process changes the state from new to ready, then there is use of long-term scheduler.

Short-term Scheduler

It is also called as CPU scheduler. Its main objective is to increase system performance in accordance with the chosen set of criteria. It is the change of ready state to running state of the process. CPU scheduler selects a process among the processes that are ready to execute and allocates CPU to one of them.

Short-term schedulers, also known as dispatchers, make the decision of which process to execute next. Short-term schedulers are faster than long-term schedulers.

Medium-term Scheduler

Medium-term scheduling is a part of swapping. It removes the processes from the memory. It reduces the degree of multiprogramming. The medium-term scheduler is in-charge of handling the swapped out-processes.

A running process may become suspended if it makes an I/O request. A suspended processes cannot make any progress towards completion. In this condition, to remove the process from memory and make space for other processes, the suspended process is moved to the secondary storage. This process is called swapping, and the process is said to be swapped out or rolled out. Swapping may be necessary to improve the process mix.

Comparison Among Scheduler

S.No.	Long-Term Scheduler	Short-Term Scheduler	Medium-Term Scheduler
1	It is a job scheduler.	It is a CPU scheduler	It is a process swapping scheduler.
2	Speed is lesser than short term scheduler.	Speed is fastest among other two.	Speed is in between both short and long term scheduler.
3	It controls the degree of multiprogramming.	It provides lesser control over degree of multiprogramming.	It reduces the degree of multiprogramming.
4	It is almost absent or minimal in time sharing system.	It is also minimal in time sharing system	It is a part of Time sharing systems.
5	It selects processes from pool and loads them into memory for execution.	It selects those processes which are ready to execute.	It can re-introduce the process into memory and execution can be continued.

Context Switch

A context switch is the mechanism to store and restore the state or context of a CPU in Process Control block so that a process execution can be resumed from the same point at a later time. Using this technique, a context switcher enables multiple processes to share a single CPU. Context switching is an essential part of a multitasking operating system features.

When the scheduler switches the CPU from executing one process to execute another, the state from the current running process is stored into the process control block. After this, the state for the process to run next is loaded from its own PCB and used to set the PC, registers, etc. At that point, the second process can start executing.

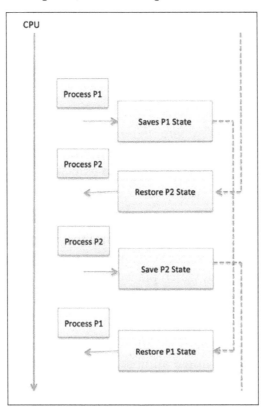

Context switches are computationally intensive since register and memory state must be saved and restored. To avoid the amount of context switching time, some hardware systems employ two or more sets of processor registers. When the process is switched, the following information is stored for later use:

- Program Counter.

- Scheduling information.

- Base and limit register value.

- Currently used register.

- Changed State.

- I/O State information.

- Accounting information.

Memory Management

In order for programs to be executed by the processor, they must be loaded into main memory, which are several orders of magnitude faster than secondary storage in terms of its access time. Historically, main memory has always been significantly more expensive than secondary storage, and system designers have tried to optimise its use. Although costs have fallen steadily, this is still the case today, and modern operating systems and applications require large amounts of memory in order to run.

The memory management component of an operating system is concerned with the organisation and management of system memory. It determines how memory is allocated to processes, responds to constantly changing demands, and interacts with memory management hardware (if present) to maximise efficiency.

Overlays

One of the main limitations imposed on programmers in the early days of computing was the size of the computer's memory. If the program was larger than the available memory, it could not be loaded, which placed severe restrictions on program size. The obvious solution would be to increase the amount of memory available, but this would significantly increase the cost of the computer system.

One way for a programmer to overcome these limitations was to use overlays. The programmer divided the program into a number of logical sections. A small portion of the program had to remain in memory at all times, but the remaining sections (or overlays) were loaded only when they were needed. The use of overlays allowed programmers to write programs that were much larger than physical memory, although responsibility for managing memory usage rested with the programmer rather than the operating system.

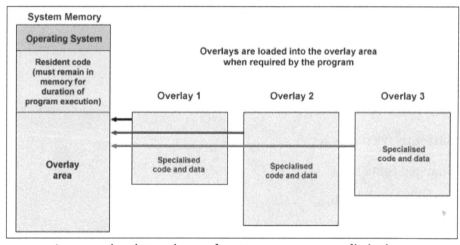

A program is written using overlays to overcome memory limitations.

Partitions and Protected Memory

Another issue that must be dealt with in terms of memory management is that of memory protection. In a single-user, single-tasking system, this is relatively easy, since it is simply a matter of protecting the operating system's memory space from the user's program. Memory is effectively split into two partitions – one partition is reserved for the operating system, while the other is available for user programs.

Protection can be implemented using a boundary register built into the processor. The boundary register contains the base memory address of the user program, effectively, defining the lower bounds of the memory space available to user processes. Each time a user process references a memory address, the system checks the referenced address against the value stored in the boundary register. If the user process has attempted to reference a memory location with a lower address, the process is terminated with an appropriate error message.

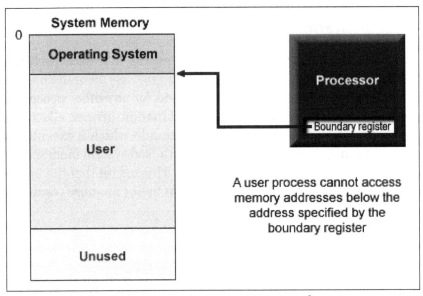

Operating system memory is protected.

In a multi-programming environment, matters are inevitably going to be far more complicated. In early multi-programming systems, the memory management function had to protect the operating system memory space from all user processes loaded into memory as before, but it now also had to protect those user processes from each other.

These early multi-programming systems used fixed partitions to allocate memory to user processes, each of which could hold a single process. Each partition was defined by two boundary registers – a base register and a limit register for the for the lower and upper memory addresses respectively. Although more complex than systems in which only a single user process was allowed to run, memory management was still relatively simple because each process ran within a pre-defined partition.

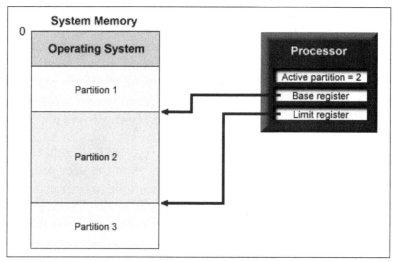

A multi-programming system with fixed partitions.

Internal Fragmentation

The main problem with the fixed-partition system was that each partition could accommodate only a single process. If the process did not use all of the memory within a partition, the remaining memory could not be used for any other process. The loss of available memory within a partition due to the fact that the process allocated to the partition may be significantly smaller than the partition in which it executes is known as internal fragmentation. Often, there was enough unused system memory to run another process, but there were no available partitions. This meant that the unused memory could not be utilised, and was plainly an inefficient use of memory resources.

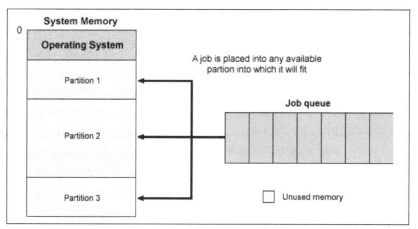

Processes are queued awaiting an available partition.

Variable Partitions

The main problem with fixed partitions is that they are rarely if ever exactly the right size for a particular process. If the partition is too small, a process cannot be loaded into it and must await the availability of a large partition. If the partition is too large, the process may be loaded but significant amounts of the available memory within the partition will be wasted.

The idea of a variable-size partition allows the operating system to create partitions of exactly the right size for a particular process wherever there is sufficient space available. Internal fragmentation is thus eliminated, but a new problem emerges. Processes are initially added to the system using contiguous memory space. As each process completes, however, it is removed from the system leaving a hole in memory. This hole can be used for a new process, providing it will fit into the space made available. Since it highly unlikely that any new processes will fit exactly into the gaps left by the old processes, the only processes able to use these gaps in memory will be smaller than their predecessors.

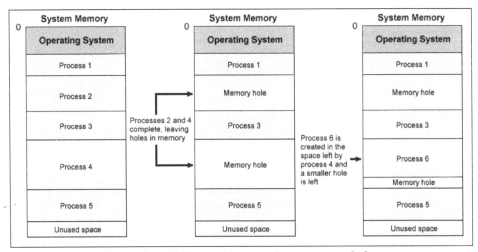

Process in variable partitions can leave memory holes.

The operating system must also determine where to place incoming programs when there may be a number of holes large enough to accommodate the newly created process. There are three memory placement strategies that have been commonly used for this purpose:

- First-fit: The process is placed in first available hole large enough to hold it, al-lowing the operating system to make a decision quickly.

- Best-fit: The process is placed in the hole that fits it most closely, leaving little space unused but creating additional management overhead (searching for the best fit) and leaving small holes that cannot be used by other processes.

- Worst-fit: The process is placed in the largest possible hole regardless of size, potentially leaving enough space for another program but again creating additional management overhead (searching for the worst fit) and potentially leaving smaller holes that cannot be used by other processes.

Over time and regardless of the memory placement strategy used, a number of small holes will be created in memory that cannot be utilised by new processes because they are simply too small. This is referred to as external fragmentation. In order to counter this, operating systems evolved the ability to relocate partitions so that the holes were effectively moved to the top of memory and merged into one much larger unused memory space. This procedure is sometimes called compaction, and while it enables memory to be used far more efficiently, it increases yet again the complexity of the memory management function. The additional system overhead required to implement a compaction scheme is considerable.

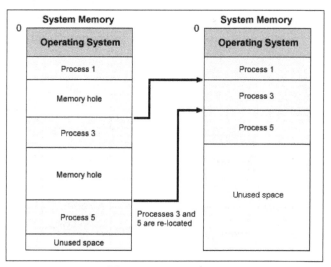

Memory compaction.

In early single-tasking operating systems, only one process could reside in memory at any one time. This did not allow for particularly efficient use of the processor, since each time execution of the resident process was halted awaiting the completion of some I/O operation such as reading from or writing to disk, the processor was effectively idle.

As the amount of available memory increased it became possible to load multiple processes into memory simultaneously, enabling the processor to be quickly switched between them to provide the illusion that a number of processes were executing at the same time. It also enabled the processor to be immediately allocated to a waiting process in the event of the current process being halted to await the completion of an I/O request.

In multitasking systems, numerous processes now compete for the available memory, and one or more of the resident processes may have to give up memory to accommodate an incoming process with a higher priority. A process that relinquishes its memory before it has completed in order to make way for another process is temporarily stored on disk (in what is often referred to as *virtual memory*) until system memory is once more available (or until it achieves a sufficiently high priority level to enable it to replace another process currently stored in main memory).

The movement of processes back and forth between system memory and secondary storage in this way is called "swapping", and may occur several times during the execution of a single process. Inevitably, swapping incurs additional operating system overhead and adds complexity to the business of managing memory. It should also be fairly self-evident that the degree to which swapping must occur can be reduced by increasing the amount of memory available.

Paging and Segmentation

The need to load an entire program into memory in one contiguous block places severe restrictions on memory usage. The use of overlays overcame the limitations imposed by the physical size of memory, but in order to make efficient use of the processor, several processes needed to be in memory at one time.

As physical memory became larger this was certainly possible, but the memory space required by each process could vary widely, and for the operating system, the main problem was trying to find the most suitable memory space for a particular process. Inevitably, some of the memory could not be used, and in many cases a process would be too big to fit into any of the available spaces.

One answer was to break each process down into a number of relatively small fixed-size blocks, called pages, which could be loaded into memory as and when required. The memory itself was also organised into blocks of the same size, called page-frames. Each page could be loaded into any available page frame, which meant that the entire available memory space could be used for user processes, and allowed far more processes to be in memory at the same time. This was a far more efficient use of computer memory, but also imposed a much greater burden on the operating system in terms of memory management overhead, since it must now keep track of multiple pages for each user process.

One of the benefits of a paging system is that only a relatively small subset of the pages belonging to a particular process need to be loaded at any one time. In fact theoretically, only the page that is currently executing needs to reside in memory. When a process references a page that is not in main memory, it generates a page fault, which prompts the operating system to load the missing page into memory from secondary storage.

The frequency with which this occurs will depend on the size of the page, and the total number of pages which make up a process. In practice, there will be a minimum number of pages that should reside in memory at any given time for a particular process. This number is known as the minimum working set, and will be determined to a large extent by the overall size of the user program.

Another method of utilising memory, called segmentation, is also based on the notion of splitting a process into blocks, but the size of the blocks (or segments) is variable. A scheme that allows the use of variable size segments can be useful from a programmer's point of view, since it lends itself to the creation of modular programs, but the operating system now not only has to keep track of the starting address of each segment, but since they are variable in size, must also calculate the offset to the end of each segment. Some systems combine paging and segmentation by implementing segments as variable-size blocks composed of fixed-size pages.

Virtual Memory

The concept of virtual memory is closely associated with that of paging. Virtual memory effectively extends the amount of memory available to applications by using some of the system's secondary storage space (i.e. the hard disk drive) as working memory. All or part of a process may be swapped between real memory and this virtual memory. This both allows more processes to co-exist on the system and eliminates the limitations on overall process size.

The only factor that limits process size, in fact, is the amount of secondary storage that is made available for virtual memory. In a sense, virtual memory systems create the illusion that there is more working memory available than is actually the case.

The use of a paging scheme, in conjunction with the use of virtual memory, leads to a situation where the individual pages of a process may be located in a number of different locations in both real memory and virtual memory. In fact, during the course of process execution, an individual page may be swapped between real and virtual memory a number of times, and is unlikely to occupy the same address twice.

This presents the operating system with a seemingly monumental task in terms of keeping track of the whereabouts of each page, for each process on the system. Furthermore, the process of swapping pages in and out of memory creates additional system overhead. It is generally accepted that the more random access memory (RAM) a system has the better it will perform, since less time will be spent swapping pages between real and virtual memory.

In a system that employs virtual memory, the size of the pages can have an effect on system efficiency. If the pages are small, the operating system will require more tracking information for each process because there will be more pages. If, on the other hand, the size of the pages is large, it will take longer to transfer each page between real memory and virtual memory, and vice versa, when swapping occurs.

Memory Mapping

In a paged virtual memory system, there are actually two different kinds of address. A program instruction within a process, for example, will have an internal (or virtual) address that will be used to reference it from within the process. A virtual address will consist of a page number and an offset from the start of the page.

When the process is loaded into memory, however, the same program instruction will also have a physical address in memory. When a virtual address is referenced by a process, therefore, the operating system must translate this virtual address to a physical address. This is further complicated by the fact that the various pages of a process may be loaded into non-contiguous page frames, and may be swapped in and out of memory several times during the lifetime of the process.

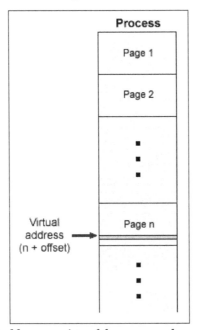

A virtual address consists of the page number and offset.

The operating system creates a page table in memory for each process. The table contains a page table entry for each page of the process, and the entries are ordered sequentially by page number. When a process is assigned to the processor, the address of the page table in memory is loaded into a special purpose register called the *page map origin register*.

Each time the process references a virtual address; the system interrogates this register to obtain the base address of the page table, and adds the page number to give it the address of the page table entry. The entry will hold the starting address in memory of the page. Adding the offset will provide the required physical address.

The diagram below illustrates how a virtual address referenced by a process is translated into a physical address in memory. The mapping is performed dynamically by a high-speed, special-purpose hardware unit called the memory management unit (MMU).

Note that only some of the pages belonging to a particular process will be loaded into memory at any given time. The page table entry for each page must therefore indicate whether or not the page currently resides in memory. This is achieved using a 1-bit field in the entry called the *resident bit*. If the resident bit is set to 1, the entry gives the page frame number. If it is set to 0, the entry provides the location of the page in secondary storage.

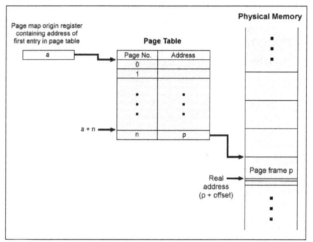

Virtual address translation (memory mapping).

Input Output (IO) System

An I/O system is required to take an application I/O request and send it to the physical device, then take whatever response comes back from the device and send it to the application. I/O devices can be divided into two categories:

- Block devices: A block device is one with which the driver communicates by sending entire blocks of data. For example, Hard disks, USB cameras, Disk-On-Key etc.

- Character devices: A character device is one with which the driver communicates by sending and receiving single characters (bytes, octets). For example, serial ports, parallel ports, sounds cards etc.

Device Controllers

Device drivers are software modules that can be plugged into an OS to handle a particular device. Operating System takes help from device drivers to handle all I/O devices.

The Device Controller works like an interface between a device and a device driver. I/O units (Keyboard, mouse, printer, etc.), typically, consist of a mechanical component and an electronic component where electronic component is called the device controller.

There is always a device controller and a device driver for each device to communicate with the Operating Systems. A device controller may be able to handle multiple devices.

As an interface its main task is to convert serial bit stream to block of bytes, perform error correction as necessary.

Any device connected to the computer is connected by a plug and socket, and the socket is connected to a device controller. Following is a model for connecting the CPU, memory, controllers, and I/O devices where CPU and device controllers all use a common bus for communication.

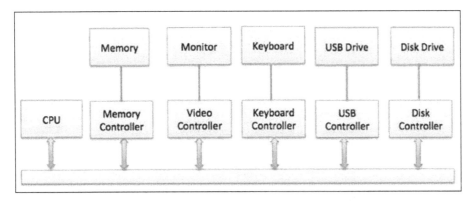

Synchronous vs. Asynchronous I/O

- Synchronous I/O – In this scheme CPU execution waits while I/O proceeds.

- Asynchronous I/O – I/O proceeds concurrently with CPU execution.

Communication to I/O Devices

The CPU must have a way to pass information to and from an I/O device. There are three approaches available to communicate with the CPU and Device:

- Special Instruction I/O.

- Memory-mapped I/O.

- Direct memory access (DMA).

Special Instruction I/O

This uses CPU instructions that are specifically made for controlling I/O devices. These instructions typically allow data to be sent to an I/O device or read from an I/O device.

Memory-mapped I/O

When using memory-mapped I/O, the same address space is shared by memory and I/O devices. The device is connected directly to certain main memory locations so that I/O device can transfer block of data to/from memory without going through CPU.

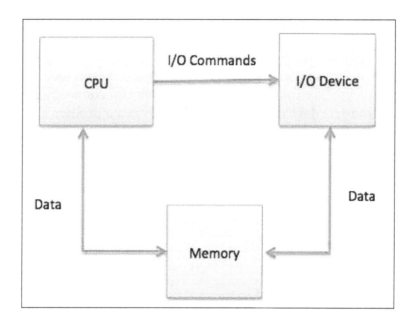

While using memory mapped IO, OS allocates buffer in memory and informs I/O device to use that buffer to send data to the CPU. I/O device operates asynchronously with CPU, interrupts CPU when finished.

The advantage to this method is that every instruction which can access memory can be used to manipulate an I/O device. Memory mapped IO is used for most high-speed I/O devices like disks, communication interfaces.

Direct Memory Access (DMA)

Slow devices like keyboards will generate an interrupt to the main CPU after each byte is transferred. If a fast device such as a disk generated an interrupt for each byte, the operating system would spend most of its time handling these interrupts. So, a typical computer uses direct memory access (DMA) hardware to reduce this overhead.

Direct Memory Access (DMA) means CPU grants I/O module authority to read from or write to memory without involvement. DMA module itself controls exchange of data between main memory and the I/O device. CPU is only involved at the beginning and end of the transfer and interrupted only after entire block has been transferred.

Direct Memory Access needs a special hardware called DMA controller (DMAC) that manages the data transfers and arbitrates access to the system bus. The controllers are programmed with source and destination pointers (where to read/write the data), counters to track the number of transferred bytes, and settings, which includes I/O and memory types, interrupts and states for the CPU cycles.

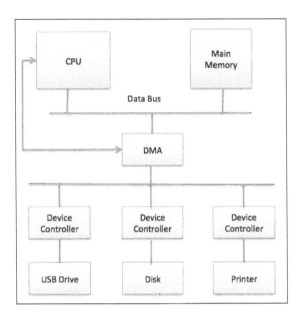

The operating system uses the DMA hardware as follows:

Step	Description
1	Device driver is instructed to transfer disk data to a buffer address X.
2	Device driver then instruct disk controller to transfer data to buffer.
3	Disk controller starts DMA transfer.
4	Disk controller sends each byte to DMA controller.
5	DMA controller transfers bytes to buffer, increases the memory address, decreases the counter C until C becomes zero.
6	When C becomes zero, DMA interrupts CPU to signal transfer completion.

Polling vs. Interrupts I/O

A computer must have a way of detecting the arrival of any type of input. There are two ways that this can happen, known as polling and interrupts. Both of these techniques allow the processor to deal with events that can happen at any time and that are not related to the process it is currently running.

Polling I/O

Polling is the simplest way for an I/O device to communicate with the processor. The process of periodically checking status of the device to see if it is time for the next I/O operation is called polling. The I/O device simply puts the information in a Status register, and the processor must come and get the information.

Most of the time, devices will not require attention and when one does it will have to wait until it is next interrogated by the polling program. This is an inefficient method and much of the processors time is wasted on unnecessary polls.

Compare this method to a teacher continually asking every student in a class, one after another, if they need help. Obviously the more efficient method would be for a student to inform the teacher whenever they require assistance.

Interrupts I/O

An alternative scheme for dealing with I/O is the interrupt-driven method. An interrupt is a signal to the microprocessor from a device that requires attention.

A device controller puts an interrupt signal on the bus when it needs CPU's attention when CPU receives an interrupt. It saves its current state and invokes the appropriate interrupt handler using the interrupt vector (addresses of OS routines to handle various events). When the interrupting device has been dealt with, the CPU continues with its original task as if it had never been interrupted.

References

- Operating-system-processes, operating-system: studytonight.com, Retrieved 13 May, 2019

- Osdev24, resources: brokenthorn.com, Retrieved 25 February, 2019

- Process-management, operating-systems, computer-software, computing: technologyuk.net, Retrieved 16 January, 2019

- Os-process-scheduling, operating-system: tutorialspoint.com, Retrieved 29 March, 2019

- Memory-management, operating-systems, computing: technologyuk.net, Retrieved 30 April, 2019

- Os-io-hardware, operating-system: tutorialspoint.com, Retrieved 29 June, 2019

Types of Operating Systems

There are various types of operating systems which can be categorized as serial processing operating system, batch processing operating system, network operating system, distributed operating system, real time operating system, embedded operating system, etc. This chapter has been carefully written to provide an easy understanding of these types of operating systems.

Mobile Operating System

A mobile operating system (Mobile OS) is a software platform on top of which other programs called application programs, can run on mobile devices such as personal digital assistant (PDA), tablets, cellular devices phones, smartphones and so on. Over the years, Mobile OS design has experienced a three-phase evolution: from the PC-based operating system to an embedded operating system to the current smartphone-oriented operating system in the past decade. Throughout the process, Mobile OS architecture has gone from complex to simple to something in-between. The evolution process is naturally driven by the technology advancements in hardware, software, and the Internet:

- Hardware: The industry has been reducing the factor size of microprocessors and peripherals to design actual mobile devices. Before the form factor size was reduced enough, the mobile device could not achieve both small size and processing capability at the same time. We had either a PC-sized laptop computer or a much weaker personal data assistant (PDA) in phone size. Mobile operating systems for PDAs usually did not have full multitasking or 3D graphics support. Features like sensors, such as accelerometers, and capacitor-based touch screens were not available in the past mobile operating systems.

- Software: With a laptop computer, the software is mainly focused on the user's productivity, where support for keyboard and mouse that have precise inputs are essential. The software for a personal data assistant, as its name implies, helps the user to manage personal data such as contacts information, email, and so on. The mobile operating systems were not designed for good responsiveness or smoothness with a rich user interface (UI) including both touch screen and other sensors.

- Internet: Along with Internet development, especially after Web 2.0, there is abundant information in the network waiting to be searched, organized, mined, and brought to users. People are increasingly living with the Internet instead of just browsing the Web. More and more people are involved in the development, including information contribution, application development, and social interactions. The mobile operating systems cannot be self-contained, but have to be open systems.

Windows Phone

Windows Phone is a proprietary smartphone operating system developed by Microsoft. It is the successor to Windows Mobile, although it is incompatible with the earlier platform. It was launched in 2010 under the name Windows Phone 7. Various hardware manufacturers including HTC, Samsung, LG, and Nokia are developing Windows Phone devices. In February 2011, Nokia and Microsoft devices announced that Windows Phone 7 would be the primary OS for all future Nokia smartphones. Windows Phone 7 received a major upgrade (7.5 Mango) in February 2011, adding features that had been missing in the original release. The second generation Windows Phone 8 was released in October 2012.

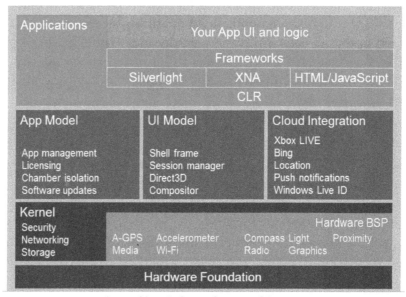

Microsoft's Windows Phone Architecture.

Windows Phone 7's architecture required a hardware layer that meets Microsoft's minimum system requirements: an ARM7 CPU, a DirectX 9-capable GPU, 256MB RAM and 8GB of flash memory, a 5-megapixel camera, a multi-touch capacitive display, an A-GPS, an accelerometer, a compass, proximity and light devices sensors, and six physical buttons: back, start, and search; camera, power/sleep, and volume. The Windows Phone kernel handles low-level device driver access as well as basic security, networking, and storage. Three libraries: an App Model for application management, a UI model for user interface management, and a Cloud Integration module for web search via Bing, location services, push notifications, and so on sit above the kernel. Application-facing APIs include Sliverlight, XNA, HTML/JavaScript and the Common Language Runtime (CLR) that supports C# or VB Net applications. The kernel itself is a proprietary Windows OS design for embedded devices that combines Windows Embedded CE 6.0 R3 and Windows Embedded Compact 77. Windows Phone 8 replaced the Windows CE kernel with one based on Windows NT. This is meant in part to mimic the Windows 8 desktop OS, allowing for easier porting of applications between the two operating systems.

webOS

webOS is a proprietary mobile operating system running on the Linux kernel, initially developed by Palm, which launched with the Palm Pre. The webOS interface revolves around "cards," individual applications that are presented one-at-a-time and can be scrolled through horizontally like a deck of cards to move applications from the foreground to the background. On startup, a launcher screen with a grid of icons is presented, together with a quick-launch bar holding commonly-used applications. The UI supports standard touch and gesture commands like tap, swipe, and pinch. webOS's Core OS is built on a Linux 2.6 kernel, with device drivers, an ext3 file system, network communication, and bluetooth. Above this sits the UI System Manager, which is responsible for window, UI and application management. The Mojo JavaScript framework provides application facing APIs, and the webOS Services Manager offers access to location, phone, camera, and so on. webOS applications are programmed in HTML, CSS, and JavaScript, and use Mojo and webOS services for UI and OS support.

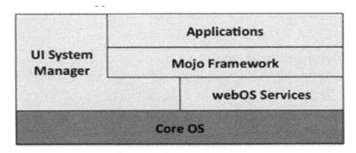

Simplified webOS Architecture.

iOS

iOS (formerly iPhone OS) is a mobile operating system created and developed by Apple Inc. exclusively for its hardware. It is the operating system that presently powers many of the company's mobile devices, including the iPhone, and iPod Touch; it also powered the iPad prior to the introduction of iPadOS in 2019. It is the second most popular mobile operating system globally after Android.

Originally unveiled in 2007 for the iPhone, iOS has been extended to support other Apple devices such as the iPod Touch (September 2007) and the iPad (January 2010). As of March 2018, Apple's App Store contains more than 2.1 million iOS applications, 1 million of which are native for iPads. These mobile apps have collectively been downloaded more than 130 billion times.

The iOS user interface is based upon direct manipulation, using multi-touch gestures. Interface control elements consist of sliders, switches, and buttons. Interaction with the OS includes gestures such as swipe, tap, pinch, and reverse pinch, all of which have specific definitions within the context of the iOS operating system and its multi-touch interface. Internal accelerometers are used by devices some applications to respond to shaking the device (one common result is the undo command) or rotating it in three dimensions (one common result is switching between portrait and landscape mode). Apple has been significantly praised for incorporating thorough accessibility functions into iOS, enabling users with vision and hearing disabilities to properly use its products.

Major versions of iOS are released annually. On all recent iOS devices, iOS regularly checks on the availability of an update, and if one is available, will prompt the user to permit its automatic installation. The current version, iOS 13 was released to the public on 19 September 2019, introducing user interface tweaks and a dark mode, along with features such as a redesigned Reminders app, a swipe keyboard, and an enhanced Photos app. iOS 13 does not support devices with less than 2 GB of RAM, including the iPhone 5s, iPod Touch (6th generation), and the iPhone 6 and iPhone 6 Plus, which still make up over 10% of all iOS devices. iOS 13 is exclusively for the iPhone and iPod touch as the iPad variant is now called iPadOS.

Features

Home Screen

The home screen, rendered by SpringBoard, displays application icons and a dock at the bottom where users can pin their most frequently used apps. The home screen appears whenever the user unlocks the device or presses the physical "Home" button whilst in another app. Before iOS 4 on the iPhone 3GS (or later), the screen's background could be customized only through jailbreaking, but can now be changed out-of-the-box. The screen has a status devices bar across the top to display data, such as time, battery level, and signal strength. The rest of the screen is devoted to the current application. When a passcode is set and a user switches on the device, the passcode must be entered at the Lock Screen before access to the Home screen is granted.

In iPhone OS 3, Spotlight was introduced, allowing users to search media, apps, emails, contacts, messages, reminders, calendar events, and similar content. In iOS 7 and later, Spotlight is accessed by pulling down anywhere on the home screen (except for the top and bottom edges that open Notification Center and Control Center). In iOS 9, there are two ways to access Spotlight. As with iOS 7 and 8, pulling down on any homescreen will show Spotlight. However, it can also be accessed as it was in iOS 3 – 6. This gives a Spotlight endowed with Siri suggestions, which include app suggestions, contact suggestions and news. In iOS 10, Spotlight is at the top of the now-dedicated "Today" panel.

Since iOS 3.2, users are able to set a background image for the Home screen. This feature is only available on third-generation devices—iPhone 3GS, third-generation iPod touch (iOS 4.0 or newer), all iPad models (since iOS 3.2)—or newer.

Researchers found that users organize icons on their homescreens based on usage-frequency and relatedness of the applications, as well as for reasons of usability and aesthetics.

System Font

iOS originally used Helvetica as the system font. Apple switched to Helvetica Neue exclusively for the iPhone 4 and its Retina Display, and retained Helvetica as the system font for older iPhone devices on iOS 4. With iOS 7, Apple announced that they would change the system font to Helvetica Neue Light, a decision that sparked criticism for inappropriate usage of a light, thin typeface for low-resolution mobile screens. Apple eventually chose Helvetica Neue instead. The release of iOS 7 also introduced the ability to scale text or apply other forms of text accessibility changes through settings. With iOS 9, Apple changed the font to San Francisco, an Apple-designed font aimed at maximum legibility and font consistency across its product lineup.

Folders

iOS 4 introduced folders, which can be created by dragging an application on top of another, and from then on, more items can be added to the folder using the same procedure. A title for the folder is automatically selected by the category of applications inside, but the name can also be edited by the user. When apps inside folders receive notification badges, the individual numbers of notifications are added up and the total number is displayed as a notification badge on the folder itself. Originally, folders on an iPhone could include up to 12 apps, while folders on iPad could include 20. With increasing display sizes on newer iPhone hardware, iOS 7 updated the folders with pages similar to the home screen layout, allowing for a significant expansion of folder functionality. Each page of a folder can contain up to nine apps, and there can be 15 pages in total, allowing for a total of 135 apps in a single folder. In iOS 9, Apple updated folder sizes for iPad hardware, allowing for 16 apps per page, still at 15 pages maximum, increasing the total to 240 apps.

Notification Center

Before iOS 5, notifications were delivered in a modal window and couldn't be viewed after being dismissed. In iOS 5, Apple introduced Notification Center, which allows users to view a history of notifications. The user can tap a notification to open its corresponding app, or clear it. Notifications are now delivered in banners that appear briefly at the top of the screen. If a user taps a received notification, the application that sent the notification will be opened. Users can also choose to view notifications in modal alert windows by adjusting the application's notification settings. Introduced with iOS 8, widgets are now accessible through the Notification Center, defined by 3rd parties.

When an app sends a notification while closed, a red badge appears on its icon. This badge tells the user, at a glance, how many notifications that app has sent. Opening the app clears the badge.

Accessibility

iOS offers various accessibility features to help users with vision and hearing disabilities. One major feature, VoiceOver, provides voice reading information on the screen, including contextual buttons, icons, links and other user interface elements, and allows the user to navigate the operating system through gestures. Any apps with default controls and developed with a UIKit framework gets VoiceOver functionality built in. One example includes holding up the iPhone to take a photo, with VoiceOver describing the photo scenery. As part of a "Made for iPhone" program, introduced with the release of iOS 7 in 2013, Apple has developed technology to use Bluetooth and a special technology protocol to let compatible third-party equipment connect with iPhones and iPads for streaming audio directly to a user's ears. Additional customization available for Made for iPhone products include battery tracking and adjustable sound settings for different environments. Apple made further efforts for accessibility for the release of iOS 10 in 2016, adding a new pronunciation editor to VoiceOver, adding a Magnifier setting to enlarge objects through the device's camera, software TTY support for deaf people to make phone calls from the iPhone, and giving tutorials and guidelines for third-party developers to incorporate proper accessibility functions into their apps.

In 2012, Liat Kornowski from *The Atlantic* wrote that "the iPhone has turned out to be one of the most revolutionary developments since the invention of Braille", and in 2016, Steven Aquino of *TechCrunch* described Apple as "leading the way in assistive technology", with Sarah Herrlinger, Senior Manager for Global Accessibility Policy and Initiatives at Apple, stating that "We see accessibility as a basic human right. Building into the core of our products supports a vision of an inclusive world where opportunity and access to information are barrier-free, empowering individuals with disabilities to achieve their goals".

Multitasking

Multitasking for iOS was first released in June 2010 along with the release of iOS 4. Only certain devices—iPhone 4, iPhone 3GS, and iPod Touch 3rd generation—were able to multitask. The iPad did not get multitasking until iOS 4.2.1 in that November. Currently, multitasking is supported on iPhone 3GS+, iPod Touch 3rd generation+, and all iPad models.

Implementation of multitasking in iOS has been criticized for its approach, which limits the work that applications in the background can perform to a limited function set and requires application developers to add explicit support for it.

Before iOS 4, multitasking was limited to a selection of the applications Apple included on the device. Users could, however "jailbreak" their device in order to unofficially multitask. Starting with iOS 4, on third-generation and newer iOS devices, multitasking is supported through seven background APIs:

- Background audio: Application continues to run in the background as long as it is playing audio or video content.

- Voice over IP: Application is suspended when a phone call is not in progress.

- Background location: Application is notified of location changes.

- Push notifications.

- Local notifications: Application schedules local notifications to be delivered at a predetermined time.

- Task completion: Application asks the system for extra time to complete a given task.

- Fast app switching: Application does not execute any code and may be removed from memory at any time.

In iOS 5, three new background APIs were introduced:

- Newsstand: Application can download content in the background to be ready for the user.

- External Accessory: Application communicates with an external accessory and shares data at regular intervals

- Bluetooth Accessory: Application communicates with a bluetooth accessory and shares data at regular intervals.

In iOS 7, Apple introduced a new multitasking feature, providing all apps with the ability to perform background updates. This feature prefers to update the user's most frequently used apps and prefers to use WiFi networks over a cellular network, without markedly reducing the device's battery life.

Switching Applications

In iOS 4.0 to iOS 6.x, double-clicking the home button activates the application switcher. A scrollable dock-like interface appears from the bottom, moving the contents of the screen up. Choosing an icon switches to an application. To the far left are icons which function as music controls, a rotation lock, and on iOS 4.2 and above, a volume controller.

With the introduction of iOS 7, double clicking the home button also activates the application switcher. However, unlike previous versions it displays screenshots of open applications on top of the icon and horizontal scrolling allows for browsing through previous apps, and it is possible to close applications by dragging them up, similar to how webOS handled multiple cards.

With the introduction of iOS 9, the application switcher received a significant visual change; whilst still retaining the card metaphor introduced in iOS 7, the application icon is smaller, and appears above the screenshot (which is now larger, due to the removal of "Recent and Favorite Contacts"), and each application "card" overlaps the other, forming a rolodex effect as the user scrolls. Now, instead of the home screen appearing at the leftmost of the application switcher, it appears rightmost. In iOS 11, the application switcher receives a major redesign. In the iPad, the Control Center and app switcher are combined. The app switcher in the iPad can also be accessed by swiping up from the bottom. In the iPhone, the app switcher cannot be accessed if there are no apps in the RAM.

Ending Tasks

In iOS 4.0 to iOS 6.x, briefly holding the icons in the application switcher makes them "jiggle" (similarly to the homescreen) and allows the user to *force* quit the applications by tapping the red minus circle that appears at the corner of the app's icon. Clearing applications from multitasking stayed the same from iOS 4.0 through 6.1.6, the last version of iOS 6.

As of iOS 7, the process has become faster and easier. In iOS 7, instead of holding the icons to close them, they are closed by simply swiping them upwards off the screen. Up to three apps can be cleared at a time compared to one in versions up to iOS 6.1.6.

Task Completion

Task completion allows apps to continue a certain task after the app has been suspended. As of iOS 4.0, apps can request up to ten minutes to complete a task in the background. This doesn't extend to background up- and downloads though (e.g. if you start a download in one application, it won't finish if you switch away from the application).

Siri

Siri is an intelligent personal assistant integrated into iOS. The assistant uses voice queries and a natural language user interface to answer questions, make recommendations, and perform actions by delegating requests to a set of Internet services. The software adapts to users' individual language usages, searches, and preferences, with continuing use. Returned results are individualized.

Originally released as an app for iOS in February 2010, it was acquired by Apple two months later, and then integrated into iPhone 4S at its release in October 2011. At that time, the separate app was also removed from the iOS App Store.

Siri supports a wide range of user commands, including performing phone actions, checking basic information, scheduling events and reminders, handling device settings, searching the Internet, navigating areas, finding information on entertainment, and is able to engage with iOS-integrated apps. With the release of iOS 10 in 2016, Apple opened up limited third-party access to Siri, including third-party messaging apps, as well as payments, ride-sharing, and Internet calling apps. With the release of iOS 11, Apple updated Siri's voices for more clear, human voices, it now supports follow-up questions and language translation, and additional third-party actions.

Game Center

Game Center is an online multiplayer "social gaming network" released by Apple. It allows users to "invite friends to play a game, start a multiplayer game through matchmaking, track their achievements, and compare their high scores on a leaderboard." iOS 5 and above adds support for profile photos.

Game Center was announced during an iOS 4 preview event hosted by Apple on April 8, 2010. A preview was released to registered Apple developers in August. It was released on September 8, 2010 with iOS 4.1 on iPhone 4, iPhone 3GS, and iPod Touch 2nd generation through 4th generation. Game Center made its public debut on the iPad with iOS 4.2.1. There is no support for the iPhone 3G, original iPhone and the first-generation iPod Touch (the latter two devices did not have Game Center because they did not get iOS 4). However, Game Center is unofficially available on the iPhone 3G via a hack.

Hardware

The main hardware platform for iOS is the ARM architecture. iOS releases before iOS 7 can only be run on iOS devices with 32-bit ARM processors (ARMv6 and ARMv7-A architectures). In 2013, iOS 7 was released with full 64-bit support (which includes native 64-bit kernel, libraries, drivers as well as all built-in applications), after Apple announced that they were switching to 64-bit ARMv8-A processors with the introduction of the Apple A7 chip. 64-bit support was also enforced for all apps in the App Store; All new apps submitted to the App Store with a deadline of February 2015, and all app up-dates submitted to the App Store with a deadline of June 1, 2015. iOS 11 drops support for all iOS devices with 32-bit ARM processors as well as 32-bit applications, making iOS 64-bit only.

Development

The iOS SDK (Software Development Kit) allows for the development of mobile apps on iOS.

While originally developing iPhone prior to its unveiling in 2007, Apple's then-CEO Steve Jobs did not intend to let third-party developers build native apps for iOS, in-stead directing them to make web applications for the Safari web browser. However, backlash from developers prompted the company to reconsider, with Jobs announcing in October 2007 that Apple would have a software development kit available for devel-opers by February 2008. The SDK was released on March 6, 2008.

The SDK is a free download for users of Mac personal computers. It is not available for Microsoft Windows PCs. The SDK contains sets giving developers access to various functions and services of iOS devices, such as hardware and software attributes. It also contains an iPhone simulator to mimic the look and feel of the device on the computer while developing. New versions of the SDK accompany new versions of iOS. In order to test applications, get technical support, and distribute apps through App Store, devel-opers are required to subscribe to the Apple Developer Program.

Combined with Xcode, the iOS SDK helps developers write iOS apps using officially supported programming languages, including Swift and Objective-C. Other companies have also created tools that allow for the development of native iOS apps using their respective programming languages.

Market Share

iOS is the second most popular mobile operating system in the world, after Android. Sales of iPads in recent years are also behind Android, while, by web use (a proxy for all use), iPads (using iOS) are still most popular.

By the middle of 2012, there were 410 million devices activated. At WWDC 2014, Tim Cook said 800 million devices had been sold by June 2014.

During Apple's quarterly earnings call in January 2015, the company announced that they had sold over one billion iOS devices since 2007.

By late 2011, iOS accounted for 60% of the market share for smartphones and tablets. By the end of 2014, iOS accounted for 14.8% of the smartphone market and 27.6% of the tablet and two-in-one market. In February 2015, StatCounter reported iOS was used on 23.18% of smartphones and 66.25% of tablets worldwide, measured by internet usage instead of sales.

In the third quarter of 2015, research from Strategy Analytics showed that iOS adoption of the worldwide smartphone market was at a record-low 12.1%, attributed to lackluster performance in China and Africa. Android accounted for 87.5% of the market, with Windows Phone and BlackBerry accounting for the rest.

Jailbreaking

Since its initial release, iOS has been subject to a variety of different hacks centered around adding functionality not allowed by Apple. Prior to the 2008 debut of Apple's native iOS App Store, the primary motive for jailbreaking was to bypass Apple's purchase mechanism for installing the App Store's native applications. Apple claimed that it will not release iOS software updates designed specifically to break these tools (other than applications that perform SIM unlocking); however, with each subsequent iOS update, previously un-patched jailbreak exploits are usually patched.

Since, the arrival of Apple's native iOS App Store, and—along with it—third-party applications, the general motives for jailbreaking have changed. People jailbreak for many different reasons, including gaining filesystem access, installing custom device themes, and modifying SpringBoard. An additional motivation is that it may enable the installation of pirated apps. On some devices, jailbreaking also makes it possible to install alternative operating systems, such as Android and the Linux kernel. Primarily, users jailbreak their devices because of the limitations of iOS. Depending on the method used, the effects of jailbreaking may be permanent or temporary.

In 2010, the Electronic Frontier Foundation (EFF) successfully convinced the U.S. Copyright Office to allow an exemption to the general prohibition on circumvention of copyright protection systems under the Digital Millennium Copyright Act (DMCA). The exemption allows jailbreaking of iPhones for the sole purpose of allowing legally obtained applications to be added to the iPhone. The exemption does not affect the contractual relations between Apple and an iPhone owner, for example, jailbreaking voiding the iPhone warranty; however, it is solely based on Apple's discretion on whether they will fix jailbroken devices in the event that they need to be repaired. At the same time, the Copyright Office exempted unlocking an iPhone from DMCA's anticircumvention prohibitions. Unlocking an iPhone allows the iPhone to be used with any wireless carrier using the same GSM or CDMA technology for which the particular phone model was designed to operate.

Unlocking

Initially most wireless carriers in the US did not allow iPhone owners to unlock it for use with other carriers. However AT&T allowed iPhone owners who have satisfied contract requirements to unlock their iPhone. Instructions to unlock the device are available from Apple, but it is ultimately the sole discretion of the carrier to authorize the device to be unlocked. This allows the use devices of a carrier-sourced iPhone on other networks. Modern versions of iOS and the iPhone fully support LTE across multiple carriers despite where the phone was originally purchased from. There are programs to remove SIM lock restrictions, but are not supported by Apple and most often not a permanent unlock – a soft-unlock.

Digital Rights Management

The closed and proprietary nature of iOS has garnered criticism, particularly by digital rights advocates such as the Electronic Frontier Foundation, computer engineer and activist Brewster Kahle, Internet-law specialist Jonathan Zittrain, and the Free Software Foundation who protested the iPad's introductory event and have targeted the iPad with their "Defective by Design" campaign. Competitor Microsoft, via a PR spokesman, criticized Apple's control over its platform.

At issue are restrictions imposed by the design of iOS, namely digital rights management (DRM) intended to lock purchased media to Apple's platform, the development model (requiring a yearly subscription to distribute apps developed for the iOS), the centralized approval process for apps, as well as Apple's general control and lockdown of the platform itself. Particularly at issue is the ability for Apple to remotely disable or delete apps at will.

Some in the tech community have expressed concern that the locked-down iOS represents a growing trend in Apple's approach to computing, particularly Apple's shift away from machines that hobbyists can "tinker with" and note the potential for such restrictions to stifle software innovation. Former Facebook developer Joe Hewitt protested against Apple's control over its hardware as a "horrible precedent" but praised iOS's sandboxing of apps.

Kernel

The iOS kernel is the XNU kernel of Dawin. The original iPhone OS (1.0) up to iPhone OS 3.1.3 used Darwin 9.0.0d1. iOS 4 was based on Darwin 10. iOS 5 was based on Darwin 11. iOS 6 was based on Darwin 13. iOS 7 and iOS 8 are based on Darwin 14. iOS 9 is based on Darwin 15. iOS 10 is based on Darwin 16. iOS 11 is based on Darwin 17. iOS 12 is based on Darwin 18.

Security

iOS utilizes many security features in both hardware and software. Below are summaries of the most prominent features.

Secure Boot

Before fully booting into iOS, there is low-level code that runs from the Boot ROM. Its task is to verify that the Low-Level Bootloader is signed by the Apple Root CA public key before running it. This process is to ensure that no malicious or otherwise unauthorized software can be run on an iOS device. After the Low-Level Bootloader finishes its tasks, it runs the higher level bootloader, known as iBoot. If all goes well, iBoot will then proceed to load the iOS kernel as well as the rest of the operating system.

Secure Enclave

The Secure Enclave is a coprocessor found in iOS devices that contain Touch ID or Face ID. It has its own secure boot process to ensure that it is completely secure. A hardware random number generator is also devices included as a part of this coprocessor. Each device's Secure Enclave has a unique ID that is given to it when it is made and cannot be changed. This identifier is used to create a temporary key that encrypts the memory in this portion of the system. The Secure Enclave also contains an anti-replay counter to prevent brute force attacks.

Passcode

iOS devices can have a passcode that is used to unlock the device, make changes to system settings, and encrypt the device's contents. Until recently, these were typically four numerical digits long. However, since unlocking the devices with a fingerprint by using Touch ID has become more widespread; six-digit passcodes are now the default on iOS with the option to switch back to four or use an alphanumeric passcode.

Touch ID

Touch ID is a fingerprint scanner that is embedded in the home button and can be used to unlock the device, make purchases, and log into applications among other functions. When used, Touch ID only temporarily stores the fingerprint data in encrypted memory in the Secure Enclave, as described above. There is no way for the device's main processor or any other part of the system to access the raw fingerprint data that is obtained from the Touch ID sensor.

Address Space Layout Randomization

Address Space Layout Randomization (ASLR) is a low-level technique of preventing memory corruption attacks such as buffer overflows. It involves placing data in randomly selected locations in memory in order to make it harder to predict ways to corrupt the system and create exploits. ASLR makes app bugs more likely to crash the app than to silently overwrite memory, regardless of whether the behavior is accidental or malicious.

Non-executable Memory

iOS utilizes the ARM architecture's Execute Never (XN) feature. This allows some portions of the memory to be marked as non-executable, working alongside ASLR to prevent buffer overflow attacks including return-to-libc attacks.

Encryption

One use of encryption in iOS is in the memory of the Secure Enclave. When a passcode is utilized on an iOS device, the contents of the device are encrypted. This is done by using a hardware AES 256 implementation that is very efficient because it is placed directly between the flash storage and RAM.

iOS, in combination with its specific hardware, uses crypto-shredding when erasing all content and settings by obliterating all the keys in 'effaceable storage'. This renders all user data on the device cryptographically inaccessible.

Keychain

The iOS keychain is a database of login information that can be shared across apps written by the same person or organization. This service is often used for storing passwords for web applications.

App Security

Third-party applications such as those distributed through the App Store must be code signed with an Apple-issued certificate. In principle, this continues the chain of trust all the way from the Secure Boot process as mentioned above to the actions of the applications installed on the device by users. Applications are also sandboxed, meaning that they can only modify the data within their individual home directory unless explicitly given permission to do otherwise. For example, they cannot access data that is owned by other user-installed applications on the device. There is a very extensive set of privacy controls contained within iOS with options to control apps' ability to access a wide variety of permissions such as the camera, contacts, background app refresh, cellular data, and access to other data and services. Most of the code in iOS, including third-party applications, runs as the "mobile" user which does not have root privileges. This ensures that system files and other iOS system resources remain hidden and inaccessible to user-installed applications.

App Store Bypasses

Companies can apply to Apple for enterprise developer certificates. These can be used to sign apps such that iOS will install them directly (sometimes called "sideloading"), without the app needing to be distributed via the App Store. The terms under which they are granted make clear that they are only to be used for companies who wish to distribute apps directly to their employees.

Circa January–February 2019, it emerged that a number of software developers were misusing enterprise developer certificates to distribute software directly to non-employees, thereby bypassing the App Store. Facebook was found to be abusing an Apple enterprise developer certificate to distribute an application to underage users that would give Facebook access to all private data on their devices. Google was abusing an Apple enterprise developer certificate to distribute an app to adults to collect data from their devices, including unencrypted data belonging to third parties. TutuApp, Panda Helper, AppValley, and TweakBox were abusing enterprise developer certificates to distribute apps that offered pirated software.

Network Security

iOS supports TLS with both low- and high-level APIs for developers. By default, the App Transport Security framework requires that servers use at least TLS 1.2. However, developers are free to override this framework and utilize their own methods of communicating over networks. When Wi-Fi is enabled, iOS uses a randomized MAC address so that devices cannot be tracked by anyone sniffing wireless traffic.

Two-Factor Authentication

Two-factor authentication is an option in iOS to ensure that even if an unauthorized person knows an Apple ID and password combination, they cannot gain access to the account. It works by requiring not only the Apple ID and password, but also a verification code that is sent to a device that is already known to be trusted. If an unauthorized user attempts to sign in using another user's Apple ID, the owner of the Apple ID receives a notification that allows them to deny access to the unrecognized device.

Android (Operating System)

Android is a Linux based operating system it is designed primarily for touch screen mobile devices such as smart phones and tablet computers.

The android is a powerful operating system and it supports large number of applications in Smartphones. These applications are more comfortable and advanced for the users. The hardware that supports android software is based on ARM architecture platform. The android is an open source operating system means that it's free and any one can use it. The android has got millions of apps available that can help you managing your life one or other way and it is available low cost in market at that reasons android is very popular.

The android development supports with the full java programming language. Even other packages that are API and JSE are not supported. The first version 1.0 of android development kit (SDK) was released in 2008 and latest updated version is jelly bean.

Android Architecture

The android is an operating system and is a stack of software components which is divided into five sections and four main layers that is:

- Linux kernel,

- Libraries,

- Android runtime.

Application Frame Work

Linux Kernel

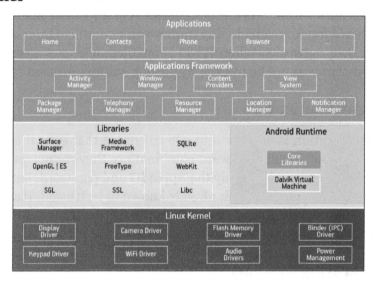

The android uses the powerful Linux kernel and it supports wide range of hardware drivers. The kernel is the heart of the operating system that manages input and output requests from software. This provides basic system functionalities like process management, memory management, basic mangement like camera, keypad, display etc the kernel handles all the things. The Linux is really good at networking and it is not necessary to interface it to the peripheral hardware. The kernel itself does not interact directly with the user but rather interacts with the shell and other programs as well as with the hard ware devices on the system.

Libraries

The on top of a Linux kennel there is a set of libraries including open source web browser such as webkit, library libc. These libraries are used to play and record audio and video. The SQLite is a data base which is useful for storage and sharing of application data. The SSL libraries are responsible for internet security etc.

Android Runtime

The android runtime provides a key component called Dalvik Virtual Machine which is a kind of java virtual machine. It is specially designed and optimized for android. The Dalvik VM is the process virtual machine in the android operating system. It is software that runs apps on android devices.

The Dalvik VM makes use of Linux core features like memory management and multithreading which is in a java language. The Dalvik VM enables every android application to run its own process. The Dalvik VM executes the files in the .dex format.

Application Frame Work

The application frame work layer provides many higher level services to applications such as windows manager, view system, package manager, resource manager etc. The application developers are allowed to make use of these services in their application.

Applications and Features

You will find all the android applications at the top layer and you will write your application and install on this layer. Example of such applications are contacts, books, browsers, services etc. Each application perform a different role in the overall applications.

Features:

- Head set layout,

- Storage,

- Connectivity: GSM/EDGE, IDEN, CDMA, Bluetooth, WI-FI, EDGE,3G,NFC, LTE,GPS,

- Messaging: SMS, MMS, C2DM (could to device messaging), GCM (Google could messaging),

- Multilanguage support,

- Multi touch,

- Video calling,

- Screen capture,

- External storage,

- Streaming media support,

- Optimized graphics.

Android Emulator

The Emulator is a new application in android operating system. The emulator is a new prototype that is used to develop and test android applications without using any physical device.

The android emulator has all of the hardware and software features like mobile device except phone calls. It provides a variety of navigation and control keys. It also provides a screen to display your application. The emulators utilize the android virtual device configurations. Once your application is running on it, it can use services of the android platform to help other applications, access the network, play audio, video, store and retrieve the data.

Application of Android- Android Application Controlled Remote Robot

Operation

It controls the robotic vehicle using an android application. The Bluetooth device is interfaced to control unit on the robot for sensing the signals transmitted by the android application. The remote operation is achieved by any smart-phone or table etc. with android OS based on touch screen operation. The transmitting end uses an android application device remote through which commands are transmitted and at the receiver side , these commands are used for controlling the robot in all directions such as forward, backward and left or right etc.

The receiver end movement is achieved by two motors that are interfaced to the micro-controller. The serial communication data sent from the android application is received by a Bluetooth receiver that is interfaced to the microcontroller.

Advantages

- Android is Linux based open source operating system, it can be developed by any one.

- Easy access to the android apps.

- You can replace the battery and mass storage, disk drive and UDB option.

- Its supports all Google services.

- The operating system is able to inform you of a new SMS and Emails or latest updates.

- It supports Multitasking.

- Android phone can also function as a router to share internet.

- It's free to customize.

- Can install a modified ROM.

- Its supports 2D and 3D graphics.

Serial Processing Operating System

The Serial Processing Operating Systems are those which Performs all the instructions into a sequence manner or the instructions those are given by the user will be executed by using the FIFO manner means first in first out. All the instructions those are entered first in the system will be executed first and the instructions those are entered later will be executed later. For running the instructions the Program Counter is used which is used for executing all the instructions.

In this the program counter will determines which instruction is going to execute and the which instruction will be execute after this. Mainly the punch cards are used for this. In this all the jobs are firstly prepared and stored on the card and after that card will be entered in the system and after that all the instructions will be executed one by one. But the main problem is that a user doesn't interact with the system while he is working on the system, means the user can't be able to enter the data for execution.

Batch Processing Operating System

The batch processing operating systems were introduced to avoid the problems of early systems. The problem of early systems was more setup time. So the problem of more set up time was reduced by processing the jobs in batches, known as batch processing system. In this approach similar jobs were submitted to the CPU for processing and were run together.

The main function of a batch processing system is to automatically keep executing the jobs in a batch. This is the important task of a batch processing system i.e. performed by the 'Batch Monitor' resided in the low end of main memory.

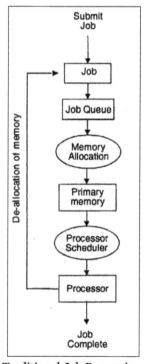

Traditional Job Processing.

This technique was possible due to the invention of hard-disk drives and card readers. Now the jobs could be stored on the disk to create the pool of jobs for its execution as a batch. First the pooled jobs are read and executed by the batch monitor, and then these jobs are grouped; placing the identical jobs (jobs with the similar needs) in the same batch, So, in the batch processing system, the batched jobs were executed automatically one after another saving its time by performing the activities (like loading of compiler) only for once. It resulted in improved system utilization due to reduced turnaround time.

In the early job processing systems, the jobs were placed in a job queue and the memory allocator managed the primary memory space, when space was available in the main memory, a job was selected from the job queue and was loaded into memory.

Once the job loaded into primary memory, it competes for the processor. When the processor became available, the processor scheduler selects job that was loaded in the memory and execute it.

In batch strategy is implemented to provide a batch file processing. So in this approach files of the similar batch are processed to speed up the task.

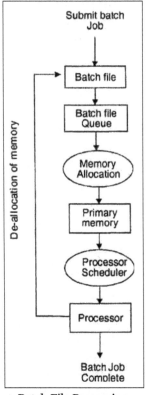

Batch File Processing.

In batch processing the user were supposed to prepare a program as a deck of punched cards. The header cards in the deck were the "job control" cards which would indicate that which compiler was to be used (like FORTRAN, COBOL compilers etc). The deck of cards would be handed in to an operator who would collect such jobs from various users. Then the submitted jobs were grouped as FORTRAN jobs, COBOL jobs etc. In addition, these jobs were classified as 'long jobs' that required more processing time or short jobs which required a short processing time. Each set of jobs was considered as a batch and the processing would be done for a batch. For instance, there may be a batch of short FORTRAN jobs. The output for each job would be separated and turned over to users in a collection area. So in this approach, files of the similar batch were processed to speed up the task.

In this environment there was no interactivity and the users had no direct control. In this system, only one job could engage the processor at a time and if there was any input/ output operation the processor had to sit idle till the completion of I/O job. So, it resulted to the underutilization of CPU time.

In batch processing system, earlier; the jobs were scheduled in the order of their arrival i.e. First Come First Served (FCFS).Even though this scheduling method was easy and simple to implement but unfair for the situations where long jobs are queued ahead of the short jobs. To overcome this problem, another scheduling method named as 'Shortest Job First' was used. As memory manaement is concerned, the main memory was partitioned into two fixed partitions. The lower end of this partition was assigned to the resident portion of the OS i.e. named as Batch Monitor. Whereas, the other partition (higher end) was assigned to the user programs.

Though, it was an improved technique in reducing the system setup time but still there were some limitations with this technique like as under-utilization of CPU time, non-interactivity of user with the running jobs etc. In batch processing system, the jobs of a batch were executed one after another. But while these jobs were performing I/O operations; meantime the CPU was sitting idle resulting to low degree of resource utilization.

Time Sharing Operating System

A time sharing system allows many users to share the computer resources simultaneously. In other words, time sharing refers to the allocation of computer resources in time slots to several programs simultaneously. For example a mainframe computer that has many users logged on to it. Each user uses the resources of the mainframe i.e., memory, CPU etc. The users feel that they are exclusive user of the CPU, even though this is not possible with one CPU i.e., shared among different users.

The time sharing systems were developed to provide an interactive use of the computer system. A time shared system uses CPU scheduling and multiprogramming to provide each user with a small portion of a time-shared computer. It allows many users to share the computer resources simultaneously. As the system switches rapidly from one user to the other, a short time slot is given to each user for their executions.

The time sharing system provides the direct access to a large number of users where CPU time is divided among all the users on scheduled basis. The OS allocates a set of time to each user. When this time is expired, it passes control to the next user on the system. The time allowed is extremely small and the users are given the impression that they each have their own CPU and they are the sole owner of the CPU. This short period of time during that a user gets attention of the CPU; is known as a time slice or a quantum. The concept of time sharing system is shown in figure.

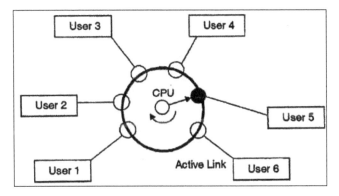

In above figure the user 5 is active but user 1, user 2, user 3, and user 4 are in waiting state whereas user 6 is in ready status.

As soon as the time slice of user 5 is completed, the control moves on to the next ready user i.e. user 6. In this state user 2, user 3, user 4, and user 5 are in waiting state and user 1 is in ready state. The process continues in the same way and so on.

The time-shared systems are more complex than the multi-programming systems. In time-shared systems multiple processes are managed simultaneously which requires an adequate management of main memory so that the processes can be swapped in or swapped out within a short time.

Network Operating System

Network Operating System is an operating system that includes special functions for connecting computers and devices into a local-area network (LAN) or Inter-network. Short form of Network Operating system is NOS. Some popular network operating systems are Novell Netware, Windows NT/2000, Linux, Sun Solaris, UNIX, and IBM OS/2. The network operating system which was first developed is Novell Netware. It was developed in 1983.

An operating system that provides the connectivity among a number of autonomous computers is called a network operating system. A typical configuration for a network operating system is a collection of personal computers along with a common printer, server and file server for archival storage, all tied together by a local network.

Some of the features of Network Operating System are to:

- It allows multiple computers to connect so that they can share data, files and hardware devices.

- Provide basic operating system features such as support for processors, protocols, automatic hardware detection and support multi-processing of applications.

- Provide security features such as authentication, logon restrictions and access control.

- Provide name and directory services.

- Provide file, print, web services and back-up services.

- Support Internetworking such as routing and WAN ports.

- User management and support for logon and logoff, remote access; system management, administration and auditing tools with graphical interfaces.

- It has clustering capabilities.

- It has internetworking features. Example: Routing.

- In this, the users can remotely access each other.

- It also includes security features. Example: Authentication of data, restrictions on required data, authorisations of users etc.

- It can also manage directory and name services.

- It also provides basic network administration utilities like access to the user.

- It also provides priority to the printing jobs which are in the queue in the network.

- It detects the new hardware whenever it is added to the system.

Types of Network Operating Systems

Peer-to-peer network operating systems allow users to share resources and files located on their computers and to access shared resources found on other computers. In a peer-to-peer network, all computers are considered equal; they all have the same privileges to use the resources available on the network. Peer-to-peer networks are designed primarily for small to medium local area networks. Windows for Workgroups is an example of the program that can function as peer-to-peer network operating systems.

Advantages of Peer-to-Peer(P2P) Operating System are as follows:

- Less requirement of hardware is there.

- No server needs to be established.

- Its setup process is natural.

Disadvantages of Peer-to-Peer(P2P) Operating System are as follows:

- It has no central location for storage, i.e. different systems have different storage capacity.

- It has less security as compared to the client-server model.

Client/server network operating systems allow the network to centralise functions and applications in one or more dedicated file servers. The file servers become the heart of the system, providing access to resources and providing security. The workstations (clients) have access to the resources available on the file servers. The network operating system allows multiple users to share the same resources irrespective of physical location simultaneously. Novell Netware and Windows 2000 Server are examples of client/ server network operating systems.

Each computer in the workgroup run an autonomous operating system; yet cooperate to allow a variety of facilities including sharing of files, sharing of hardware resources and execution of remote machines etc.

Network operating systems are implementations of loosely coupled operating systems on top of loosely coupled hardware. Network operating/systems is the software that supports the use of a network of machines and provides users that are aware of using a set of computers, with facilities designed to ease the use of remote resources located over the network. These resources are made available as services and might be printers, processors, file systems or other devices. Some resources, of which dedicated hardware devices such as printers, tape drives are connected to and managed by a particular machine and are made available to other machines in the network via a service. A typical example of such a system is a set of workstations connected through a local area network (LAN). Every workstation has its operating system every user has its workstation in exclusive use and cooperates to allow a variety of facilities including sharing of files, sharing of hardware resources and execution of remote machines etc. A user can execute a login command to connect to another station and also can access a set of shared files maintained by a workstation named/ file server.

Advantages of Client Server Operating System are as follows:

- In this, security to the machines is provided through the server.

- Here, hardware can be easily connected to the system.

- Also, new technology is easily integrated into the system.

- The central server is more stable in a client-server model.

- Hardware and the operating system can be specialised.

- In this model, different machines can remotely access the server from different locations.

Disadvantages Client Server Operating System are as follows:

- It seems to be costly as buying and running a server is cost effective.

- Also, here we always have to depend on the central location for any type of operation like for storage, for accessing of data etc.

- It requires regular maintenance.

- Daily updating is required as per requirement.

Distributed Operating System

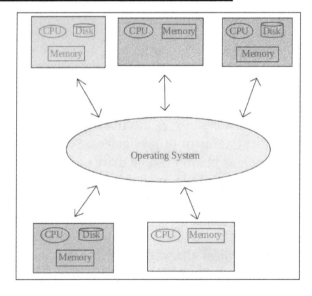

These types of operating system is a recent advancement in the world of computer technology and are being widely accepted all-over the world and, that too, with a great pace.

Various autonomous interconnected computers communicate each other using a shared communication network. Independent systems possess their own memory unit and CPU. These are referred as loosely coupled systems or distributed systems. These system's processors differ in size and function. The major benefit of working with these types of operating system is that it is always possible that one user can access the files or software which are not actually present on his system but on some other system connected within this network i.e., remote access is enabled within the devices connected in that network.

Advantages of Distributed Operating System

- Failure of one will not affect the other network communication, as all systems are independent from each other.

- Electronic mail increases the data exchange speed.

- Since resources are being shared, computation is highly fast and durable.

- Load on host computer reduces.

- These systems are easily scalable as many systems can be easily added to the network.

- Delay in data processing reduces.

Disadvantages of Distributed Operating System

- Failure of the main network will stop the entire communication.

- To establish distributed systems the language which are used are not well defined yet.

- These types of systems are not readily available as they are very expensive. Not only that the underlying software is highly complex and not understood well yet.

Examples of Distributed Operating System are- LOCUS etc.

Multiprocessor Operating System

Multiprocessor operating systems are the server operating systems with special features for the communication and the connectivity. Multiprocessor operating systems are used where multiple CPUs connected into a single system.

Multiprocessor operating system (OS) is almost a regular OS as they also handle system calls, do memory management, provide file system, and also manage input/output devices.

But, there are some extra features available in multiprocessor operating systems, those extra features are listed below:

- Process synchronization,

- Resource management,

- Scheduling.

Here is the list of some various organizations of multiprocessor operating systems:

- Each CPU has its own OS,

- Master-Slave multiprocessors,

- Symmetric multiprocessors.

Each CPU has its own OS

To statically divide the memory into as many partitions as there are central processing units and given central processing unit its own private memory and its own private copy of the OS is basically the simplest way to organize a multiprocessor OS or multi-processor operating system.

Master-Slave Multiprocessors

The master-slave models basically solve almost all the problems of the first model. In this model, there is a single data structure that keeps track of ready processes. Now, when a central processing unit goes idle in this model, then it asks the OS for a process to run and it is assigned one.

Symmetric Multiprocessors

Symmetric multiprocessors (SMP) is the third model. In this model, there is one copy of the OS in memory, but any central processing unit can run it.

Now, when a system call is made, then the central processing unit on which the system call was made traps to the kernel and then processes that system call.

This model balances processes and memory dynamically.

Parallel Processing Systems

Parallel Processing Systems are designed to speed up the execution of programs by dividing the program into multiple fragments and processing these fragments simultaneously. Such systems are multiprocessor systems also known as tightly coupled systems. Parallel systems deal with the simultaneous use of multiple computer resources that can include a single computer with multiple processors, a number of computers connected by a network to form a parallel processing cluster or a combination of both.

Parallel computing is an evolution of serial computing where the jobs are broken into discrete parts that can be executed concurrently. Each part is further broken down to a series of instructions. Instructions from each part execute simultaneously on different CPUs.

Parallel systems are more difficult to program than computers with a single processor because the architecture of parallel computers varies accordingly and the processes of multiple CPUs must be coordinated and synchonized. Several models for connecting processors and memory modules exist, and each topology requires a different programming model. The three models that are most commonly used in building parallel computers include synchronous processors each with its own memory, asynchronous processors each with its own memory and asynchronous processors with a common, shared memory. Flynn has classified the computer systems based on parallelism in the instructions and in the data streams. These are:

- Single instruction stream, single data stream (SISD).

- Single instruction stream, multiple data stream (SIMD).

- Multiple instruction streams, single data stream (MISD).

- Multiple instruction stream, multiple data stream (MIMD).

The above classification of parallel computing system is focused in terms of two independent factors: the number of data streams that can be simultaneously processed, and the number of instruction streams that can be simultaneously processed. Here 'instruction stream' we mean an algorithm that instructs the computer what to do whereas 'data stream' (i.e. input to an algorithm) we mean the data that are being operated upon.

Even though Flynn has classified the computer 'systems into four types based on parallelism but only two of them are relevant to parallel computers. These are SIMD and MIMD computers.

SIMD computers are consisting of 'n' processing units receiving a single stream of instruction from a central control unit and each processing unit operates on a different piece of data. Most SIMD computers operate synchronously using a single global dock. The block diagram of SIMD computer is shown below.

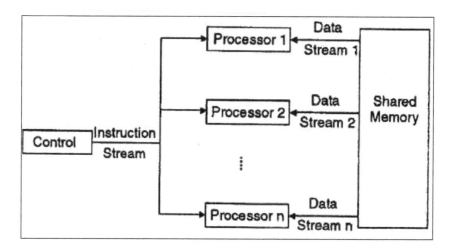

MIMD computers are consisting of 'n' processing units; each with its own stream of instruction and each processing unit operate on unit operates on a different piece of data. MIMD is the most powerful computer system that covers the range of multiprocessor systems. The block diagram of MIMD computer is shown.

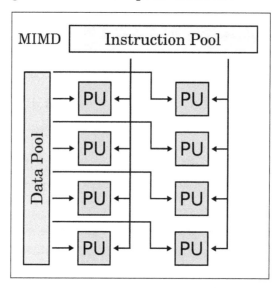

The SIMD systems are easier to program because it deals with single thread of execution. On the hand, the MIMD machines are more efficient because you can utilize the full machine power.

Parallel operating systems are primarily concerned with managing the resources of parallel machines. A parallel computer is a set of processors that are able to work cooperatively to solve a computational problem. So, a parallel computer may be a supercomputer with hundreds or thousands of processors or may be a network of workstations.

A few years ago, parallel computers could be found only in research laboratories and they were used mainly for computation intensive applications like numerical simulations of complex systems. Today, there are a lot of parallel computers available in the market; used to execute both data intensive applications in commerce and computation intensive applications in science and engineering.

Today, new applications arise and demand faster computers. Commercial applications are the most used on parallel computers. A computer that runs such an application; should be able to process large amount in data of sophisticated ways. These applications include graphics, virtual reality, and decision support, parallel databases, medicine diagnosis and so on. We can say with no doubt that commercial applications will define future parallel computers architecture but scientific applications will remain important users of parallel computing technology.

Concurrency becomes a fundamental requirement for algorithms and programs. A program has to be able to use a variable number of processors and also has to be able to run on multiple processors computer architecture. According to Tanenbaum, a distributed system is a set of independent computers that appear to the user like a single one. So, the computers have to be independent and the software has to hide individual computers to the users. MIMD computers and workstations connected through LAN and WAN are examples of distributed systems. The main difference between parallel systems and distributed systems is the way in which these systems are used. A parallel system uses a set of processing units to solve a single problem. A distributed system is used by many users together.

Real Time Operating System (RTOS)

A Real Time Operating System (RTOS) is an operating system developed for real-time embedded applications evolved around processors or controllers. It allows priorities to be changed instantly and data to be processed rapidly enough that the results may be used in response to another process taking place at the same time, as in transaction processing. It has the ability to immediately respond in a predetermined and predictable way to external events. Overall a mode of action and reaction by RTOS and application software handles the entire embedded application.

Let us consider the role of RTOS in the mobile phone. A cell phone has several features like call processing, notifying a waiting call, maintain a phone directory, messages and other utilities like web browsers, calculator, games, apps etc. RTOS handles each of these features as a separate task. Suppose a user is playing game on his cell phone and a call arrives, immediately the caller's ID starts flashing on the screen. After completion of the call, the user can resume the game from the level/ point it has got suspended. It is observed that in this case RTOS handled the tasks using priorities and performed multitasking using context switching and scheduler.

Embedded Operating Systems

An embedded operating system is simply an operating system designed for embedded systems. The main characteristics of the embedded operating system are resource efficiency and reliability. The existence of embedded operating system comes into existence because we have a very limited amount of hardware like RAM, ROM, timer-counters and other on-chip peripherals.

So, in this case, we need some operating system that can manage all the hardware resource by leaving some unimportant features. Embedded systems generally have Real Time Operating System (RTOS) to perform the task in a given time frame.

The hardware in the embedded systems depends on the application need. So some time for getting the best results we need to customize the embedded operating system.

As we know the assembly language is more near to hardware and code are written in assembly perform better. So sometime to get the better result and speed some code or modules are programmed in assmbly language. To get the response from the system.

The embedded operating systems are generally written in the c language because c language can interact better with the hardware.

Stand-Alone Operating System

The operating system that you have used in your laptop and desktop computing. They are totally designed to use that single machine. Even it has a network capability but its main purpose is to take care of all the hardware resources of the existing system. This is called stand-alone operating system.

Stand-Alone Operating System Example

- Windows 95,

- Windows NT Workstation,

- Windows 98,

- Windows 2000 Professional,

- Windows Millennium Edition,

- Windows XP Home Edition,

- Windows XP Professional Edition,

- Windows 7, 8 & 10,

- Mac OS,

- OS/2 Warp Client,

- UNIX,

- Linux.

Types of Embedded Operating Systems

- Single System Control Loop.

- Multi-Tasking Operating System.

- Rate Monotonic Operating System.

- Preemptive Operating System.

- Real-Time Operating System.

Single System Control Loop

This is the very basic type of operating system that performs only a single function at a time. This is still not clear that such a simple operating system could be an embedded operating system. Because generally operating systems perform multiple tasks to manage the system resource.

Multi-Tasking Operating System

This type of operating system can perform multiple tasks at a time. The multiple tasks can run simultaneously. The operating system can keep track of each task and can switch between it without losing the information.

In multitasking actually, the overall time of a problem is divided into small tasks. Each divided subtask gets the CPU time based on a fixed interval.

Only current executing process get the entire CPU time. The remaining task executing in a virtual environment. Where they get a register, program counter (PC), stack memory and a stack pointer. The task is excuting in a virtual environment. This all goes in runtime. When a higher priority task is coming to the currently executing task is saved into memory.

Rate Monotonic Operating System

In this type of operating system, a rate monotonic priority algorithm is used in real-time operating systems (RTOS). It is a priority-based scheduling algorithm. In this operating system, the scheduling is preemptive. Means the task gets interrupted or suspended by another task with a short period.

The execution time of the task is set in such a way that all task gets an equal amount of execution time or at least the task get the chance to execute when it is expected to run. This type of operating system always gives the shorter task a higher priority.

Preemptive Operating System

In this type of operating system, the currently executing task may be interrupted by the other higher priority task and can be resumed later.

The system has a scheduler that receives the interrupt that is received from the external calls. Once the interrupt is received scheduler pause the runing task and start the higher priority task. The control of the CPU passes from one task to another. This is called preemption. The main concept here is to manage the higher priority task that is more important and critical.

Features of Embedded Operating Systems

Real-Time Operation

Real-time embedded systems have a time constrained to execute the task. This time is called a deadline. The soft-real-time system may vary the deadline. But the hard real-time system must complete the task in a given time frame.

Soft-Real-Time System

The example of the soft-real-time system could be our day to day lifer products like washing machine, microwave oven, printer and fax machine. Let's suppose we are cooking something. We put some item to cook. We set a time and temperature. As soon as we press the start button of the oven it takes some random time to start to suppose 15sec. Even after a 15sec delay, it cooked perfectly, nothing went wrong in cooking. It missed the time by approx 15sec. This is generally happening in the soft real-time system.

Hard-Real-Time System

There is some application where the systems should act in a given time otherwise some went wrong or action is not acceptable.

Like in a traffic light controller, the timing of different signals should be running in a mentioned time in the program. The variation in time is not acceptable because something wrong may happen.

In essence, the deadline is fixed according to the system application. And to make the system time critical we pause other less important tasks so the main priority task can execute on time.

Reactive Operation

A system is called reactive if it acts on certain input by the user in the form of switch press or by some sensor. For example, a motion sensor security sensor triggers the alarm when someone comes in the range of the sensor. Here system is reacting based on the sensor input.

Configurability

As we know that embedded systems are designed as per the application requirement. And according to the hardware we need to customize the embedded operating system. So the operating system should be designed in such a way that an embedded developer can configure the operating system as per the need.

In some operating system facility of conditional compilation is available. Where the developer compiles the only required module from the overall modules. And it is best suitable if we are using the object-oriented approach.

I/O Device Flexibility

There is no generalise hardware that is suitable or adjustable for all operating system versions.

Direct use of Interrupts

The embedded operating system provides the use of interrupts to give them more control over the peripheral. The general purpose operating system does not provide such kind of facility to the user directly.

In the embedded system we need more control on the individual hardware so there is the demand of the interrupts. The interrupt also has the priority. And according to that priority, the task is serviced by the CPU.

Fast and Lightweight

As the embedded systems have small CPU with limited processing power. It should be customised perfectly so that it can execute fast.

It the embedded system developer task to understand the existing hardware and remove the unwanted software modules at the time of compilation. This will give a lightweight operating system results a faster execution speed.

Small Size

The size is every time considered in an embedded system. Because it has very limited resources like RAM, ROM and CPU power. So keep the embedded operating system small as possible to fit into given memory space.

Embedded Operating Systems Applications

Once the embedded operating system is compiled it can be used in a variety of application. The list is for mobile using the embedded operating system.

- Symbian,

- Embedded Linux,

- Palm OS,

- Windows Mobile,

- iOS,

- BlackBerry OS.

References

- Mobile-operating-systems-and-application-development-platforms-a-survey: researchgate.net, Retrieved 14 July, 2019

- Juli clover (november 18, 2019). "apple releases ios and ipados 13.2.3 with bug fixes for messages, mail and more". Macrumors. Retrieved november 18,2019

- Saylor, michael (2012). The mobile wave: how mobile intelligence will change everything. Vanguard press. P. 33. Isbn 1-59315-720-7

- What-is-android-introduction-features-applications: elprocus.com, Retrieved 11 January, 2019

- Types-of-operating-system, disk-operating-system, fundamental: ecomputernotes.com, Retrieved 18 April, 2019

- Time-sharing-operating-system, disk-operating-system, fundamental: ecomputernotes.com, Retrieved 27 May, 2019

- Types-of-operating-systems: geeksforgeeks.org, Retrieved 21 July, 2019

- Multiprocessor-operating-system, operating-system: codescracker.com, Retrieved 13 July, 2019

Distributed Operating System

The system which runs distributed applications on multiple computers linked by communications is termed as distributed operating system. It has five different architectural styles namely layered architecture, object based architecture, data-centered architecture, event based architecture and hybrid architecture. This chapter discusses in detail these different styles of distributed operating system.

Distributed Operating System is a model where distributed applications are running on multiple computers linked by communications. A distributed operating system is an extension of the network operating system that supports higher levels of communication and integration of the machines on the network.

This system looks to its users like an ordinary centralized operating system but runs on multiple, independent central processing units (CPUs).

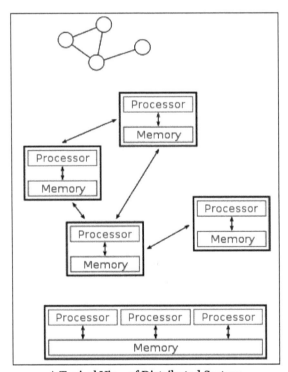

A Typical View of Distributed System.

These systems are referred as loosely coupled systems where each processor has its own local memory and processors communicate with one another through various communication lines, such as high speed buses or telephone lines. By loosely coupled systems, we mean that such computers possess no hardware connections at the CPU - memory bus level, but are connected by external interfaces that run under the control of software.

The Distributed Os involves a collection of autonomous computer systems, capable of communicating and cooperating with each other through a LAN / WAN. A Distributed Os provides a virtual machine abstraction to its users and wide sharing of resources like as computational capacity, I/O and files etc.

The structure shown in fig contains a set of individual computer systems and workstations connected via communication systems, but by this structure we cannot say it is a distributed system because it is the software, not the hardware, that determines whether a system is distributed or not.

The users of a true distributed system should not know, on which machine their programs are running and where their files are stored. LOCUS and MICROS are the best examples of distributed operating systems.

Using LOCUS operating system it was possible to access local and distant files in uniform manner. This feature enabled a user to log on any node of the network and to utilize the resources in a network without the reference of his/her location. MICROS provided sharing of resources in an automatic manner. The jobs were assigned to different nodes of the whole system to balance the load on different nodes.

Below given are some of the examples of distributed operating systems:

- IRIX operating system; is the implementation of UNIX System V, Release 3 for Silicon Graphics multiprocessor workstations.

- DYNIX operating system running on Sequent Symmetry multiprocessor computers.

- AIX operating system for IBM RS/6000 computers.

- Solaris operating system for SUN multiprocessor workstations.

- Mach/OS is a multithreading and multitasking UNIX compatible operating system.

- OSF/1 operating system developed by Open Foundation Software: UNIX compatible.

Distributed systems provide the following advantages:

- Sharing of resources,

- Reliability,

- Communication,

- Computation speedup.

Distributed systems are potentially more reliable than a central system because if a system has only one instance of some critical component, such as a CPU, disk, or network interface, and that component fails, the system will go down. When there are multiple instances, the system may be able to continue in spite of occasional failures. In addition to hardware failures, one can also consider software failures. Distributed systems allow both hardware and software errors to be dealt with.

A distributed system is a set of computers that communicate and collaborate each other using software and hardware interconnecting components. Multiprocessors (MIMD computers using shared memory architecture), multi-computers connected through static or dynamic interconnection networks (MIMD computers using message passing architecture) and workstations connected through local area network are examples of such distributed systems.

A distributed system is managed by a distributed operating system. A distributed operating system manages the system shared resources used by multiple processes, the process scheduling activity (how processes are allocating on available processors), the communication and synchronization between running processes and so on. The software for parallel computers could be also tightly coupled or loosely coupled. The loosely coupled software allows computers and users of a distributed system to be independent each other but having a limited possibility to cooperate. An example of such a system is a group of computers connected through a local network. Every computer has its own memory, hard disk. There are some shared resources such files and printers. If the interconnection network broke down, individual computers could be used but without some features like printing to a non-local printer.

Amoeba Distributed Operating System

Amoeba is a general-purpose distributed operating system. It is designed to take a collection of machines and make them act together as a single integrated system. In general, users are not aware of the number and location neither of the processors that run their commands, nor of the number and location of the file servers that store their files. To the casual user, an Amoeba system looks like a single old-fashioned time-sharing system.

Amoeba is an ongoing research project. It should be thought of as a platform for doing research and development in distributed and parallel systems, languages, protocols and applications. Although it provides some UNIX emulation, and has a definite UNIX-like flavor (including over 100 UNIX-like utilities), it is NOT a plug-compatible replacement for UNIX. It should be of interest to educators and researchers who want the source code of a distributed operating system to inspect and tinker with, as well as to those who need a base to run distributed and parallel applications.

Amoeba is intended for both "distributed" computing (multiple independent users working on different projects) and "parallel" computing (e.g., one user using 50 CPUs to play chess in parallel). Amoeba provides the necessary mechanism for doing both distributed and parallel applications, but the policy is entirely determined by user-level programs. For example, both a traditional (i.e. sequential) 'make' and a new parallel 'amake' are supplied.

Design Goals

The basic design goals of Amoeba are:

- Distribution: Connecting together many machines.

- Parallelism: Allowing individual jobs to use multiple CPUs easily.

- Transparency: Having the collection of computers act like a single system.

- Performance: Achieving all of the above in an efficient manner.

Amoeba is a distributed system, in which multiple machines can be connected together. These machines need not all be of the same kind. The machines can be spread around a building on a LAN. Amoeba uses the high performance FLIP network protocol for LAN communication. If an Amoeba machine has more than one network interface it will automatically act as a FLIP router between the various networks and thus connect the various LANs together.

Amoeba is also a parallel system. This means that a single job or program can use multiple processors to gain speed. For example, a branch and bound problem such as the Traveling Salesman Problem can use tens or even hundreds of CPUs, if available, all working together to solve the problem more quickly. Large "back end" multiprocessors, for example, can be harnessed this way as big "compute engines."

Another key goal is transparency. The user need not know the number or the location of the CPUs, nor the place where the files are stored. Similarly, issues like file replication are handled largely automatically, without manual intervention by the users.

Put in different terms, a user does not log into a specific machine, but into the system as a whole. There is no concept of a "home machine." Once logged in, the user does not have to give special remote login commands to take advantage of multiple processors or do special remote mount operations to access distant files. To the user, the whole system looks like a single conventional timesharing system.

Performance and reliability are always key issues in operating systems, so substantial effort has gone into dealing with them. In particular, the basic communication mechanism has been optimized to allow messages to be sent and replies received with a minimum of delay, and to allow large blocks of data to be shipped from machine to machine at high bandwidth. These building blocks serve as the basis for implementing high performance subsystems and applications on Amoeba.

System Architecture

Since distributed and parallel computing is different from personal computing, it is worthwhile first describing the kind of hardware configuration for which Amoeba was designed. A typical Amoeba system will consist of three functional classes of machines:

- First, each user has a workstation for running the user interface, the X window system. This workstation can be a typical engineering workstation, or a specialized X terminal. It is entirely dedicated to running the user interface, and does not have to do other computing.

- Second, there exists a pool of processors that are dynamically allocated to users as required. These processors can be part of a multiprocessor or multicomputer, be a collection of single-board computers or be a group of workstations allocated for this purpose. Usually, each pool processor has several megabytes of private memory, that is, pool processors need not have any shared memory (but it is not forbidden). Communication is performed by sending packets over the LAN. All the heavy computing happens in the processor pool.

- Third, there are specialized servers, such as file servers and directory servers that run all the time. They may run on processor pool processors, or on dedicated hardware, as desired.

All these components must be connected by a fast LAN. At present only Ethernet is supported, but ports to other LANs are possible.

Fundamental Concepts in Amoeba

Microkernel + Server Architecture

Amoeba was designed with what is currently termed a microkernel architecture. This means that every machine in an Amoeba system runs a small, identical piece of software called the kernel. The kernel supports the basic process, communication, and object primitives. It also handles raw device I/O and memory management. Everything else is built on top of these fundamentals, usually by user-space server processes.

Thus, the system is structured as a collection of independent processes. Some of these are user processes, running application programs. Such processes are called clients. Others are server processes, such as the Bullet file server or the directory server. The basic function of the microkernel is to provide an environment in which clients and servers can run and communicate with one another.

This modular design makes it easier to understand, maintain, and modify the system. For example, since the file server is an isolated server, rather than being an integral part of the operating system, it is possible for users to implement new file servers for specialized purposes (e.g. NFS, database). In conventional systems, such as UNIX, adding additional user-defined file systems is infeasible.

Threads

In many traditional operating systems, a process consists of an address space and a single thread of control. In Amoeba, each process has its own address space, but it may contain multiple "threads of control" (threads). Each thread has its own program counter and its own stack, but shares code and global data with all the other threads in its process.

Having multiple threads inside each process is convenient for many purposes and fits into the model of distributed and parallel computing very well. For example, a file server may have multiple threads, each thread initially waiting for a request to come in. When a request comes in, it is accepted by some thread, which then begins processing it. If that thread subsequently blocks waiting for disk I/O, other threads can continue. Despite their independent control, however, all the threads can access a common block cache, using semaphores to provide inter-thread synchronization. This design makes programming servers and parallel applications much easier.

Not only are user processes structured as collections of threads communicating by RPC, but the kernel is as well. In particular, threads in the kernel provide access to memory management services.

Remote Procedure Call

Threads often need to communicate with one another. Threads within a single process can just communicate via the shared memory, but threads located in different processes need a different mechanism. The basic Amoeba communication mechanism is the remote procedure call (RPC). Communication consists of a client thread sending a message to a server thread, then blocking until the server thread sends back a return message, at which time the client is unblocked.

To shield the naive user from these details, special library procedures, called stubs, are provided to access remote services. Amoeba has a special language called Amoeba Interface Language (AIL) for automatically generating these stub procedures. They marshal parameters and hide the details of the communication from the users.

Group Communication

For many applications, one-to-many communication is needed, in which a single sender wants to send a message to multiple receivers. For example, a group of cooperating servers may need to do this when a data structure is updated. It is also frequently needed for parallel programming. Amoeba provides a basic facility for reliable, totally-ordered group communication, in which all receivers are guaranteed to get all group messages in exactly the same order. This mechanism simplifies many distributed and parallel programming problems.

Objects and Capabilities

There are two fundamental concepts in Amoeba: objects and capabilities. All services and communication are built around them.

An object is conceptually an abstract data type. That is, an object is a data structure on which certain operations are defined. For example, a directory is an object to which certain operations can be applied, such as "enter name" and "look up name."

Amoeba primarily supports software objects, but hardware objects also exist. Each object is managed by a server process to which RPCs can be sent. Each RPC specifies the object to be used, the operation to be performed, and any parameters to be passed.

When an object is created, the server doing the creation constructs a 128-bit value called a capability and returns it to the caller. Subsequent operations on the object require the user to send its capability to the server to both specify the object and prove the user has permission to manipulate the object. Capabilities are protected cryptographically to prevent tampering. All objects in the entire system are named and protected using this one simple, transparent scheme.

Memory Management

The Amoeba memory model is simple and efficient. A process' address space consists of one or more segments mapped onto user-specified virtual addresses. When a process is executing, all its segments are in memory. There is no swapping or paging at present, thus Amoeba can only run programs that fit in physical memory. The primary advantage of this scheme is simplicity and high performance. The primary disadvantage is that it is not possible to run programs larger than physical memory.

Input/Output

I/O is also handled by kernel threads. To read raw blocks from a disk, for example, a user process having the appropriate authorization, does RPCs with a disk I/O thread in the kernel. The caller is not aware that the server is actually a kernel thread, since the interface to kernel threads and user threads is identical. Generally speaking, only file servers and similar system-like processes communicate with kernel I/O threads.

Software Outside the Kernel

The job of the Amoeba microkernel is to support threads, RPC, memory management and I/O. Everything else is built on top of these primitives.

Bullet File Server

The standard Amoeba file server has been designed for high performance and is called the Bullet server. It stores files contiguously on disk, and caches whole files contiguously in core. Except for very large files, when a user programs needs a file, it will request that the Bullet server send it the entire file in a single RPC. A dedicated machine with at least 16 MB of RAM is needed for the Bullet file server for installation (except on the Sun 3 where there is a maximum of 12 MB). The more RAM the better, in fact. The performance is improved with a larger file cache. The maximum file size is also limited by the amount of physical memory available to the Bullet server.

Directory Server

In contrast to most other operating systems file management and file naming are separated in Amoeba. The Bullet server just manages files, but does not handle naming. It simply reads and writes files, specified by capabilities. A capability can be thought of as a kind of handle for an object, such as a file. A directory server maps ASCII strings onto capabilities. Directories contain (ASCII string, capability) pairs; these capabilities will be for files, directories, and other objects. Since directories may contain capabilities for other directories, hierarchical file systems can be built easily, as well as more general structures.

A directory entry may contain either a single capability or a set of capabilities, to allow a file name to map onto a set of replicated files. When the user looks up a name in a directory, the entire set of capabilities is returned, to provide high availability. These replicas may be on different file servers, potentially far apart (the directory server has no idea about what kind of objects it has capabilities for or where they are located). Operations are provided for managing replicated files in a consistent way.

Compilers

Amoeba comes standard with compilers for ANSI standard C, Pascal, Modula 2, BASIC, and Fortran 77. Each of these comes with appropriate libraries. Amoeba also comes with a collection of third-party software, including the GNU C compiler.

Parallel Programming

A new language called Orca has been developed. It is for parallel programming. Orca allows programmers to create user-defined data types which processes on different machines can share in a controlled way, in effect simulating an object-based distributed shared memory over a LAN. Operations on each object are performed in such a way as to provide the illusion of there being only a single copy, shared by all machines. The Orca run-time system uses the Amoeba IPC facilities to make sharing of software objects over the network highly efficient.

Utilities

Amoeba provides a large number of utilities modeled after the programs that come with UNIX. Among others, these include awk, basename, cal, cat, cdiff, chmod, cmp, comm, compress, cp, cpdir, dd, diff, echo, ex, expr, factor, file, find, fold, fortune, grep, head, jove, kill, ksh, ln, look, ls, m4, make, mkdir, more, mv, od, pr, prep, printenv, pwd, quote, rev, rm, rmdir, sed, sh, shar, size, sleep, sort, spell, split, strings, sum, tail, tar, tee, termcap, test, time, touch, tr, treecmp, true, tset, tsort, tty, uniq, uud, uue, vi, wc, who, xargs, yacc and many other old favorites. Furthermore, a number of new programs are provided such as amake, a highly parallel configuration manager.

UNIX Emulation

To aid in porting UNIX programs to the Amoeba environment, an emulation library, called Ajax, offers major POSIX P1003.1 compatibility. Most POSIX conformant programs work without modification. They simply have to be compiled and linked on Amoeba.

TCP/IP

Although the basic communication mechanism in Amoeba is the Amoeba FLIP protocol, a special server is provided to allow TCP/IP communication, through RPCs to the TCP/IP server. In this way, machines can be accessed through the Internet.

X Windows

Amoeba's user interface is the industry standard X Window System (X11R6). For X servers running on workstations, a special version of X is available that uses the Amoeba RPC for high-performance communication. When hard-wired X terminals are used, these can be interfaced using the TCP/IP server.

Connection to UNIX

A special UNIX driver is provided with Amoeba that can be linked into a SunOS 4.1.1 (or higher) UNIX kernel, allowing UNIX programs to communicate with Amoeba programs. It is also possible, as stated before, to use TCP/IP for this communication (e.g., for non-Sun machines), but the feature described here is much faster and less complex if Sun workstations are available. Utilities are provided to transfer files between UNIX and the Bullet file server.

Advantages of Distributed System

- Sharing Data: There is a provision in the environment where user at one site may be able to access the data residing at other sites.

- Autonomy: Because of sharing data by means of data distribution each site is able to retain a degree of control over data that are stored locally.

- In distributed system there is a global database administrator responsible for the entire system. A part of global data base administrator responsibilities is delegated to local data base administrator for each site. Depending upon the design of distributed database.

- Each local database administrator may have different degree of local autonomy.

- Availability: If one site fails in a distributed system, the remaining sites may be able to continue operating. Thus a failure of a site doesn't necessarily imply the shutdown of the System.

Disadvantages of Distributed Systems

The added complexity required to ensure proper co-ordination among the sites, is the major disadvantage. This increased complexity takes various forms:

- Software Development Cost: It is more difficult to implement a distributed database system; thus it is more costly.

- Greater Potential for Bugs: Since the sites that constitute the distributed database system operate parallel, it is harder to ensure the correctness of algorithms, especially operation during failures of part of the system, and recovery from failures. The potential exists for extremely subtle bugs.

- Increased Processing Overhead: The exchange of information and additional computation required to achieve intersite co-ordination are a form of overhead that does not arise in centralized system.

Architecture of Distributed Operating System

Architectural Styles

There are four different architectural styles, plus the hybrid architecture, when it comes to distributed systems. The basic idea is to organize logically different components, and distribute those computers over the various machines.

- Layered Architecture,

- Object Based Architecture,

- Data-centered Architecture,

- Event Based Architecture,

- Hybrid Architecture.

Layered Architecture

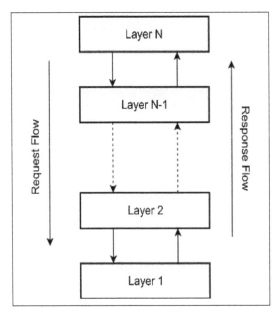

The layered architecture separates layers of components from each other, giving it a much more modular approach. A well-known example for this is the OSI model that incorporates a layered architecture when interacting with each of the components. Each interaction is sequential where a layer will contact the adjacent layer and this process continues, until the request is been catered to. But in certain cases, the implementation can be made so that some layers will be skipped, which is called cross-layer coordination. Through cross-layer coordination, one can obtain better results due to performance increase.

The layers on the bottom provide a service to the layers on the top. The request flows from top to bottom, whereas the response is sent from bottom to top. The advantage of using this approach is that, the calls always follow a predefined path, and that each layer can be easily replaced or modified without affecting the entire architecture. The following image is the basic idea of a layered architecture style.

The image given below, represents the basic architecture style of a distributed system.

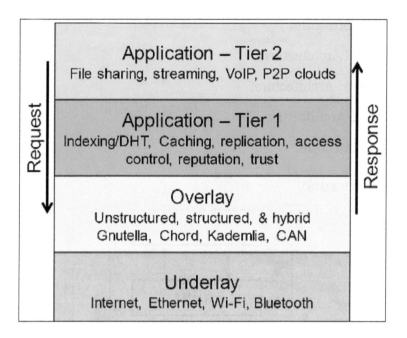

Object Based Architecture

This architecture style is based on loosely coupled arrangement of objects. This has no specific architecture like layers. Like in layers, this does not have a sequential set of steps that needs to be carried out for a given call. Each of the components is referred to as objects, where each object can interact with other objects through a given connector or interface. These are much more direct where all the different components can interact directly with other components through a direct method call.

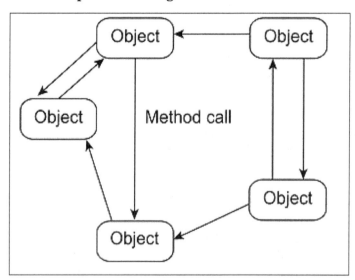

As shown in the above image, communication between object happen as method invocations. These are generally called Remote Procedure Calls (RPC). Some popular examples are Java RMI, Web Services and REST API Calls. This has the following properties:

- This architecture style is less structured.

- Component = object.

- Connector = RPC or RMI.

When decoupling these processes in space, people wanted the components to be anonymous and replaceable. And the synchronization process needed to be asynchronous, which has led to Data Centered Architectures and Event Based Architectures.

Data Centered Architecture

This architecture is based on a data center, where the primary communication happens via a central data repository. This common repository can be either active or passive. This is more like a producer consumer problem. The producers produce items to a common data store, and the consumers can request data from it. This common repository could even be a simple database. But the idea is that, the communication between objects happening through this shared common storage. This supports different components (or objects) by providing a persistent storage space for those components (such as a MySQL database). All the information related to the nodes in the system is stored in this persistent storage. In event-based architectures, data is only sent and received by those components who have already subscribed. Some popular examples are distributed file systems, producer consumer, and web based data services.

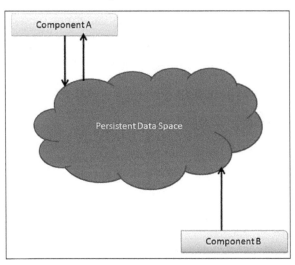

Event Based Architecture

The entire communication in this kind of a system happens through events. When an event is generated, it will be sent to the bus system. With this, everyone else will be notified telling that such an event has occurred. So, if anyone is interested, that node can pull the event from the bus and use it. Sometimes these events could be data, or even URLs to resources. So, the receiver can access whatever the information is given in the event and process accordingly. Processes communicate through the propagation of events.

These events occasionally carry data. An advantage in this architectural style is that, components are loosely coupled. So it is easy to add, remove and modify components in the system. Some examples are publisher - subscriber system, Enterprise Services Bus (ESB) and akka.io.

One major advantage is that, these heterogeneous components can contact the bus, through any communication protocol. But an ESB or a specific bus has the capability to handle any type of incoming request and process accordingly.

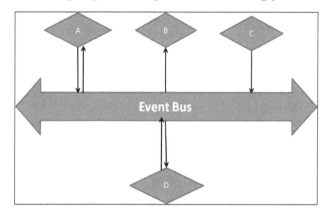

This architectural style is based on the publisher-subscriber architecture. Between each node there is no direct communication or coordination. Instead, objects which are subscribed to the service communicate through the event bus.

The event based architecture supports, several communication styles:

- Publisher-subscriber,

- Broadcast,

- Point-to-Point.

The major advantages of this architecture is that the Components are decoupled in space-loosely coupled.

System Level Architecture

The two major system level architectures that we use today are Client-server and Peer-to-peer (P2P). We use these two kinds of services in our day to day lives, but the difference between these two is often misinterpreted.

Client Server Architecture

The client server architecture has two major components. The client and the server. The Server is where all the processing, computing and data handling is happening, whereas the Client is where the user can access the services and resources given by the Server (Remote Server). The clients can make requests from the Server, and the Server will respond accordingly. Generally, there is only one server that handles the remote side. But to be on the safe side, we do use multiple servers will load balancing techniques.

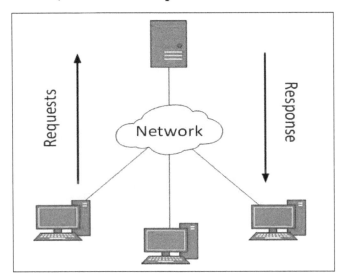

As one common design feature, the Client Server architecture has a centralized security database. This database contains security details like credentials and access details. Users can't log in to a server, without the security credentials. So, it makes this architecture a bit more stable and secure than Peer to Peer. The stability comes where the security database can allow resource usage in a much more meaningful way. But on the other hand, the system might get low, as the server only can handle a limited amount of workload at a given time.

Advantages

- Easier to Build and Maintain,

- Better Security,

- Stable.

Disadvantages

- Single point of failure,

- Less scalable.

Peer-to-Peer (P2P)

The general idea behind peer-to-peer is where there is no central control in a distributed system. The basic idea is that, each node can either be a client or a server at a given time. If the node is requesting something, it can be known as a client, and if some node is providing something, it can be known as a server. In general, each node is referred to as a Peer.

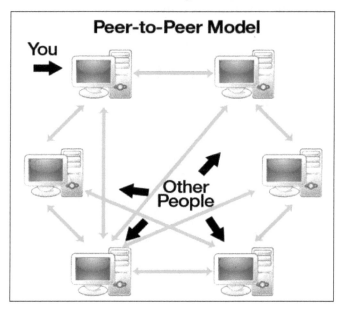

In this network, any new node has to first join the network. After joining in, they can either request a service or provide a service. The initiation phase of a node (Joining of a node), can vary according to implementation of a network. There are two ways in how a new node can get to know, what other nodes are providing:

- Centralized Lookup Server: The new node has to register with the centralized look up server and mention the services it will be providing, on the network. So, whenever you want to have a service, you simply have to contact the centralized look up server and it will direct you to the relevant service provider.

- Decentralized System: A node desiring for specific services must, broadcast and ask every other node in the network, so that whoever is providing the service will respond.

A Comparison Between Client Server and Peer-to-Peer Architectures

Basis For Comparison	Client-Server	Peer-To-Peer
Basic	There is a specific server and specific clients connected to the server.	Clients and server are not distinguished; each node act as client and server.

Service	The client request for service and server respond with the service.	Each node can request for services and can also provide the services.
Focus	Sharing the information.	Connectivity.
Data	The data is stored in a Centralized server.	Each peer has its own data.
Server	When several clients request for the services simultaneously, a server can get bottlenecked.	As the services are provided by several servers distributed in the peer-to-peer system, a server in not bottlenecked.
Expense	The client-server is expensive to implement.	Peer-to-peer is less expensive to implement.
Stability	Client-Server is more stable and scalable.	Peer-to Peer suffers if the number of peers increases in the system.

Centralized Architectures

In the basic client-server model, processes in a distributed system are divided into two (possibly overlapping) groups. A server is a process implementing a specific service, for example, a file system service or a database service. A client is a process that requests a service from a server by sending it a request and subsequently waiting for the server's reply. This client-server interaction, also known as request-reply behavior is shown in figure.

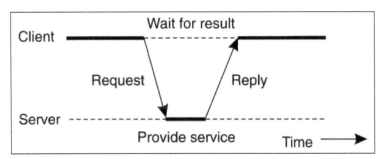

General interaction between a client and a server.

Communication between a client and a server can be implemented by means of a simple connectionless protocol when the underlying network is fairly reliable as in many local-area networks. In these cases, when a client requests a service, it simply packages a message for the server, identifying the service it wants, along with the necessary input data. The message is then sent to the server. The latter, in turn, will always wait for an incoming request, subsequently process it, and package the results in a reply message that is then sent to the client.

Using a connectionless protocol has the obvious advantage of being efficient. As long as messages do not get lost or corrupted, the request/reply protocol just sketched works fine. Unfortunately, making the protocol resistant to occasional transmission failures is not trivial. The only thing we can do is possibly let the client resend the request when no reply message comes in. The problem, however, is that the client cannot detect whether the original request message was lost, or that transmission of the reply failed. If the reply was lost, then resending a request may result in performing the operation twice. If the operation was something like "transfer $10,000 from my bank account," then clearly, it would have been better that we simply reported an error instead. On the other hand, if the operation was "tell me how much money we have left," it would be perfectly acceptable to resend the request. When an operation can be repeated multiple times without harm, it is said to be idempotent. Since, some requests are idempotent and others are not it should be clear that there is no single solution for dealing with lost messages.

As an alternative, many client-server systems use a reliable connection-oriented protocol. Although this solution is not entirely appropriate in a local-area network due to relatively low performance, it works perfectly fine in wide-area systems in which communication is inherently unreliable. For example, virtually all internet application protocols are based on reliable TCP/IP connections. In this case, whenever a client requests a service, it first sets up a connection to the server before sending the request. The server generally uses that same connection to send the reply message, after which the connection is torn down. The trouble is that setting up and tearing down a connection is relatively costly, especially when the request and reply messages are small.

Application Layering

The client-server model has been subject to many debates and controversies over the years. One of the main issues was how to draw a clear distinction between a client and a server. Not surprisingly, there is often no clear distinction. For example, a server for a distributed database may continuously act as a client because it is forwarding requests to different file servers responsible for implementing the database tables. In such a case, the database server itself essentially does no more than process queries.

However, considering that many client-server applications are targeted toward supporting user access to databases, many people have advocated a distinction between the following three levels, essentially following the layered architectural style we discussed previously:

- The user-interface level.

- The processing level.

- The data level.

The user-interface level contains all that is necessary to directly interface with the user, such as display management. The processing level typically contains the applications. The data level manages the actual data that is being acted on.

Clients typically implement the user-interface level. This level consists of the programs that allow end users to interact with applications.

The simplest user-interface program is nothing more than a character-based screen. Such an interface has been typically used in mainframe environments. In those cases where the mainframe controls all interaction, including the keyboard and monitor, one can hardly speak of a client-server environment. However, in many cases, the user's terminal does some local processing such as echoing typed keystrokes, or supporting form-like interfaces in which a complete entry is to be edited before sending it to the main computer.

Nowadays, even in mainframe environments, we see more advanced user interfaces. Typically, the client machine offers at least a graphical display in which pop-up or pull-down menus are used, and of which many of the screen controls are handled through a mouse instead of the keyboard. Typical examples of such interfaces include the X-Windows interfaces as used in many UNIX environments, and earlier interfaces developed for MS-DOS PCs and Apple Macintoshes.

Modern user interfaces offer considerably more functionality by allowing applications to share a single graphical window, and to use that window to exchange data through user actions. For example, to delete a file, it is usually possible to move the icon representing that file to an icon representing a trash can. Likewise, many word processors allow a user to move text in a document to another position by using only the mouse.

Many client-server applications can be constructed from roughly three different pieces: a part that handles interaction with a user, a part that operates on a database or file system, and a middle part that generally contains the core functionality of an application. This middle part is logically placed at the processing level. In contrast to user interfaces and databases, there are not many aspects common to the processing level. Therefore, we shall give several examples to make this level clearer.

As a first example, consider an internet search engine. Ignoring all the animated banners, images, and other fancy window dressing, the user interface of a search engine is very simple: a user types in a string of keywords and is subsequently presented with a list of titles of web pages. The back end is formed by a huge database of web pages that have been prefetched and indexed. The core of the search engine is a program that transforms the user's string of keywords into one or more database queries. It subsequently ranks the results into a list, and transforms that list into a series of HTML pages. Within the client-server model, this information retrieval part is typically placed at the processing level.

As a second example, consider a decision support system for a stock brokerage. Analogous to a search engine, such a system can be divided into a front end implementing the user interface, a back end for accessing a database with the financial data, and the analysis programs between these two. Analysis of financial data may require sophisticated methods and techniques from statistics and artificial intelligence. In some cases, the core of a financial decision support system may even need to be executed on high-performance computers in order to achieve the throughput and responsiveness that is expected from its users.

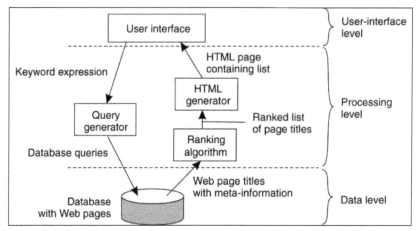

The simplified organization of an Internet search engine into three different layers.

As a last example, consider a typical desktop package, consisting of a word processor, a spreadsheet application, communication facilities, and so on. Such "office" suites are generally integrated through a common user interface that supports compound documents, and operates on files from the user's home directory (In an office environment, this home directory is often placed on a remote file server.) In this example, the processing level consists of a relatively large collection of programs, each having rather simple processing capabilities.

The data level in the client-server model contains the programs that maintain the actual data on which the applications operate. An important property of this level is that data are often persistent, that is, even if no application is running, data will be stored somewhere for next use. In its simplest form, the data level consists of a file system, but it is more common to use a full-fledged database. In the client-server model, the data level is typically implemented at the server side.

Besides merely storing data, the data level is generally also responsible for keeping data consistent across different applications. When databases are being used, maintaining consistency means that metadata such as table descriptions, entry constraints and application-specific metadata are also stored at this level. For example, in the case of a bank, we may want to generate a notification when a customer's credit card debt reaches a certain value. This type of information can be maintained through a database trigger that activates a handler for that trigger at the appropriate moment.

In most business-oriented environments, the data level is organized as a relational database. Data independence is crucial here. The data are organized independent of the applications in such a way that changes in that organization do not affect applications, and neither do the applications affect the data organization. Using relational databases in the client-server model helps separate the processing level from the data level, as processing and data are considered independent.

However, relational databases are not always the ideal choice. A characteristic feature of many applications is that they operate on complex data types that are more easily modeled in terms of objects than in terms of relations. Examples of such data types range from simple polygons and circles to representations of aircraft designs, as is the case with computer-aided design (CAD) systems.

In those cases where data operations are more easily expressed in terms of object manipulations, it makes sense to implement the data level by means of an object-oriented or object-relational database. Notably the latter type has gained popularity as these databases build upon the widely dispersed relational data model, while offering the advantages that object-orientation gives.

Multi-tiered Architectures

The distinction into three logical levels suggests a number of possibilities for physically distributing a client-server application across several machines. The simplest organization is to have only two types of machines:

- A client machine containing only the programs implementing (part of) the user-interface level.

- A server machine containing the rest, that is the programs implementing the processing and data level.

In this organization everything is handled by the server while the client is essentially no more than a dumb terminal, possibly with a pretty graphical interface. There are many other possibilities, of which we explore some of the more common ones in this section.

One approach for organizing the clients and servers is to distribute the programs in the application layers of the previous section across different machines. As a first step, we make a distinction between only two kinds of machines: client machines and server machines, leading to what is also referred to as a (physically) two-tiered architecture.

One possible organization is to have only the terminal-dependent part of the user interface on the client machine, as shown in figure and give the applications remote control over the presentation of their data. An alternative is to place the entire user-interface software on the client side. In such cases, we essentially divide the application into a graphical front end, which communicates with the rest of the application (residing at the server) through an application-specific protocol. In this model, the front end (the client software) does no processing other than necessary for presenting the application's interface.

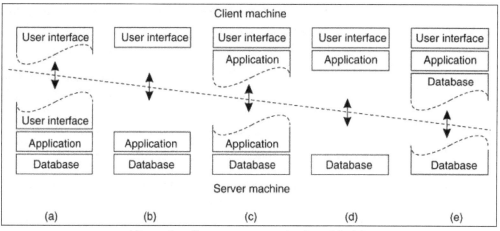

Alternative client-server organizations (a)–(e).

Continuing along this line of reasoning, we may also move part of the application to the front end, as shown in figure above. An example where this makes sense is where the application makes use of a form that needs to be filled in entirely before it can be processed. The front end can then check the correctness and consistency of the form, and where necessary interact with the user. Another example of the organization of figure is that of a word processor in which the basic editing functions execute on the client side where they operate on locally cached, or in-memory data, but where the advanced support tools such as checking the spelling and grammar execute on the server side.

In many client-server environments, the organizations shown in figures are particularly popular. These organizations are used where the client machine is a PC or workstation, connected through a network to a distributed file system or database. Essentially, most of the application is running on the client machine, but all operations on files or database entries go to the server. For example, many banking applications run on an end-user's machine where the user prepares transactions and such. Once finished, the application contacts the database on the bank's server and uploads the transactions for further processing. Figure represents the situation where the client's local disk contains part of the data. For example, when browsing the Web, a client can gradually build a huge cache on local disk of most recent inspected Web pages.

We note that for a few years there has been a strong trend to move away from the configurations shown in figure. Above in that case that client software is placed at end-user machines. In these cases, most of the processing and data storage is handled at the server side. The reason for this is simple: although client machines do a lot, they are also more problematic to manage. Having more functionality on the client machine makes client-side software more prone to errors and more dependent on the client's underlying platform (i.e., operating system and resources). From a system's management perspective, having what are called fat clients is not optimal. Instead the thin clients as represented by the organizations are much easier, perhaps at the cost of less sophisticated user interfaces and client-perceived performance.

This trend does not imply that we no longer need distributed systems. On the contrary, what we are seeing is that server-side solutions are becoming increasingly more distributed as a single server is being replaced by multiple servers running on different machines. In particular, when distinguishing only client and server machines as we have done so far, we miss the point that a server may sometimes need to act as a client, as shown in figure leading to a (physically) three-tiered architecture.

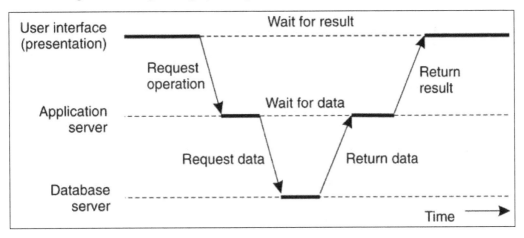

In this architecture, programs that form part of the processing level reside on a separate server, but may additionally be partly distributed across the client and server machines. A typical example of where a three-tiered architecture is used is in transaction processing.

Another, but very different example where we often see a three-tiered architecture is in the organization of web sites. In this case, a web server acts as an entry point to a site, passing requests to an application server where the actual processing takes place. This application server, in turn, interacts with a database server. For example, an application server may be responsible for running the code to inspect the available inventory of some goods as offered by an electronic bookstore. To do so, it may need to interact with a database containing the raw inventory data.

Decentralized Architectures

Multi-tiered client-server architectures are a direct consequence of dividing applications into a user-interface, processing components, and a data level. The different tiers correspond directly with the logical organization of applications. In many business environments, distributed processing is equivalent to organizing a client-server application as multitier architecture. We refer to this type of distribution as vertical distribution. The characteristic feature of vertical distribution is that it is achieved by placing logically different components on different machines. The term is related to the concept of vertical fragmentation as used in distributed relational databases, where it means that tables are split column-wise, and subsequently distributed across multiple machines.

Again, from a system management perspective, having a vertical distribution can help functions are logically and physically split across multiple machines, where each machine is tailored to a specific group of functions. However, vertical distribution is only one way of organizing client-server applications. In modern architectures, it is often the distribution of the clients and the servers that counts, which we refer to as horizontal distribution. In this type of distribution, a client or server may be physically split up into logically equivalent parts, but each part is operating on its own share of the complete data set, thus balancing the load.

From a high-level perspective, the processes that constitute a peer-to-peer system are all equal. This means that the functions that need to be carried out are represented by every process that constitutes the distributed system. As a consequence, much of the interaction between processes is symmetric each process will act as a client and a server at the same time (which is also referred to as acting as a servent).

Given this symmetric behavior, peer-to-peer architectures evolve around the question how to organize the processes in an overlay network, that is, a network in which the nodes are formed by the processes and the links represent the possible communication channels (which are usually realized as TCP connections). In general, a process cannot communicate directly with an arbitrary other process, but is required to send messages through the available communication channels. Two types of overlay networks exist: those that are structured and those that are not. These two types are surveyed extensively in Lua et al. along with numerous examples. Aberer et al. provide a reference architecture that allows for a more formal comparison of the different types of peer-to-peer systems.

Structured Peer-to-Peer Architectures

In a structured peer-to-peer architecture, the overlay network is constructed using a deterministic procedure. By far the most-used procedure is to organize the processes through a distributed hash table (DHT). In a DHT-based system, data items are assigned a random key from a large identifier space, such as a 128-bit or 160-bit identifier. Likewise, nodes in the system are also assigned a random number from the same identifier space. The crux of every DHT-based system is then to implement an efficient and deterministic scheme that uniquely maps the key of a data item to the identifier of a node based on some distance metric. Most importantly, when looking up a data item, the network address of the node responsible for that data item is returned. Effectively, this is accomplished by routing a request for a data item to the responsible node.

For example, in the Chord system the nodes are logically organized in a ring such that a data item with key k is mapped to the node with the smallest identifier idk. This node is referred to as the successor of key k and denoted as succ(k), as shown in figure below. To actually look up the data item, an application running on an arbitrary node would then call the function LOOKUP(k) which would subsequently return the network address of succ(k). At that point, the application can contact the node to obtain a copy of the data item.

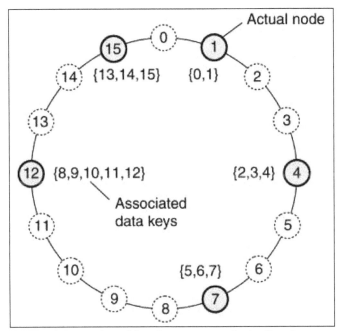

The mapping of data items onto nodes in Chord.

We will not go into algorithms for looking up a key now, Instead, let us concentrate on how nodes organize themselves into an overlay network, or, in other words, membership management. In the following, it is important to realize that looking up a key does not follow the logical organization of nodes in the ring from figure. Rather, each node will maintain shortcuts to other nodes in such a way that lookups can generally be done in O(log (N)) number of steps, where N is the number of nodes participating in the overlay.

Now consider Chord again. When a node wants to join the system, it starts with generating a random identifier id. Note that if the identifier space is large enough, then provided the random number generator is of good quality, the probability of generating an identifier that is already assigned to an actual node is close to zero. Then, the node can simply do a lookup on id, which will return the network address of succ(id). At that point, the joining node can simply contact succ(id) and its predecessor and insert itself in the ring. Of course, this scheme requires that each node also stores information on its predecessor. Insertion also yields that each data item whose key is now associated with node id, is transferred from succ(id).

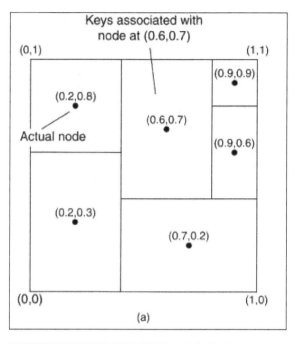

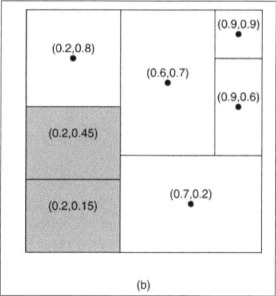

(a) The mapping of data items onto nodes in CAN. (b) Splitting a region when a node joins.

Leaving is just as simple: node id informs its departure to its predecessor and successor, and transfers its data items to succ(id).

Similar approaches are followed in other DHT-based systems. As an example, consider the Content Addressable Network (CAN), described in Ratnasamy et al. CAN deploys a d-dimensional Cartesian coordinate space, which is completely partitioned among all all the nodes that participate in the system. For purpose of illustration, let us consider only the 2-dimensional case, of which an example is shown in figure above.

Figure shows how the two-dimensional space [0,1]x[0,1] is divided among six nodes. Each node has an associated region. Every data item in CAN will be assigned a unique point in this space, after which it is also clear which node is responsible for that data (ignoring data items that fall on the border of multiple regions, for which a deterministic assignment rule is used).

When a node P wants to join a CAN system, it picks an arbitrary point from the coordinate space and subsequently looks up the node Q in whose region that point falls. This lookup is accomplished through positioned-based routing. Node Q then splits its region into two halves, as shown in figure and one half is assigned to the node P. Nodes keeps track of their neighbors, that is, nodes responsible for adjacent region. When splitting a region, the joining node P can easily come to know who its new neighbors are by asking node P. As in Chord, the data items for which node P is now responsible are transferred from node Q.

Leaving is a bit more problematic in CAN. Assume that in figure the node with coordinate (0.6, 0.7) leaves. Its region will be assigned to one of its neighbors, say the node at (0.9, 0.9), but it is clear that simply merging it and obtaining a rectangle cannot be done. In this case, the node at (0.9, 0.9) will simply take care of that region and inform the old neighbors of this fact. Obviously, this may lead to less symmetric partitioning of the coordinate space, for which reason a background process is periodically started to repartition the entire space.

Unstructured Peer-to-Peer Architectures

Unstructured peer-to-peer systems largely rely on randomized algorithms for constructing an overlay network. The main idea is that each node maintains a list of neighbors, but that this list is constructed in a more or less random way. Likewise, data items are assumed to be randomly placed on nodes. As a consequence, when a node needs to locate a specific data item, the only thing it can effectively do is flood the network with a search query.

One of the goals of many unstructured peer-to-peer systems is to construct an overlay network that resembles a random graph. The basic model is that each node maintains a list of c neighbors, where, ideally, each of these neighbors represents a randomly chosen live node from the current set of nodes. The list of neighbors is also referred to as a partial view. There are many ways to construct such a partial view. Jelasity et al. have developed a framework that captures many different algorithms for overlay construction to allow for evaluations and comparison. In this framework, it is assumed that nodes regularly exchange entries from their partial view. Each entry identifies another node in the network, and has an associated age that indicates how old the reference to that node is.

The active thread takes the initiative to communicate with another node. It selects that node from its current partial view. Assuming that entries need to be pushed to the selected peer, it continues by constructing a buffer containing c/2+1 entries, including an entry identifying itself. The other entries are taken from the current partial view.

If the node is also in pull mode it will wait for a response from the selected peer. That peer, in the meantime, will also have constructed a buffer by means the passive thread shown in figure, whose activities strongly resemble that of the active thread.

The crucial point is the construction of a new partial view. This view, for initiating as well as for the contacted peer, will contain exactly c entries, part of which will come from received buffer. In essence, there are two ways to construct the new view. First, the two nodes may decide to discard the entries that they had sent to each other. Effectively, this means that they will swap part of their original views. The second approach is to discard as many old entries as possible. In general, it turns out that the two approaches are complementary. It turns out that many membership management protocols for unstructured overlays fit this framework. There are a number of interesting observations to make.

First, let us assume that when a node wants to join it contacts an arbitrary other node, possibly from a list of well-known access points. This access point is just a regular member of the overlay, except that we can assume it to be highly available. In this case, it turns out that protocols that use only push mode or only pull mode can fairly easily lead to disconnected overlays. In other words, groups of nodes will become isolated and will never be able to reach every other node in the network. Clearly, this is an undesirable feature, for which reason it makes more sense to let nodes actually exchange entries.

The figure below shows: (a) The steps taken by the active thread. (b) The steps taken by the passive thread.

Actions by active thread (periodically repeated):

```
    select a peer P from the current partial view;

    if PUSH_MODE {

        mybuffer = [(MyAddress, 0)];

        permute partial view;

        move H oldest entries to the end;

        append first c/2 entries to mybuffer;

        send mybuffer to P;

    } else {

        send trigger to P;

    }
```

```
if PULL_MODE {

    receive P›s buffer;

}

construct a new partial view from the current one and P›s buffer;

increment the age of every entry in the new partial view;
```

Actions by passive thread:

```
receive buffer from any process Q;

if PULL_MODE {

    mybuffer = [(MyAddress, 0)];

    permute partial vie w;

    move H oldest entries to the end;

    append first c/2 entries to mybuffer;

    send mybuffer to P;

}

construct a new partial view from the current one and P›s buffer;

increment the age of every entry in the new partial view;
```

Second, leaving the network turns out to be a very simple operation provided the nodes exchange partial views on a regular basis. In this case, a node can simply depart without informing any other node. What will happen is that when a node P selects one of its apparent neighbors, say node Q, and discovers that Q no longer responds, it simply removes the entry from its partial view to select another peer. It turns out that when constructing a new partial view, a node follows the policy to discard as many old entries as possible, departed nodes will rapidly be forgotten. In other words, entries referring to departed nodes will automatically be quickly removed from partial views.

However, there is a price to pay when this strategy is followed. To explain, consider for a node P the set of nodes that have an entry in their partial view that refers to P. Technically, this is known as the indegree of a node. The higher node P's indegree is, the higher the probability that some other node will decide to contact P. In other words, there is a danger that P will become a popular node, which could easily bring it into an imbalanced position regarding workload. Systematically discarding old entries turns out to promote nodes to ones having a high indegree. There are other trade-offs in addition, for which we refer to Jelasity et al.

Topology Management of Overlay Networks

Although it would seem that structured and unstructured peer-to-peer systems form strict independent classes, this need actually not be case. One key observation is that by carefully exchanging and selecting entries from partial views, it is possible to construct and maintain specific topologies of overlay networks. This topology management is achieved by adopting a two-layered approach, as shown in figure.

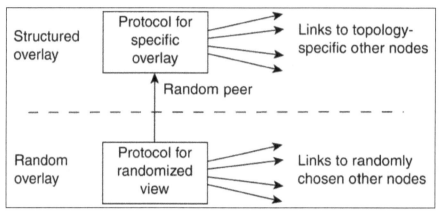

A two-layered approach for constructing and maintaining specific
overlay topologies using techniques from unstructured peer-to-peer systems.

The lowest layer constitutes an unstructured peer-to-peer system in which nodes periodically exchange entries of their partial views with the aim to maintain an accurate random graph. Accuracy in this case refers to the fact that the partial view should be filled with entries referring to randomly selected live nodes.

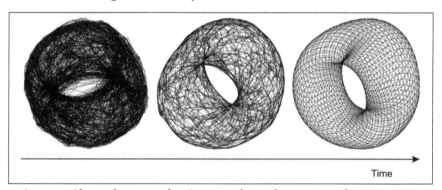

Generating a specific overlay network using a two-layered unstructured peer-to-peer system.

The lowest layer passes its partial view to the higher layer, where an additional selection of entries takes place. This then leads to a second list of neighbors corresponding to the desired topology. Jelasity and Babaoglu propose to use a ranking function by which nodes are ordered according to some criterion relative to a given node. A simple ranking function is to order a set of nodes by increasing distance from a given node P. In that case, node P will gradually build up a list of its nearest neighbors provided the lowest layer continues to pass randomly selected nodes.

As an illustration, consider a logical grid of size NxN with a node placed on each point of the grid. Every node is required to maintain a list of c nearest neighbors, where the distance between a node at (a_1, a_2) and (b_1, b_2) is defined as d_1+d_2, with $d_i=\min(N-|a_i-b_i|, |a_i-b_i|)$. If the lowest layer periodically executes the protocol as outlined in figure, the topology that will evolve is a torus.

Of course, completely different ranking functions can be used. Notably those that are related to capturing the semantic proximity of the data items as stored at a peer node are interesting. This proximity allows for the construction of semantic overlay networks that allow for highly efficient search algorithms in unstructured peer-to-peer systems.

Superpeers

Notably in unstructured peer-to-peer systems, locating relevant data items can become problematic as the network grows. The reason for this scalability problem is simple: as there is no deterministic way of routing a lookup request to a specific data item, essentially the only technique a node can resort to is flooding the request. There are various ways in which flooding can be dammed, but as an alternative many peer-to-peer systems have proposed to make use of special nodes that maintain an index of data items.

There are other situations in which abandoning the symmetric nature of peer-to-peer systems is sensible. Consider a collaboration of nodes that offer resources to each other. For example, in a collaborative content delivery network (CDN), nodes may offer storage for hosting copies of web pages allowing web clients to access pages nearby, and thus to access them quickly. In this case a node P may need to seek for resources in a specific part of the network. In that case, making use of a broker that collects resource usage for a number of nodes that are in each other's proximity will allow to quickly selecting a node with sufficient resources.

Nodes such as those maintaining an index or acting as a broker are generally referred to as superpeers. As their name suggests, superpeers are often also organized in a peer-to-peer network, leading to a hierarchical organization as explained in Yang and Garcia-Molina. A simple example of such an organization is shown in figure. In this organization, every regular peer is connected as a client to a superpeer. All communication from and to a regular peer proceeds through that peer's associated superpeer.

In many cases, the client-superpeer relation is fixed: whenever a regular peer joins the network, it attaches to one of the superpeers and remains attached until it leaves the network. Obviously, it is expected that superpeers are long-lived processes with a high availability. To compensate for potential unstable behavior of a superpeer, backup schemes can be deployed, such as pairing every superpeer with another one and requiring clients to attach to both.

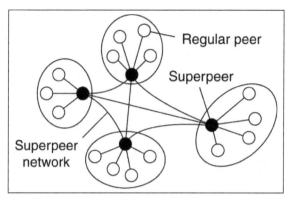

A hierarchical organization of nodes into a superpeer network.

Having a fixed association with a superpeer may not always be the best solution. For example, in the case of file-sharing networks, it may be better for a client to attach to a superpeer that maintains an index of files that the client is generally interested in. In that case, chances are bigger that when a client is looking for a specific file, its superpeer will know where to find it. Garbacki et al. describe a relatively simple scheme in which the client-superpeer relation can change as clients discover better superpeers to associate with. In particular, a superpeer returning the result of a lookup operation is given preference over other superpeers.

As we have seen, peer-to-peer networks offer a flexible means for nodes to join and leave the network. However, with superpeer networks a new problem is introduced, namely how to select the nodes that are eligible to become superpeer.

Hybrid Architectures

An important class of distributed systems that is organized according to hybrid architecture is formed by edge-server systems. These systems are deployed on the Internet where servers are placed "at the edge" of the network. This edge is formed by the boundary between enterprise networks and the actual Internet, for example, as provided by an Internet Service Provider (ISP). Likewise, where end users at home connect to the Internet through their ISP, the ISP can be considered as residing at the edge of the Internet. This leads to a general organization as shown in figure.

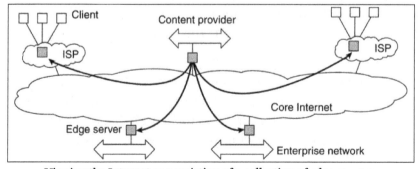

Viewing the Internet as consisting of a collection of edge servers.

End users, or clients in general, connect to the Internet by means of an edge server. The edge server's main purpose is to serve content, possibly after applying filtering and transcoding functions. More interesting is the fact that a collection of edge servers can be used to optimize content and application distribution. The basic model is that for a specific organization, one edge server acts as an origin server from which all content originates. That server can use other edge servers for replicating web pages and such.

Collaborative Distributed Systems

Hybrid structures are notably deployed in collaborative distributed systems. The main issue in many of these systems to first get started, for which often a traditional client-server scheme is deployed. Once a node has joined the system, it can use a fully decentralized scheme for collaboration.

To make matters concrete, let us first consider the BitTorrent file-sharing system. BitTorrent is a peer-to-peer file downloading system. Its principal working is shown in figure. The basic idea is that when an end user is looking for a file, he downloads chunks of the file from other users until the downloaded chunks can be assembled together yielding the complete file. An important design goal was to ensure collaboration. In most file-sharing systems, a significant fraction of participants merely download files but otherwise contribute close to nothing. To this end, a file can be downloaded only when the downloading client is providing content to someone else.

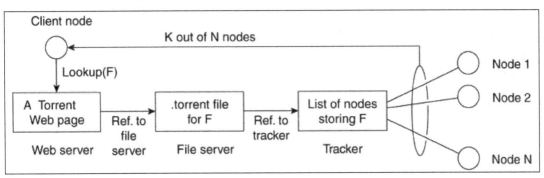

To download a file, a user needs to access a global directory, which is just one of a few well-known web sites. Such a directory contains references to what are called .torrent files. A .torrent file contains the information that is needed to download a specific file. In particular, it refers to what is known as a tracker, which is a server that is keeping an accurate account of active nodes that have (chunks) of the requested file. An active node is one that is currently downloading another file. Obviously, there will be many different trackers, although there will generally be only a single tracker per file (or collection of files).

Once the nodes have been identified from where chunks can be downloaded, the downloading node effectively becomes active. At that point, it will be forced to help others, for example by providing chunks of the file it is downloading that others do not yet have. This enforcement comes from a very simple rule: if node P notices that node Q is downloading more than it is uploading, P can decide to decrease the rate at which it sends data to Q. This scheme works well provided P has something to download from Q. For this reason, nodes are often supplied with references to many other nodes putting them in a better position to trade data.

Clearly, BitTorrent combines centralized with decentralized solutions. As it turns out, the bottleneck of the system is, not surprisingly, formed by the trackers.

As another example, consider the Globule collaborative content distribution network. Globule strongly resembles the edge-server architecture mentioned above. In this case, instead of edge servers, end users (but also organizations) voluntarily provide enhanced web servers that are capable of collaborating in the replication of web pages. In its simplest form, each such server has the following components:

- A component that can redirect client requests to other servers.

- A component for analyzing access patterns.

- A component for managing the replication of web pages.

The server provided by Alice is the web server that normally handles the traffic for Alice's Web site and is called the origin server for that site. It collaborates with other servers, for example, the one provided by Bob, to host the pages from Bob's site. In this sense, Globule is a decentralized distributed system. Requests for Alice's Web site are initially forwarded to her server, at which point they may be redirected to one of the other servers. Distributed redirection is also supported.

However, Globule also has a centralized component in the form of its broker. The broker is responsible for registering servers, and making these servers known to others. Servers communicate with the broker completely analogous to what one would expect in a client-server system.

Middleware in Distributed Applications

If we look at Distributed systems today, they lack the uniformity and consistency. Various heterogeneous devices have taken over the world where distributed system caters to all these devices in a common way. One way distributed systems can achieve uniformity is through a common layer to support the underlying hardware and operating systems. This common layer is known as a middleware, where it provides services beyond what is already provided by Operating systems, to enable various features and components of a distributed system to enhance its functionality better. This layer provides a certain data structures and operations that allow processes and users on far-flung machines to inter-operate and work together in a consistent way. The image given below depicts the usage of a middleware to inter-connect various kinds of nodes together. According to Andrew Tannenbaum, middleware is like the operating system of distributed systems.

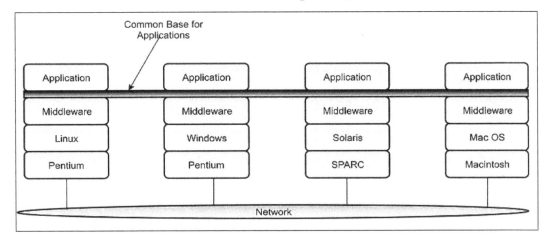

Use

Middleware services provide a more functional set of application programming interfaces to allow an application to:

- Locate transparently across the network, thus providing interaction with another service or application.

- Filter data to make them friendly usable or public via anonymization process for privacy protection (for example).

- Be independent from network services.

- Be reliable and always available.

- Add complementary attributes like semantics.

when compared to the operating system and network services.

Middleware offers some unique technological advantages for business and industry. For example, traditional database systems are usually deployed in closed environments where users access the system only via a restricted network or intranet (e.g., an enterprise's internal network). With the phenomenal growth of the World Wide Web, users can access virtually any database for which they have proper access rights from anywhere in the world. Middleware addresses the problem of varying levels of interoperability among different database structures. Middleware facilitates transparent access to legacy database management systems (DBMSs) or applications via a web server without regard to database-specific characteristics.

Businesses frequently use middleware applications to link information from departmental databases, such as payroll, sales, and accounting, or databases housed in multiple geographic locations. In the highly competitive healthcare community, laboratories make extensive use of middleware applications for data mining, laboratory information system (LIS) backup, and to combine systems during hospital mergers. Middleware helps bridge the gap between separate LISs in a newly formed healthcare network following a hospital buyout.

Middleware can help software developers avoid having to write application programming interfaces (API) for every control program, by serving as an independent programming interface for their applications. For Future Internet network operation through traffic monitoring in multi-domain scenarios, using mediator tools (middleware) is a powerful help since they allow operators, searchers and service providers to supervise quality of service and analyse eventual failures in telecommunication services.

Finally, e-commerce uses middleware to assist in handling rapid and secure transactions over many different types of computer environments. In short, middleware has become a critical element across a broad range of industries, thanks to its ability to bring together resources across dissimilar networks or computing platforms.

In 2004, members of the European Broadcasting Union (EBU) carried out a study of Middleware with respect to system integration in broadcast environments. This involved system design engineering experts from 10 major European broadcasters working over a 12-month period to understand the effect of predominantly software-based products to media production and broadcasting system design techniques. The resulting reports Tech 3300 and Tech 3300s were published and are freely available from the EBU web site.

Types

Message-oriented Middleware

Message-oriented middleware (MOM) is middleware where transactions or event notifications are delivered between disparate systems or components by way of messages, often via an enterprise messaging system. With MOM, messages sent to the client are collected and stored until they are acted upon, while the client continues with other processing.

Enterprise Messaging

An enterprise messaging system is a type of middleware that facilitates message passing between disparate systems or components in standard formats, often using XML, SOAP or web services. As part of an enterprise messaging system, message broker software may queue, duplicate, translate and deliver messages to disparate systems or components in a messaging system.

Enterprise Service Bus

Enterprise service bus (ESB) is defined by the Burton Group as "some type of integration middleware product that supports both message-oriented middleware and Web services".

Intelligent Middleware

Intelligent Middleware (IMW) provides real-time intelligence and event management through intelligent agents. The IMW manages the real-time processing of high volume sensor signals and turns these signals into intelligent and actionable business information. The actionable information is then delivered in end-user power dashboards to individual users or is pushed to systems within or outside the enterprise. It is able to support various heterogeneous types of hardware and software and provides an API for interfacing with external systems. It should have a highly scalable, distributed architecture which embeds intelligence throughout the network to transform raw data systematically into actionable and relevant knowledge. It can also be packaged with tools to view and manage operations and build advanced network applications most effectively.

Content-centric Middleware

Content-centric middleware offers a simple *provider-consumer* abstraction through which applications can issue requests for uniquely identified content, without worrying about where or how it is obtained. Juno is one example, which allows applications to generate content requests associated with high-level delivery requirements. The middleware then adapts the underlying delivery to access the content from sources that are best suited to matching the requirements. This is therefore similar to publish/subscribe middleware, as well as the Content-centric networking paradigm.

Remote Procedure Call

Remote procedure call middleware enables a client to use services running on remote systems. The process can be synchronous or asynchronous.

Object Request Broker

With object request broker middleware, it is possible for applications to send objects and request services in an object-oriented system.

SQL-oriented Data Access

SQL-oriented Data Access is middleware between applications and database servers.

Embedded Middleware

Embedded middleware provides communication services and software/firmware integration interface that operates between embedded applications, the embedded operating system, and external applications.

Other

Other sources include these additional classifications:

- Transaction processing monitors – provides tools and an environment to develop and deploy distributed applications.

- Application servers – software installed on a computer to facilitate the serving (running) of other applications.

Architectures versus Middleware

Middleware forms a layer between applications and distributed platforms, as shown in figure. An important purpose is to provide a degree of distribution transparency, that is, to a certain extent hiding the distribution of data, processing, and control from applications.

What is comonly seen in practice is that middleware systems actually follow a specific architectural sytle. For example, many middleware solutions have adopted an object-based architectural style, such as CORBA. Others, like TIB/Rendezvous provide middleware that follows the event-based architectural style.

Having middleware molded according to a specific architectural style has the benefit that designing applications may become simpler. However, an obvious drawback is that the middleware may no longer be optimal for what an application developer had in mind. For example, CORBA initially offered only objects that could be invoked by remote clients. Later, it was felt that having only this form of interaction was too restrictive, so that other interaction patterns such as messaging were added. Obviously, adding new features can easily lead to bloated middle-ware solutions.

In addition, although middleware is meant to provide distribution transparency, it is generally felt that specific solutions should be adaptable to application requirements. One solution to this problem is to make several versions of a middleware system, where each version is tailored to a specific class of applications. An approach that is generally considered better is to make middleware systems such that they are easy to configure, adapt, and customize as needed by an application. As a result, systems are now being developed in which a stricter separation between policies and mechanisms is being made. This has led to several mechanisms by which the behavior of middleware can be modified.

Interceptors

Conceptually, an interceptor is nothing but a software construct that will break the usual flow of control and allow other (application specific) code to be executed. To make interceptors generic may require a substantial implementation effort, as illustrated in Schmidt et al., and it is unclear whether in such cases generality should be preferred over restricted applicability and simplicity. Also, in many cases having only limited interception facilities will improve management of the software and the distributed system as a whole.

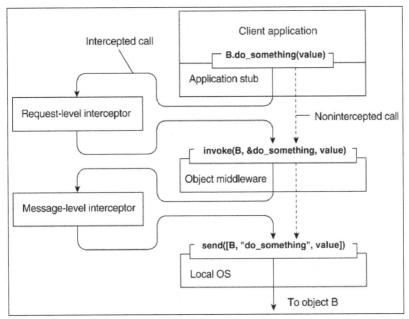

Using interceptors to handle remote-object invocations.

To make matters concrete, consider interception as supported in many object-based distributed systems. The basic idea is simple: an object A can call a method that belongs to an object B, while the latter resides on a different machine than A. Such a remote-object invocation is carried as a three-step approach:

- Object A is offered a local interface that is exactly the same as the interface offered by object B. A simply calls the method available in that interface.

- The call by A is transformed into a generic object invocation, made possible through a general object-invocation interface offered by the middleware at the machine where A resides.

- Finally, the generic object invocation is transformed into a message that is sent through the transport-level network interface as offered by A's local operating system.

After the first step, the call B.do_something(value) is transformed into a generic call such as invoke(B, &do_something, value) with a reference to B's method and the parameters that go along with the call. Now imagine that object B is replicated. In that case, each replica should actually be invoked. This is a clear point where interception can help. What the request-level interceptor will do is simply call invoke(B, &do_something, value) for each of the replicas. The beauty of this all is that the object A need not be aware of the replication of B, but also the object middleware need not have special components that deal with this replicated call. Only the request-level interceptor, which may be added to the middleware needs to know about B's replication.

In the end, a call to a remote object will have to be sent over the network. In practice, this means that the messaging interface as offered by the local operating system will need to be invoked. At that level, a message-level interceptor may assist in transferring the invocation to the target object. For example, imagine that the parameter value actually corresponds to a huge array of data. In that case, it may be wise to fragment the data into smaller parts to have it assembled again at the destination. Such a fragmentation may improve performance or reliability. Again, the middleware need not be aware of this fragmentation; the lower-level interceptor will transparently handle the rest of the communication with the local operating system.

Challenges in Distributed Operating System

The major challenges in distributed systems are listed below:

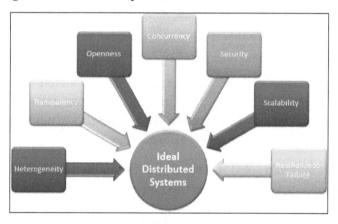

Heterogeneity

The Internet enables users to access services and run applications over a heterogeneous collection of computers and networks. Heterogeneity (that is, variety and difference) applies to all of the following:

- Hardware devices: Computers, tablets, mobile phones, embedded devices, etc.

- Operating System: Ms Windows, Linux, Mac, Unix, etc.

- Network: Local network, the Internet, wireless network, satellite links, etc.

- Programming languages: Java, C/C++, Python, PHP, etc.

- Different roles of software developers, designers, system managers.

Different programming languages use different representations for characters and data structures such as arrays and records. These differences must be addressed if programs written in different languages are to be able to communicate with one another. Programs written by different developers cannot communicate with one another unless they use common standards, for example, for network communication and the representation of primitive data items and data structures in messages. For this to happen, standards need to be agreed and adopted – as have the Internet protocols.

Middleware: The term middleware applies to a software layer that provides a programming abstraction as well as masking the heterogeneity of the underlying networks, hardware, operating systems and programming languages. Most middleware is implemented over the Internet protocols, which themselves mask the differences of the underlying networks, but all middleware deals with the differences in operating systems and hardware.

Heterogeneity and mobile code: The term mobile code is used to refer to program code that can be transferred from one computer to another and run at the destination – Java applets are an example. Code suitable for running on one computer is not necessarily suitable for running on another because executable programs are normally specific both to the instruction set and to the host operating system.

Transparency

Transparency is defined as the concealment from the user and the application programmer of the separation of components in a distributed system, so that the system is perceived as a whole rather than as a collection of independent components. In other words, distributed systems designers must hide the complexity of the systems as much as they can. Some terms of transparency in distributed systems are:

- Access: Hide differences in data representation and how a resource is accessed.

- Location: Hide where a resource is located.

- Migration: Hide that a resource may move to another location.

- Relocation: Hide that a resource may be moved to another location while in use.

- Replication: Hide that a resource may be copied in several places.

- Concurrency: Hide that a resource may be shared by several competitive users.

- Failure: Hide the failure and recovery of a resource.

- Persistence: Hide whether a (software) resource is in memory or a disk.

Openness

The openness of a computer system is the characteristic that determines whether the system can be extended and reimplemented in various ways. The openness of distributed systems is determined primarily by the degree to which new resource-sharing services can be added and be made available for use by a variety of client programs. If the well-defined interfaces for a system are published, it is easier for developers to add new features or replace sub-systems in the future. Example: Twitter and Facebook have API that allows developers to develop their own software interactively.

Concurrency

Both services and applications provide resources that can be shared by clients in a distributed system. There is therefore a possibility that several clients will attempt to access a shared resource at the same time. For example, a data structure that records bids for an auction may be accessed very frequently when it gets close to the deadline time. For an object to be safe in a concurrent environment, its operations must be synchronized in such a way that its data remains consistent. This can be achieved by standard techniques such as semaphores, which are used in most operating systems.

Security

Many of the information resources that are made available and maintained in distributed systems have a high intrinsic value to their users. Their security is therefore of considerable importance. Security for information resources has three components:

- Confidentiality (protection against disclosure to unauthorized individuals).

- Integrity (protection against alteration or corruption).

- Availability for the authorized (protection against interference with the means to access the resources).

Scalability

Distributed systems must be scalable as the number of user increases. The scalability is defined by B. Clifford Neuman as;

A system is said to be scalable if it can handle the addition of users and resources without suffering a noticeable loss of performance or increase in administrative complexity.

Scalability has 3 dimensions:

- Size: Number of users and resources to be processed. Problem associated is overloading.

- Geography: Distance between users and resources. Problem associated is communication reliability.

- Administration: As the size of distributed systems increases, many of the system need to be controlled. Problem associated is administrative mess.

Failure Handling

Computer systems sometimes fail. When faults occur in hardware or software, programs may produce incorrect results or may stop before they have completed the intended computation. The handling of failures is particularly difficult.

References

- Distributed-operating-system, disk-operating-system, fundamental: ecomputernotes.com, Retrieved 1 June, 2019

- Gerndt, michael (2002). Performance-oriented application development for distributed architectures: perspectives for commercial and scientific environments. Ios pr, inc. Isbn 978-1586032678

- Distributed-system: imfrosty.com, Retrieved 12 April, 2019

- Bagwell, h. (2008). Middleware: providing value beyond autoverificationarchived 2009-10-12 at the wayback machine. Ivdt. Retrieved march 3, 2009. "archived copy". Archived from the original on 2009-10-12. Retrieved 2009-03-09

- Distributed-system-architectures-and-architectural-styles, single-post, keetmalin: wixsite.com, Retrieved 3 August, 2019

- Challenges-for-a-distributed-system, distributed-systems: ejbtutorial.com, Retrieved 23 June, 2019

Threads in Operating Systems

A thread refers to a single sequence stream within a process that allows multiple executions of streams. Thread libraries are used by programmers for the creation and management of threads. The topics elaborated in this chapter will help in gaining a better perspective about threads used in operating systems.

A thread is a single sequence stream within in a process. Because threads have some of the properties of processes, they are sometimes called lightweight processes. In a process, threads allow multiple executions of streams. An operating system that has thread facility, the basic unit of CPU utilization is a thread.

- A thread can be in any of several states (Running, Blocked, Ready or Terminated).

- Each thread has its own stack.

- A thread has or consists of a program counter (PC), a register set, and a stack space. Threads are not independent of one other like processes as a result threads shares with other threads their code section, data section, OS resources also known as task, such as open files and signals.

Process Model with Consideration of Threads

In a multithreaded environment, a process, as the unit of resource ownership and protection, is associated with:

- A virtual address space that holds the process image.

- Protected access to I/O devices, files, and other resources that are owned by other processes.

A thread otherwise has:

- A thread execution state.

- A saved thread context when not running. A simple way to view a thread is as an independent program counter within a process, indicating the position of the instruction that the thread is working on.

- A stack tracing the execution path.

- Some space for local variables.

Figure illustrates the distinction between single-threaded process model and multi-threaded process model. As we stated before, a process image includes its PCB, user address space for global variables and code, as well as user and kernel stacks tracing procedural invocations. In a multi-threading environment, there is still a single PCB and user address space associated with each single process, but multiple user stacks and kernel stacks are needed for multiple threads. A separate control block for each thread is also necessary to record the execution context, priority, and state information. Thus all threads within a process share the state of the process, reside in the same address space, and have access to the same collection of data. If the value of a global variable is altered by one thread, other threads can see the result by visiting the same variable.

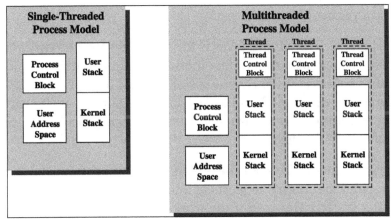

Single threaded and multithreaded process models.

Benefits of Multi-threading

The introduction of thread is not to seek a perfection of a theoretical model, but does bring benefits:

- It takes far less time to create a new process in an existing process than to create a brand new process.

- It takes less time to terminate a thread.

- It takes less time to do control switching between two threads within a same process than process switching.

- Threads make it easier to communicate between different execution traces. Sharing the same user address space enables the communication naturally but process communication demands special supports from the operating system.

Thus if there is a function that should be implemented as a set of related units of execution, it is far more efficient to do so as a collection of threads rather than a collection of separate processes.

Many systems or facilities in the real world are in nature concurrent systems. That is different parts of a system run at the same time. But due to the limitation of early computer systems, the parallel structures are forced to be implemented in a serial fashion. The availability of threads provides more bullets for the computers to reflect the real world in a straightforward way.

Application of Threads

Take web servers as an example. Let's consider the way how the client requests are processed and responded by a web server in terms of the model of the execution traces inside it. With the development of technologies, the following models have been practised in turn by a variety of web servers:

- Blocked model: The simplest way is to set up only one process, which processes one user request at a time. Thus if another request arrives over the Internet while the process is still busy processing and not listening, the new request will simply not be received. This blocked model is similar as the early batch-processing operating systems, where a job will not be processed until all previous ones have been finished.

- Multiplexing model: To solve the problem in the blocked model, a single process may respond to multiple requests in a time-sharing fashion like a time-sharing operating system. However if the work-load of the server is heavy, then each single request will have to wait a long time until completely served.

- Forking model: Since the requests come in independently, a natural way to respond is to create a new process for each newly coming request. This is usually done by the invocation of the UNIX routine fork(), so this model is called forking model. But this model also has its problems. Each process created requires its own address space but main memory is a limited resource. Though the appearance of virtual memory technique allows the suspension of processes, but a process has to be in main memory to be executed. The swapping out and in consumes much time. And the creation of process also takes much time, so the performance of such a web server may be greatly impaired.

- Process-pool model: This model is an improvement to the forking model. Instead of creating a process when a request arrives and terminating it when the process finishes, a set of processes may be created in the first place when the web server is launched at the very beginning. These processes are managed as a process pool and whenever a process is needed for processing a request, the pool will allocate a process for the task. When the processing is finished, the process is returned to the pool for future requests. This model to much extent avoids the overhead of process creation and termination.

- Process-pool with multithreading: The story has not ended yet. Limited resource of the computer system cannot afford a number of processes in the pool. With the introduction of multithreading, the process pool model may be revised to let a single process responsible for multiple requests (e.g. from a same user) with one thread for each request. In this way, the number of processes needed in the pool may be reduced significantly. The sharing of user address space among the threads also fits well the relevance between the requests.

From this abstract example, we can see how processes and threads work together to solve real problems.

Thread Functionality

Thread States

Although a thread embodies the dynamic behavior of processes, and is the unit of scheduling and dispatching, there are however several actions that affect all of the threads in a process and the operating system must manage at the process level.

- Suspension means swapping the process image out of main memory. Since all threads share the same address space, all the threads must enter a Suspend state at the same time.

- Termination of a process terminates all threads within that process. For example, if a Java thread calls `System.exit(0)`, then the JVM process will exit and all the threads will be terminated.

Thus the key states for a thread are Running, Ready, and Blocked. Accordingly there are events that cause a thread state transition:

- Spawn: When a new process is created, typically a thread for this process is also spawned. Later on, other threads may be spawned within the same address space. Every new thread is provided with its own register context and stack space and placed on the ready queue.

- Block: When a thread needs to wait for an event, it will be blocked and its thread context is saved in its thread control block. The processor may then schedule another thread to run.

- Unblock: Similar to the case regarding process, when a desired event occurs, the waiting thread will then be unblocked and moved to the ready queue.

- Finish: When a thread completes, the space allocated for it will be deallocated.

Note that with multithreading the Blocked state of a process makes no more sense. While a thread is blocked, another thread in the same process may still run on the processor. For example, Figure shows a program that performs two remote procedure call (RPC) to two different hosts to obtain a combined result.

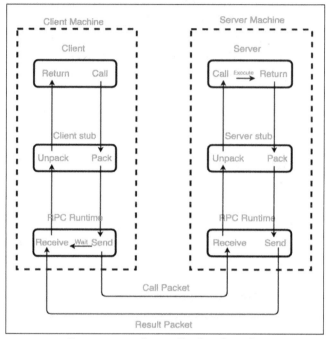

Remote procedure call using threads.

An RPC is similar to a regular procedure call except that the RPC caller and the RPC callee may reside on different hosts. The transfer of parameters and results involves data transmission over the network instead merely local stack push and pop operations. The RPC mechanism is illustrated in figure.

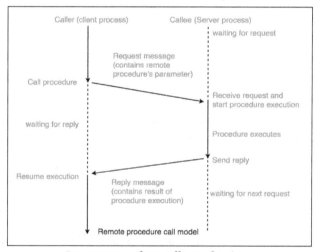

Remote procedure calls mechanism.

In a single-threaded system, the two requests have to be done in sequence, while in a multithreaded environment, each request may be made by separate threads. Although on a uniprocessor system at any moment only one thread may be running, and the requests still have to be generated sequentially, the process however waits concurrently for the two replies.

Thread Synchronization

Since threads in a processor share the same address space, the result of a thread's operation is visible to other threads. This enables the communication between threads, but may cause problems as well.

User-level and Kernel-level Threads

We move on to consider the implementation issues of threads. There are two common ways to support threads: user-level threads and kernel-level threads. Figure respectively show the two approaches and their combination.

User-level Threads

In this approach, all of the work of thread management is done by the user application, and the operating system kernel is not aware of the existence of threads. Typically a thread library is available providing routines for manipulating threads (creating, terminating, scheduling, and saving and restoring thread context) and communication between threads as well. JVM implementations on Windows platform fall into this category.

Same as we have said, when a user process is created, a single thread is spawned and begins running in the process space. This thread may spawn a new thread sometime in the same process by invoking the spawn utility in the threads library. The threads library creates a data structure for the new thread and then dispatch control to one of the threads in the currently running process. When the control switches between individual threads and the library, the thread context is also saved or restored accordingly.

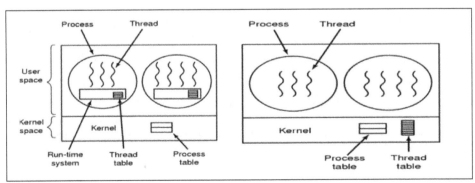

User-level and kernel-level threads.

The above activities all happen within the user address space. The kernel has no idea of these and always schedule the process as a unit and assign a single execution state to it.

But how the thread state transition and process state transition work together consistently? Figure gives an example. Suppose process B is executing in thread 2; the state of the process and the two threads are shown in figure. Now let's see what will happen in the following three occasions:

- Thread 2 makes a system call that blocks process B, e.g. an I/O call. This causes control to transfer to the kernel. The kernel then starts the I/O operation, places process B in the Blocked state, and switches control to another process. Meanwhile, the information the threads maintained by the threads library remains unchanged, so thread 2 is still perceived as running though it is not. The new snapshot is illustrated in figure.

- A timeout event occurs: The kernel determines that process B has exhausted its time slice, so places it in the Ready state and dispatches another process. Similar to the first case, the thread states are still the same.

- Thread 2 has reached a point where it has to wait until thread 1 has performed a specific action. Thus, thread 2 enters a Blocked state and thread 1 becomes active and begins to run. The process itself remains in the Running state.

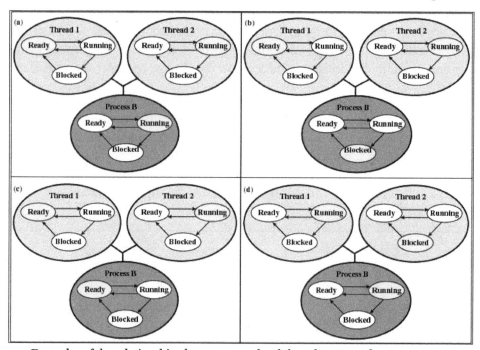

Examples of the relationships between user-level thread states and process states.

Kernel-level Threads

With a kernel-level thread implementation, all of the thread management work is done by the kernel. The operating system may also provide an application programming interface (API) to the user application, similar to the above threads library, but there is no thread management code in user address space. The examples include Windows 2000, Linux, and some implementation of JVM on Solaris.

Figure depicts this approach. The kernel maintains context information for every process and for individual threads within processes. Scheduling by the kernel is done on a thread basis.

Comparison between User-level and Kernel-level Threads

Compared with the kernel-level implementation, the user-level one has the following advantages:

- No mode switching: Thread switching does not require mode switching, whose overhead is huge. The threads library works in the user address and there is no need to switch to the kernel mode. Some experiments have shown that there may be an order of magnitude or more of difference between user-level threads and kernel threads regarding the time needed for various thread operations.

- Customizable thread scheduling: Thread scheduling can be tailored according to the nature of the application so that better performance may be achieved.

- System independent: User-level implementation may be easily ported to other platforms since the threads library is a set of application-level utilities.

On the other side of the story, user-level threads also possess explicit disadvantages:

- Process-level blocking: A blocking system call made by a thread in a process will cause all the threads in the process to be blocked.

- Undistributable threads: In a multi-processor system, the kernel assigns one process to only one processor at a time. Thus the multiple threads in a single process have no chance to run simultaneously.

The kernel-level threads do not have the above problems, but thread switching causes mode switching and may greatly impair the performance.

Thus some systems tried to combine the two approaches together, e.g. Solaris and some good results have been achieved in this direction.

Thread Libraries

A thread library provides the programmer an API for creating and managing threads. There are two primary ways of implementing a thread library. The first approach is to provide a library entirely in user space with no kernel support. All code and data structures for the library exist in user space. This means that invoking a function in the library results in a local function call in user space and not a system call.

The second approach is to implement a kernel-level library supported directly by the operating system. In this case, code and data structures for the library exist in kernel space. Invoking a function in the API for the library typically results in a system call to the kernel.

Three main thread libraries are in use today:

- POSIX Pthreads,

- Win32, and

- Java. Pthreads.

The threads extension of the POSIX standard, may be provided as either a user- or kernel-level library. The Win32 thread library is a kernel-level library available on Windows systems. The Java thread API allows thread creation and management directly in Java programs. However, because in most instances the JVM is running on top of a host operating system, the Java thread API is typically implemented using a thread library available on the host system. This means that on Windows systems, Java threads are typically implemented using the Win32 API; UNIX and Linux systems often use Pthreads.

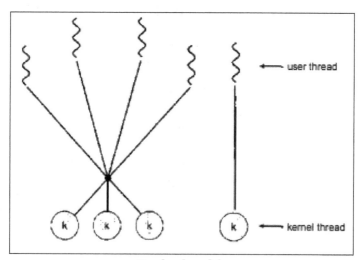

Two level model.

As an illustrative example, we design a multithreaded program that performs the summation of a non-negative integer in a separate thread using the well-known summation function. For example, if N were 5, this function would represent the summation from 0 to 5, which is 15. Each of the three programs will be run with the upper bounds of the summation entered on the command line; thus, if the user enters 8, the summation of the integer values from 0 to 8 will be output.

Pthreads

Pthreads refers to the POSIX standard (IEEE 1003.1c) defining an API for thread creation and synchronization. This is a specification for thread behavior, not an implementation. Operating system designers may implement the specification in any way they wish. Numerous systems implement the Pthreads specification, including Solaris, Linux, Mac OS X, and Tru64 UNIX. Shareware implementations are available in the public domain for the various Windows operating systems as well. In a Pthreads program, separate threads begin execution in a specified function, this is the runner () function. When this program begins, a single thread of control begins in main().

After some initialization, main() creates a second thread that begins control in the runner () function. Both threads share the global data sum. Let's look more closely at this program. All Pthreads programs must include the pthread.h header file. The statement pthreadjt tid declares the identifier for the thread we will create. Each thread has a set of attributes, including stack size and scheduling information. The pthread_attr_t attr declaration represents the attributes for the thread. We set the attributes in the function call pthread_attr_init C&attr). Because we did not explicitly set any attributes, we use the default attributes provided. A separate thread is created with the pthread_create () function call. In addition to passing the thread identifier and the attributes for the thread, we also pass the name of the function where the new thread will begin execution - in this case, the runner () function. Last, we pass the integer parameter that was provided on the command line, argv. At this point, the program has two threads: the initial (or parent) thread in main() and the summation (or child) thread performing the summation operation in the runner () function. After creating the summation thread, the parent thread will wait for it to complete by calling the pthread_join() function. The summation thread will complete when it calls the function pthread.exit(). Once the summation thread has returned, the parent thread will output the value of the shared data sum.

Win32 Threads

The technique for creating threads using the Win32 thread library is similar to the Pthreads technique in several ways. We must include the windows.h header file when using the Win32 API. Just as in the Pthreads, data shared by the separate threads—in this case, Sum—are declared globally the DWORD data type is an unsigned 32-bit integer. We also define the SummationO function that is to be performed in a separate thread. This function is passed a pointer to a void, which Win32 defines as LPVOID. The thread performing this function sets the global data Sum to the value of the summation from 0 to the parameter passed to SummationO.

Threads are created in the Win32 API using the CreateThreadO function and—just as in Pthreads—a set of attributes for the thread is passed to this function. These attributes include security information, the size of the stack, and a flag that can be set to indicate if the thread is to start in a suspended state. In this program, we use the default values for these attributes (which do not initially set the thread to a suspended state and instead make it eligible to be run by the CPU scheduler). Once the summation thread is created, the parent must wait for it to complete before outputting the value of Sum, as the value is set by the summation thread. Recall that the Pthread program had the parent thread wait for the summation thread using the pthread join() statement. We perform the equivalent of this in the Win32 API using the WaitForSingleObject () function, which causes the creating thread to block until the summation thread has exited.

Thread in Java

Every java application has at least one thread – main thread. Although, there are so many other java threads running in background like memory management, system management, signal processing etc. But from application point of view – main is the first java thread and we can create multiple threads from it.

Multithreading refers to two or more threads executing concurrently in a single program. A computer single core processor can execute only one thread at a time and time slicing is the OS feature to share processor time between different processes and threads.

Java Thread Benefits

- Java Threads are lightweight compared to processes; it takes less time and resource to create a thread.

- Threads share their parent process data and code.

- Context switching between threads is usually less expensive than between processes.

- Thread intercommunication is relatively easy than process communication.

Java provides two ways to create a thread programmatically.

- Implementing the java.lang.Runnable interface.

- Extending the java.lang.Thread class.

Java Thread Example – Implementing Runnable Interface

To make a class runnable, we can implement java.lang.Runnable interface and provide implementation in public void run() method. To use this class as Thread, we need to create a Thread object by passing object of this runnable class and then call start() method to execute the run() method in a separate thread.

Here is a java thread example by implementing Runnable interface.

```java
package com.journaldev.threads;

public class HeavyWorkRunnable implements Runnable {

    @Override

    public void run() {

        System.out.println("Doing heavy processing - START "+Thread.
currentThread().getName());

        try {

            Thread.sleep(1000);

            //Get database connection, delete unused data from DB

            doDBProcessing();

        } catch (InterruptedException e) {

            e.printStackTrace();

        }

        System.out.println("Doing heavy processing - END "+Thread.cur-
rentThread().getName());

    }

    private void doDBProcessing() throws InterruptedException {

        Thread.sleep(5000);

    }

}
```

Java Thread Example – Extending Thread Class

We can extend java.lang.Thread class to create our own java thread class and override run() method. Then we can create it's object and call start() method to execute our custom java thread class run method.

Here is a simple java thread example showing how to extend Thread class.

```java
package com.journaldev.threads;

public class MyThread extends Thread {

    public MyThread(String name) {
```

```java
        super(name);

    }

    @Override

    public void run() {

        System.out.println("MyThread - START "+Thread.currentThread().
getName());

        try {

            Thread.sleep(1000);

            //Get database connection, delete unused data from DB

            doDBProcessing();

        } catch (InterruptedException e) {

            e.printStackTrace();

        }

        System.out.println("MyThread - END "+Thread.currentThread().
getName());

    }

    private void doDBProcessing() throws InterruptedException {

        Thread.sleep(5000);

    }


}
```

Test Program

```java
package com.journaldev.threads;

public class ThreadRunExample {

    public static void main(String[] args){

        Thread t1 = new Thread(new HeavyWorkRunnable(), "t1");

        Thread t2 = new Thread(new HeavyWorkRunnable(), "t2");

        System.out.println("Starting Runnable threads");

        t1.start();
```

```
          t2.start();

          System.out.println("Runnable Threads has been started");

          Thread t3 = new MyThread("t3");

          Thread t4 = new MyThread("t4");

          System.out.println("Starting MyThreads");

          t3.start();

          t4.start();

          System.out.println("MyThreads has been started");


      }

}
```

Output of the above java thread example program is:

```
Starting Runnable threads

Runnable Threads has been started

Doing heavy processing - START t1

Doing heavy processing - START t2

Starting MyThreads

MyThread - START Thread-0

MyThreads has been started

MyThread - START Thread-1

Doing heavy processing - END t2

MyThread - END Thread-1

MyThread - END Thread-0

Doing heavy processing - END t1
```

Once we start any thread, it's execution depends on the OS implementation of time slicing and we can't control their execution. However, we can set threads priority but even then it doesn't guarantee that higher priority thread will be executed first.

Thread in Python

There are two modules which support the usage of threads in Python - thread and threading.

The thread module has been considered as "deprecated" for quite a long time. Users have been encouraged to use the threading module instead. So, in Python 3 the module "thread" is not available anymore. But that's not really true: It has been renamed to "_thread" for backwards incompatibilities in Python3.

The module "thread" treats a thread as a function, while the module "threading" is implemented in an object oriented way, i.e. every thread corresponds to an object.

The Thread Module

It's possible to execute functions in a separate thread with the module Thread. To do this, we can use the function thread.start_new_thread:

```
thread.start_new_thread(function, args[, kwargs])
```

This method starts a new thread and return its identifier. The thread executes the function "function" (function is a reference to a function) with the argument list args (which must be a list or a tuple). The optional kwargs argument specifies a dictionary of keyword arguments. When the function returns, the thread silently exits. When the function terminates with an unhandled exception, a stack trace is printed and then the thread exits (but other threads continue to run).

Example for a Thread in Python:

```
from thread import start_new_thread

def heron(a):

    """Calculates the square root of a"""

    eps = 0.0000001

    old = 1

    new = 1

    while True:

        old,new = new, (new + a/new) / 2.0

        print old, new

        if abs(new - old) < eps:

            break

    return new

start_new_thread(heron, (99,))

start_new_thread(heron, (999,))
```

```
start_new_thread(heron,(1733,))

c = raw_input("Type something to quit.")
```

The raw_input() in the previous example is necessary, because otherwise all the threads would be exited, if the main program finishes. raw_input() waits until something has been typed in.

We expand the previous example with counters for the threads.

```
from thread import start_new_thread


num_threads = 0

def heron(a):

    global num_threads

    num_threads += 1


    # code has been left out, see above

    num_threads -= 1

    return new


start_new_thread(heron,(99,))

start_new_thread(heron,(999,))

start_new_thread(heron,(1733,))

start_new_thread(heron,(17334,))


while num_threads > 0:

    pass
```

The script above doesn't work the way we might expect it to work. What is wrong? The problem is that the final while loop will be reached even before one of the threads could have incremented the counter num_threads.

But there is another serious problem:

The problem arises by the assignments to num_thread,

```
num_threads += 1
```

and

```
num_threads -= 1
```

These assignment statements are not atomic. Such an assignment consists of three actions:

- Reading the value of num_thread.

- A new int instance will be incremented or decremented by 1.

- The new value has to be assigned to num_threads.

Errors like this happen in the case of increment assignments: The first thread reads the variable num_threads, which still has the value 0. After having read this value, the thread is put to sleep by the operating system. Now, it is the second thread's turn: It also reads the value of the variable num_threads, which is still 0, because the first thread has been put to sleep too early, i.e. before it had been able to increment its value by 1. Now the second thread is put to sleep. Now, it is the third thread's turn, which again reads a 0, but the counter should have been 2 by now. Each of these threads assigns now the value 1 to the counter. Similiar problems occur with the decrement operation.

Problems of this kind can be solved by defining critical sections with lock objects. These sections will be treated atomically, i.e. during the execution of such a section a thread will not be interrupted or put to sleep.

The method thread.allocate_lock is used to create a new lock object:

```
lock_object = thread.allocate_lock()
```

The beginning of a critical section is tagged with lock_object.acquire() and the end with lock_object.release(). The solution with locks looks like this:

```
from thread import start_new_thread, allocate_lock

num_threads = 0

thread_started = False

lock = allocate_lock()

def heron(a):
    global num_threads, thread_started
    lock.acquire()
    num_threads += 1
    thread_started = True
```

```
        lock.release()


        ...


        lock.acquire()
        num_threads -= 1
        lock.release()
        return new


start_new_thread(heron,(99,))
start_new_thread(heron,(999,))
start_new_thread(heron,(1733,))


while not thread_started:
        pass
while num_threads > 0:
        pass
```

Threading Module

We want to introduce the threading module with an example. The Thread of the example doesn't do a lot, essentially it just sleeps for 5 seconds and then prints out a message:

```
import time
from threading import Thread
def sleeper(i):
        print "thread %d sleeps for 5 seconds" % i
        time.sleep(5)
        print "thread %d woke up" % i


for i in range(10):
        t = Thread(target=sleeper, args=(i,))
        t.start()
```

Method of operation of the threading. Thread has a method start(), which can start a Thread. It triggers off the method run(), which has to be overloaded. The join() method makes sure that the main program waits until all threads have terminated.

The previous script returns the following output:

```
thread 0 sleeps for 5 seconds

thread 1 sleeps for 5 seconds

thread 2 sleeps for 5 seconds

thread 3 sleeps for 5 seconds

thread 4 sleeps for 5 seconds

thread 5 sleeps for 5 seconds

thread 6 sleeps for 5 seconds

thread 7 sleeps for 5 seconds

thread 8 sleeps for 5 seconds

thread 9 sleeps for 5 seconds

thread 1 woke up

thread 0 woke up

thread 3 woke up

thread 2 woke up

thread 5 woke up

thread 9 woke up

thread 8 woke up

thread 7 woke up

thread 6 woke up

thread 4 woke up
```

The next example shows a thread, which determines, if a number is prime or not. The Thread is defined with the threading module:

```
import threading


class PrimeNumber(threading.Thread):

  def __init__(self, number):

    threading.Thread.__init__(self)
```

```
    self.Number = number


  def run(self):

    counter = 2

    while counter*counter < self.Number:

      if self.Number % counter == 0:

        print "%d is no prime number, because %d = %d * %d" % ( self.
Number, self.Number, counter, self.Number / counter)

              return

          counter += 1

      print "%d is a prime number" % self.Number
threads = []
while True:

    input = long(raw_input("number: "))

    if input < 1:

        break


    thread = PrimeNumber(input)

    threads += [thread]

    thread.start()


for x in threads:

    x.join()
```

With locks it should look like this:

```
class PrimeNumber(threading.Thread):

    prime_numbers = {}

    lock = threading.Lock()

    def __init__(self, number):

        threading.Thread.__init__(self)
```

```python
        self.Number = number

        PrimeNumber.lock.acquire()

        PrimeNumber.prime_numbers[number] = "None"

        PrimeNumber.lock.release()


    def run(self):
        counter = 2
        res = True
        while counter*counter < self.Number and res:
            if self.Number % counter == 0:
                res = False
            counter += 1
        PrimeNumber.lock.acquire()
        PrimeNumber.prime_numbers[self.Number] = res
        PrimeNumber.lock.release()
threads = []
while True:
    input = long(raw_input("number: "))
    if input < 1:
        break

    thread = PrimeNumber(input)
    threads += [thread]
    thread.start()


for x in threads:
    x.join()
```

Pinging with Threads

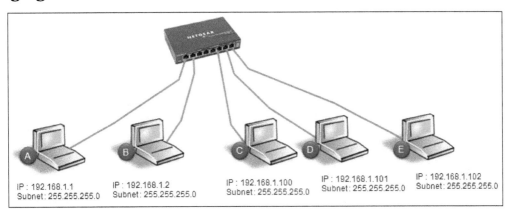

IP : 192.168.1.1   IP : 192.168.1.2   IP : 192.168.1.100   IP : 192.168.1.101   IP : 192.168.1.102
Subnet: 255.255.255.0   Subnet: 255.255.255.0   Subnet: 255.255.255.0   Subnet: 255.255.255.0   Subnet: 255.255.255.0

The following example shows an interesting application, which can be easily used. If you want to determine in a local network which addresses are active or which computers are active, this script can be used. But you have to be careful with the range, because it can jam the network, if too many pings are started at once. Manually we would do the following for a network 192.168.178.x: We would ping the addresses 192.168.178.0, 192.168.178.1, 192.168.178.3 until 192.168.178.255 in turn. Every time we would have to wait a few seconds for the return values. This can be programmed in Python with a for loop over the address range of the IP addresses and a os.popen("ping -q -c2 "+ip,"r").

A solution without threads is highly inefficient, because the script will have to wait for every ping.

Solution with threads:

```
import os, re


received_packages = re.compile(r"(\d) received")

status = ("no response","alive but losses","alive")


for suffix in range(20,30):

    ip = "192.168.178."+str(suffix)

    ping_out = os.popen("ping -q -c2 "+ip,"r")

    print "... pinging ",ip

    while True:

        line = ping_out.readline()
```

```
        if not line: break

        n_received = received_packages.findall(line)

        if n_received:

            print ip + ": " + status[int(n_received[0])]
```

To understand this script, we have to look at the results of a ping on a shell command line:

```
$ ping -q -c2 192.168.178.26

PING 192.168.178.26 (192.168.178.26) 56(84) bytes of data.


--- 192.168.178.26 ping statistics ---

2 packets transmitted, 2 received, 0% packet loss, time 999ms

rtt min/avg/max/mdev = 0.022/0.032/0.042/0.010 ms
```

If a ping doesn't lead to success, we get the following output:

```
$ ping -q -c2 192.168.178.23

PING 192.168.178.23 (192.168.178.23) 56(84) bytes of data.


--- 192.168.178.23 ping statistics ---

2 packets transmitted, 0 received, +2 errors, 100% packet loss, time
1006ms
```

This is the fast solution with threads:

```
import os, re, threading


class ip_check(threading.Thread):

    def __init__(self,ip):

        threading.Thread.__init__(self)

        self.ip = ip

        self.__successful_pings = -1

    def run(self):

        ping_out = os.popen("ping -q -c2 "+self.ip,"r")
```

```
    while True:

      line = ping_out.readline()

      if not line: break

      n_received = re.findall(received_packages,line)

      if n_received:

        self.__successful_pings = int(n_received[0])

  def status(self):

    if self.__successful_pings == 0:

      return "no response"

    elif self.__successful_pings == 1:

      return "alive, but 50 % package loss"

    elif self.__successful_pings == 2:

      return "alive"

    else:

      return "shouldn't occur"

received_packages = re.compile(r"(\d) received")


check_results = []

for suffix in range(20,70):

  ip = "192.168.178."+str(suffix)

  current = ip_check(ip)

  check_results.append(current)

  current.start()


for el in check_results:

  el.join()

  print "Status from ", el.ip,"is",el.status()
```

Implicit Threading and Language-based Threads

Implicit threading is the use of libraries or other language support to hide the management of threads. In the context of C, the most common implicit threading library is OpenMP. OpenMP uses the #pragma compiler directive to detect and insert additional library code at compile time. As an example, consider the prime number calculator. The following example shows the OpenMP equivalent.

```c
#include <stdio.h>

#include <stdbool.h>

#include <omp.h>


int
main (int argc, char **argv)
{
  /* Set up the overall algorithm parameters */
  unsigned long value = 2;
  unsigned long end = 100000000L;
  unsigned long iter = 0;
  unsigned long count = 0;


  /* OpenMP parallel for-loop with reduction on count. So each thread
     will have its own count, but they'll all be combined in the end. */
#pragma omp parallel for default(shared) private(iter) reduction(+:count)
  for (value = 2; value < end; value++)
    {
      bool is_prime = true;
      for (iter = 2; iter * iter <= value && is_prime; iter++)
        if (value % iter == 0) is_prime = false;


      if (is_prime) count++;
```

```
    }


    printf ("Total number of primes less than %ld: %ld\n", end, count);


    return 0;
}
```

With implicit threading, the focus of the programmer is on writing the algorithm rather than the multithreading. The OpenMP library itself takes care of managing the threads. Specifically, the #pragmaline indicates that OpenMP (omp) should parallelize a for-loop (parallel for) with some constraints on the variables. The OpenMP implementation on that system will then inject code to perform the thread creation and join.

OpenMP in C is built on top of the Pthread library. As such, any code that can be written using OpenMP can be converted into a more verbose Pthread equivalent. However, the disadvantage of OpenMP is that it only works for certain types of tasks. There are many types of programs, such as the keyboard listener example, that can be implemented in Pthreads but not OpenMP.

Threads as Objects

In other languages, traditional object-oriented languages provide explicit multithreading support with threads as objects. In these types of languages, classes are written to either extend a thread class or implement a corresponding interface. This style resembles the Pthread approach, as the code is written with explicit thread management. However, the encapsulation of data within the classes and additional synchronization features simplify the task.

Concurrency as Language Design

Languages such as C, Java, and Python were all designed before multicore architectures rose to prominence in the early 2000s. As such, multithreading support in these languages was added as a supplement to the language, rather than a core feature. These languages were originally designed for a uniprocessing procedural or object-oriented paradigm. As a result, the memory models that underly these languages are not adequate to prevent race conditions. The multithreading libraries had to provide additional features that allowed programmers to synchronize access to shared data. Or, put another way, programmers were forced to do extra work to make their programs work correctly.

Newer programming languages have avoided this problem by building assumptions of concurrent execution directly into the language design itself. For instance, Go combines a trivial implicit threading technique (goroutines) with channels, a well-defined form of message-passing communication. Rust adopts an explicit threading approach similar to Pthreads. However, Rust has very strong memory protections that require no additional work by the programmer.

Goroutines

The Go language includes a trivial mechanism for implicit threading: place the keyword go before a function call. In the example below, the line go keyboard_listener(messages) launches a new thread that will execute the keyboard listener function. The new thread is passed a connection to a message-passing channel. Then, the main thread calls success := <-messages, which performs a blocking read on the channel. Once the user has entered the correct guess of 7, the keyboard listener thread writes to the channel, allowing the main thread to progress.

Channels and goroutines are core parts of the Go language, which was designed under the assumption that most programs would be multithreaded. This design choice streamlines the development model, allowing the language itself to bear the responsibility for managing the threads and scheduling.

```go
package main


import (

        "bufio"

        "fmt"

        "os"

        "strconv"

        "strings"

)


/* Main program entry point */

func main() {

        /* Create a channel for communication */

        messages := make(chan string)


        fmt.Print("Guess a number between 1 and 10: ")
```

```
        /* Start the keyboard listener as a goroutine with the channel */
        go keyboard_listener(messages)


        /* Wait until there is data in the channel */
        success := <-messages
        if success == "true" {
                fmt.Println("You must have guess 7.")
        }
}


/* Define the keyboard listener thread with channel back to main */
func keyboard_listener(messages chan string) {
        stdin := bufio.NewReader(os.Stdin)


        /* Loop forever, reading keyboard input */
        for {
                text, _ := stdin.ReadString('\n')


                /* Try to convert the input text to an int 7 */
                value, err := strconv.ParseInt(strings.Trim(text,
"\n"), 10, 32)
                if err == nil {
                        if value == 7 {
                                /* Success. Send a message back through
the channel and exit */
                                messages <- "true"
                                return
                        }
                }
```

```
            fmt.Print("Wrong. Try again. ")
        }
}
```

Rust Concurrency

Rust is another language that has been created in recent years, with concurrency as a central design feature. The following example illustrates the use of thread::spawn() to create a new thread, which can later be joined by invoking join() on it. The argument to thread::spawn() beginning at the || is known as a *closure*, which can be thought of as an anonymous function. That is, the child thread here will print the value of x.

```
use std::thread;


fn main() {
    /* Initialize a mutable variable x to 10 */
    let mut x = 10;


    /* Spawn a new thread */
    let child_thread = thread::spawn(move || {
        /* Make the thread sleep for one second, then print x */
        x -= 1;
        println!("x = {}", x)
    });


    /* Change x in the main thread and print it */
    x += 1;
    println!("x = {}", x);


    /* Join the thread and print x again */
    child_thread.join();
}
```

However, there is a subtle point in this code that is central to Rust's design. Within the new thread (executing the code in the closure), the x variable is distinct from the x in other parts of this code. Rust enforces a very strict memory model (known as "ownership") which prevents multiple threads from accessing the same memory. In this example, the move keyword indicates that the spawned thread will receive a separate copy of x for its own use. Regardless of the scheduling of the two threads, the main and child threads cannot interfere with each other's modifications of x, because they are distinct copies. It is impossible for the two threads to share access to the same memory.

Major Issues with Multi-threaded Programs

Multithreaded programs allow the execution of multiple parts of a program at the same time. These parts are known as threads and are lightweight processes available within the process.

Threads improve the application performance using parallelism. They share information like data segment, code segment files etc. with their peer threads while they contain their own registers, stack, counter etc.

Some of the issues with multithreaded programs are as follows:

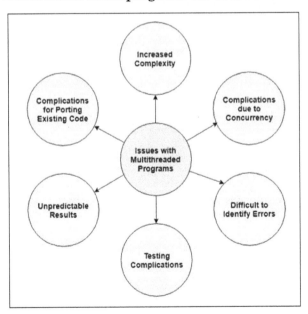

Let us see them one by one:

- Increased Complexity: Multithreaded processes are quite complicated. Coding for these can only be handled by expert programmers.

- Complications due to Concurrency: It is difficult to handle concurrency in multithreaded processes. This may lead to complications and future problems.

- Difficult to Identify Errors: Identification and correction of errors is much more difficult in multithreaded processes as compared to single threaded processes.

- Testing Complications: Testing is a complicated process i multithreaded programs as compared to single threaded programs. This is because defects can be timing related and not easy to identify.

- Unpredictable results: Multithreaded programs can sometimes lead to unpredictable results as they are essentially multiple parts of a program that are running at the same time.

- Complications for Porting Existing Code: A lot of testing is required for porting existing code in multithreading. Static variables need to be removed and any code or function calls that are not thread safe need to be replaced.

References

- Thread-libraries: padakuu.com, Retrieved 19 May, 2019

- Java-thread-example: journaldev.com, Retrieved 28 April, 2019

- Threads: python-course.eu, Retrieved 8 August , 2019

- Major-issues-with-multi-threaded-programs: tutorialspoint.com, Retrieved 9 May, 2019

Operating System Security

The process that is concerned with the protection of operating system from threats, viruses, trojans, malware, etc. is known as operation system security. Some of its policies and procedures are acceptable use policy, access control policy, information security policy, incident response policy, etc. The topics elaborated in this chapter will help in gaining a better perspective about operating system security.

Security refers to providing a protection system to computer system resources such as CPU, memory, disk, software programs and most importantly data/information stored in the computer system. If a computer program is run by an unauthorized user, then he/she may cause severe damage to computer or data stored in it. So, a computer system must be protected against unauthorized access, malicious access to system memory, viruses, worms etc.

Operating system security (OS security) is the process of ensuring OS integrity, confidentiality and availability.

OS security refers to specified steps or measures used to protect the OS from threats, viruses, worms, malware or remote hacker intrusions. OS security encompasses all preventive-control techniques, which safeguard any computer assets capable of being stolen, edited or deleted if OS security is compromised.

OS security encompasses many different techniques and methods which ensure safety from threats and attacks. OS security allows different applications and programs to perform required tasks and stop unauthorized interference.

OS security may be approached in many ways, including adherence to the following:

- Performing regular OS patch updates.

- Installing updated antivirus engines and software.

- Scrutinizing all incoming and outgoing network traffic through a firewall.

- Creating secure accounts with required privileges only (i.e., user management).

Authentication

Authentication refers to identifying each user of the system and associating the executing programs with those users. It is the responsibility of the Operating System to create a protection system which ensures that a user who is running a particular program is authentic. Operating Systems generally identifies/authenticates users using following three ways:

- Username/Password – User need to enter a registered username and password with Operating system to login into the system.

- User card/key – User need to punch card in card slot, or enter key generated by key generator in option provided by operating system to login into the system.

- User attribute - fingerprint/ eye retina pattern/signature – User need to pass his/her attribute via designated input device used by operating system to login into the system.

One Time Passwords

One-time passwords provide additional security along with normal authentication. In One-Time Password system, a unique password is required every time user tries to login into the system. Once a one-time password is used, then it cannot be used again. One-time password is implemented in various ways:

- Random numbers: Users are provided cards having numbers printed along with corresponding alphabets. System asks for numbers corresponding to few alphabets randomly chosen.

- Secret key: User are provided a hardware device which can create a secret id mapped with user id. System asks for such secret id which is to be generated every time prior to login.

- Network password: Some commercial applications send one-time passwords to user on registered mobile/email which is required to be entered prior to login.

Program Threats

Operating system's processes and kernel do the designated task as instructed. If a user program made these process do malicious tasks, then it is known as Program Threats. One of the common examples of program threat is a program installed in a computer which can store and send user credentials via network to some hacker. Following is the list of some well-known program threats.

- Trojan Horse: Such program traps user login credentials and stores them to send to malicious user who can later on login to computer and can access system resources.

- Trap Door: If a program which is designed to work as required, have a security hole in its code and perform illegal action without knowledge of user then it is called to have a trap door.

- Logic Bomb: Logic bomb is a situation when a program misbehaves only when certain conditions met otherwise it works as a genuine program. It is harder to detect.

- Virus: Virus as name suggest can replicate themselves on computer system. They are highly dangerous and can modify/delete user files, crash systems. A virus is generally a small code embedded in a program. As user accesses the program, the virus starts getting embedded in other files/programs and can make system unusable for user.

System Threats

System threats refer to misuse of system services and network connections to put user in trouble. System threats can be used to launch program threats on a complete network called as program attack. System threats create such an environment that operating system resources/user files are misused. Following is the list of some well-known system threats:

- Worm: Worm is a process which can choked down a system performance by using system resources to extreme levels. A Worm process generates its multiple copies where each copy uses system resources, prevents all other processes to get required resources. Worm processes can even shut down an entire network.

- Port Scanning: Port scanning is a mechanism or means by which a hacker can detects system vulnerabilities to make an attack on the system.

- Denial of Service: Denial of service attacks normally prevents user to make legitimate use of the system. For example, a user may not be able to use internet if denial of service attacks browser's content settings.

Computer Security Classifications

As per the U.S. Department of Defense Trusted Computer System's Evaluation Criteria there are four security classifications in computer systems: A, B, C, and D. This is widely used specifications to determine and model the security of systems and of security solutions. Following is the brief description of each classification.

Classification Type and Description	
1	Type A Highest Level. Uses formal design specifications and verification techniques. Grants a high degree of assurance of process security.

2	Type B
	Provides mandatory protection system. Have all the properties of a class C2 system. Attaches a sensitivity label to each object. It is of three types:
	• B1 – Maintains the security label of each object in the system. Label is used for making decisions to access control.
	• B2 – Extends the sensitivity labels to each system resource, such as storage objects, supports covert channels and auditing of events.
	• B3 – Allows creating lists or user groups for access-control to grant access or revoke access to a given named object.
3	Type C
	Provides protection and user accountability using audit capabilities. It is of two types:
	• C1 – Incorporates controls so that users can protect their private information and keep other users from accidentally reading / deleting their data. UNIX versions are mostly Cl class.
	• C2 – Adds an individual-level access control to the capabilities of a Cl level system.
4	Type D
	Lowest level. Minimum protection. MS-DOS, Window 3.1 fall in this category.

Secure Operating System

Secure operating systems are important because of the information that we enter into our computers. It's essential that our computers are as secure as possible so that our data is safe and sound. Find out which operating systems are the most secure so that you can protect your computer.

Is Windows Secure

Windows certainly isn't secure and there have been many reported attacks on Windows machines. Every new version of Microsoft windows has a number of security holes which need to be plugged. These vulnerabilities allow hackers easy access into the computer once they are discovered.

Mac OSX

Mac has long used the campaign stating that their operating system is much more secure than Windows. However, this isn't true either. The only reason that Mac OS seems to be more secure is because it isn't used as much.

Windows is the most popular operating system in the world and this means that it receives a lot of attention from hackers as well as computer users. Because most people use Windows, hackers will concentrate on Windows when they are writing viruses and attacking systems.

Mac and Linux are much less popular operating systems and are actually just as insecure as Windows if you study them. There are viruses which can affect Linux and Mac operating systems, although fewer than those that affect Windows, but really no system is 100% safe.

Recent studies have suggested that Mac OS could actually be less secure than other operating systems, and this is a very troubling statistic for many people.

Mac Virus

The very first Mac virus was bundled along with illegal pirated versions of iLife. If Mac users downloaded this application their computer was infected with a Trojan. This Trojan worked in exactly the same way as a PC Trojan by opening a backdoor into your computer which criminals could then use to steal information.

While Apple might claim that Mac's are fully secure, this quite obviously isn't true. Even though the virus only affects a limited number of computers, it has proved that viruses are possible on Mac computers.

Security-focused Operating System

General-purpose operating systems may be secure in practice, without being specifically "security-focused".

Similar concepts include security-evaluated operating systems that have achieved certification from an auditing organization, and trusted operating systems that provide sufficient support for multilevel security and evidence of correctness to meet a particular set of requirements.

Linux

Android-based

- PrivatOS was a hardened proprietary operating system for Blackphone.

- Replicant is a FOSS operating system based on the Android mobile platform, which aims to replace all proprietary Android components with their free software counterparts. It is available for several smartphones and tablet computers. In March 2014, the Replicant project announced the discovery of a backdoor present in a wide range of Samsung Galaxy products that allows the baseband processor to read and write the device's storage, sometimes with normal user privileges and sometimes as the root user, depending on device model. It is not generally known whether Samsung's proprietary firmware for the radio chip can be remotely instructed to use these access features and the intentions of creating such a backdoor.

Debian-based

- Subgraph is a Linux-based operating system designed to be resistant to surveillance and interference by sophisticated adversaries over the Internet. Subgraph OS is designed with features which aim to reduce the attack surface of the operating system, and increase the difficulty required to carry out certain classes of attack. This is accomplished through system hardening and a proactive, ongoing focus on security and attack resistance. Subgraph OS also places emphasis on ensuring the integrity of installed software packages through deterministic compilation. Subgraph OS features a kernel hardened with the Grsecurity and PaX patchset, Linux namespaces, and Xpra for application containment, mandatory file system encryption using LUKS, resistance to cold boot attacks, and is configured by default to isolate network communications for installed applications to independent circuits on the Tor anonymity network.

- Tails is a security-focused Linux distribution aimed at preserving privacy and anonymity. It is meant to be run as Live-CD or from a USB Drive and to not write any kind of data to a drive, unless specified or persistance is set. That way, it lives in RAM and everything is purged from the system whenever it is powered off. Tails is designed to do an emergency shutdown and erase its data from RAM if the medium where it resides is expelled.

- Whonix is an anonymous general purpose operating system based on VirtualBox, Debian GNU/Linux and Tor. By Whonix design, IP and DNS leaks are impossible. Not even Malware as Superuser can find out the user's real IP address/location. This is because Whonix consists of two (virtual) machines. One machine solely runs Tor and acts as a gateway, called Whonix-Gateway. The other machine, called Whonix-Workstation is on a completely isolated network. It is also possible to use multiple Whonix Workstations simultaneously through one Gateway that will provide stream isolation (though is not necessarily endorsed). All the connections are forced through Tor with the Whonix Gateway Virtual Machine, therefore IP and DNS leaks are impossible.

Fedora-based

Qubes OS is a desktop operating system based around the Xen hypervisor that allows grouping programs into a number of isolated sandboxes (virtual machines) to provide security. Windows for programs running within these sandboxes ("security domains") can be color coded for easy recognition. The security domains are configurable, they can be transient (changes to the file system will not be preserved), and their network connection can be routed through special virtual machines (for example one that only provides Tor networking). The operating system provides secure mechanisms for copy and paste and for copying files between the security domains.

Gentoo-based

Tin Hat Linux is derived from Hardened Gentoo Linux. It aims to provide a very secure, stable, and fast desktop environment that lives purely in RAM.

Other Linux Distributions

- Alpine Linux is a lightweight musl and BusyBox-based distribution. It uses PaX and grsecurity patches in the default kernel and compiles all packages with stack-smashing protection. Version 3.8.1 was released 11 September 2018.

- Annvix was originally forked from Mandriva to provide a security-focused server distribution that employs ProPolice protection, hardened configuration, and a small footprint. There were plans to include full support for the RSBAC mandatory access control system. However, Annvix is dormant, with the last version being released on 30 December 2007.

- EnGarde Secure Linux is a secure platform designed for servers. It has had a browser-based tool for MAC using SELinux since 2003. Additionally, it can be accompanied with Web, DNS, and email enterprise applications, specifically focusing on security without any unnecessary software. The community platform of EnGarde Secure Linux is the bleeding-edge version freely available for download.

- Immunix was a commercial distribution of Linux focused heavily on security. They supplied many systems of their own making, including StackGuard; cryptographic signing of executables; race condition patches; and format string exploit guarding code. Immunix traditionally releases older versions of their distribution free for non-commercial use. The Immunix distribution itself is licensed under two licenses: The Immunix commercial and non-commercial licenses. Many tools within are GPL, however; as is the kernel.

- Solar Designer's Openwall Project (Owl) was the first distribution to have a non-executable userspace stack, /tmp race condition protection, and access control restrictions to /proc data, by way of a kernel patch. It also features a per-user tmp directory via the pam_mktemp PAM module, and supports Blowfish password encryption.

BSD-based

- OpenBSD is a BSD-based operating system focused on code correctness and security.

- TrustedBSD is a sub-project of FreeBSD designed to add trusted operating system extensions, targeting the Common Criteria for Information Technology Security Evaluation. Its main focuses are working on access control lists, event auditing, extended attributes, mandatory access controls, and fine-grained capabilities. Since access control lists are known to be confronted with the confused deputy problem, capabilities are a different way to avoid this issue. As part of the TrustedBSD project, there is also a port of NSA's FLASK/TE implementation to run on FreeBSD. Many of these trusted extensions have been integrated into the main FreeBSD branch starting at 5.x.

Object-capability Systems

These operating systems are all engineered around the object-capabilities security paradigm, where instead of having the system deciding if an access request should be granted the bundling of authority and designation makes it impossible to request anything not legitimate.

- CapROS,

- EROS,

- Genode,

- Fiasco.OC,

- KeyKOS,

- seL4.

Solaris-based

Trusted Solaris was a security-focused version of the Solaris Unix operating system. Aimed primarily at the government computing sector, Trusted Solaris adds detailed auditing of all tasks, pluggable authentication, mandatory access control, additional physical authentication devices, and fine-grained access control. Trusted Solaris is Common Criteria certified. The most recent version, Trusted Solaris 8, received the EAL4 certification level augmented by a number of protection profiles. Telnet was vulnerable to buffer overflow exploits until patched in April 2001.

Windows Server

Starting with Windows Server 2008, Windows Server has added an installation option called "Server Core", in which the traditional graphical user interface is not installed. Administration, in Windows Server 2008, should rely on Windows Command Prompt. Roles and components are then installed individually. This option reduces the Windows Server footprint, the result of which is reduced demand on system resources and reduced number of components that could potentially be exploited via potential security vulnerabilities.

Later, with Windows Server 2016, Microsoft introduced a Nano Server installation option with even more reduced footprint. It is headless and does not support a locally connected keyboard and monitor. Nano Server in Windows Server 1709 (the constantly updated sibling of Windows Server 2016) can only be installed in a container.

Security-evaluated Operating System

In computing, security-evaluated operating systems have achieved certification from an external security-auditing organization, the most popular evaluations are Common Criteria (CC) and FIPS 140-2.

Oracle Solaris

Trusted Solaris 8 was a security-focused version of the Solaris Unix operating system. Aimed primarily at the government computing sector, Trusted Solaris adds detailed auditing of all tasks, pluggable authentication, mandatory access control, additional physical authentication devices, and fine-grained access control(FGAC). Versions of Trusted Solaris through version 8 are Common Criteria certified.

BAE Systems' STOP

BAE Systems' STOP version 6.0.E received an EAL4+ in April 2004 and the 6.1.E version received an EAL5+ certification in March 2005. STOP version 6.4 U4 received an EAL5+ certification in July 2008. Versions of STOP prior to STOP 6 have held B3 certifications under TCSEC. While STOP 6 is binary compatible with Linux, it does not derive from the Linux kernel.

Red Hat Enterprise Linux 5

Red Hat Enterprise Linux 5 achieved EAL4+ in June 2007.

Red Hat Enterprise Linux 6

Red Hat Enterprise Linux Version 6.2 on 32 bit x86 Architecture achieved EAL4+ in December 2014. Red Hat Enterprise Linux Version 6.2 with KVM Virtualization for x86 Architectures achieved EAL4+ in October 2012.

Novell SUSE Linux Enterprise Server

Novell's SUSE Linux Enterprise Server 9 running on an IBM eServer was certified at CAPP/EAL4+ in February 2005.

Microsoft Windows

The following versions of Microsoft Windows have received EAL 4 Augmented ALC_ FLR.3 certification:

- Windows 2008 Server (64-bit), Enterprise (64-bit) and Datacenter, as well as Windows Vista Enterprise (both 32-bit and 64-bit) attained EAL 4 Augmented (colloquially referred to as EAL 4+) ALC_FLR.3 status in 2009.

- Windows 2000 Server, Advanced Server, and Professional, each with Service Pack 3 and Q326886 Hotfix operating on the x86 platform were certified as CAPP/EAL 4 Augmented ALC_FLR.3 in October 2002. (This includes standard configurations as Domain Controller, Server in a Domain, Stand-alone Server, Workstation in a Domain, Stand-alone Workstation).

- Windows XP Professional and Embedded editions, with Service Pack 2, and Windows Server 2003 Standard and Enterprise editions (32-bit and 64-bit), with Service Pack 1, were all certified in December 2005.

Mac OS X

Apple's Mac OS X and Mac OS X Server running 10.3.6 both with the Common Criteria Tools Package installed were certified at CAPP/EAL3 in January 2005.

Apple's Mac OS X & Mac OS X Server running the latest version 10.4.6 has not yet been fully evaluated however the Common Criteria Tools package is available.

GEMSOS

Gemini Multiprocessing Secure Operating System is a TCSEC A1 system that runs on x86 processor type COTS hardware.

HP OpenVMS and SEVMS

The SEVMS enhancement to VMS is a CC B1/B3 system formerly of Digital Equipment Corporation (DEC) later Compaq, now Hewlett-Packard (HP).

Green Hills INTEGRITY-178B

Green Hills Software's INTEGRITY-178B real-time operating system was certified at Common Criteria EAL6+ in September 2008. Running on an embedded PowerPC processor on a Compact PCI card.

Unisys MCP

The Unisys MCP operating system includes an implementation of the DoD Orange

Book C2 specification, the controlled access protection sub-level of discretionary protection. MCP/AS obtained the C2 rating in August, 1987.

Unisys OS 2200

The Unisys OS 2200 operating system includes an implementation of the DoD Orange Book B1, Labeled security protection level specification. OS 2200 first obtained a successful B1 evaluation in September, 1989. Unisys maintained that evaluation until 1994 through the National Computer Security Center Rating Maintenance Phase (RAMP) of the Trusted Product Evaluation Program.

Trusted Operating System

Trusted Operating System (TOS) generally refers to an operating system that provides sufficient support for multilevel security and evidence of correctness to meet a particular set of government requirements.

The most common set of criteria for trusted operating system design is the Common Criteria combined with the Security Functional Requirements (SFRs) for Labeled Security Protection Profile (LSPP) and mandatory access control (MAC). The Common Criteria is the result of a multi-year effort by the governments of the U.S., Canada, United Kingdom, France, Germany, the Netherlands and other countries to develop harmonized security criteria for IT products.

Examples:

Examples of certified trusted operating systems are:

- Apple Mac OS X 10.6 (Rated EAL 3+).

- HP-UX 11i v3 (Rated EAL 4+).

- Some Linux distributions (Rated up to EAL 4+).

- Microsoft Windows 7 and Microsoft Server 2008 R2 (Rated EAL 4+).

- AIX 5L with PitBull Foundation (Rated EAL 4+).

- Trusted Solaris.

- Trusted UNICOS 8.0 (Rated B1).

- XTS-400 (Rated EAL5+).

- IBM VM (SP, BSE, HPO, XA, ESA, etc.) with RACF.

Examples of operating systems that might be certifiable are:

- FreeBSD with the TrustedBSD extensions.

- SELinux.

Companies that have created trusted operating systems include:

- Addamax (BSD, SVR3, SVR4, HP/UX).

- Argus Systems Group (Solaris, AIX, Linux).

- AT&T (System V).

- BAE Systems (XTS Unix).

- Bull (AIX).

- Data General (DG/UX).

- Digital Equipment Corporation (Ultrix).

- Gemini Computers (GEMSOS).

- General Dynamics C4 Systems (Linux).

- Harris Corporation (SVR3, SVR4).

- Hewlett-Packard (HP/UX).

- Honeywell (Multics).

- IBM (OS/390, AIX).

- SCO (SCO Unix).

- Secure Computing Corporation (LOCK, Mach, BSD).

- SecureWare (Apple A/UX, HP/UX, SCO).

- Sequent Computer Systems (Dynix/ptx).

- Silicon Graphics (IRIX).

- Sun Microsystems (SunOS, Solaris).

- Trusted Information Systems (Xenix, Mach).

Trusted Operating System Design

Operating systems by themselves (regardless of their security constraints) are very difficult to design. They handle many duties, are subject to interruptions and context switches, and must minimize overhead so as not to slow user computations and interactions. Adding the responsibility for security enforcement to the operating system substantially increases the difficulty of designing an operating system.

Trusted System Design Elements

That security consideration pervades the design and structure of operating systems implies two things. First, an operating system controls the interaction between subjects and objects, so security must be considered in every aspect of its design. That is, the operating system design must include definitions of which objects will be protected in what way, which subjects will have access and at what levels, and so on. There must be a clear mapping from the security requirements to the design, so that all developers can see how the two relate. Moreover, once a section of the operating system has been designed, it must be checked to see that the degree of security that it is supposed to enforce or provide has actually been designed correctly. This checking can be done in many ways, including formal reviews or simulations. Again, a mapping is necessary, this time from the requirements to design to tests so that developers can affirm that each aspect of operating system security has been tested and shown to work correctly.

Second, because security appears in every part of an operating system, its design and implementation cannot be left fuzzy or vague until the rest of the system is working and being tested. It is extremely hard to retrofit security features to an operating system designed with inadequate security. Leaving an operating system's security to the last minute is much like trying to install plumbing or wiring in a house whose foundation is set, structure defined, and walls already up and painted; not only must you destroy most of what you have built, but you may also find that the general structure can no longer accommodate all that is needed (and so some has to be left out or compromised). Thus, security must be an essential part of the initial design of a trusted operating system. Indeed, the security considerations may shape many of the other design decisions, especially for a system with complex and constraining security requirements. For the same reasons, the security and other design principles must be carried throughout implementation, testing, and maintenance.

Good design principles are always good for security, as we have noted above. But several important design principles are quite particular to security and essential for building a solid, trusted operating system. These principles have been articulated well by Saltzer [SAL74] and Saltzer and Schroeder:

- Least privilege: Each user and each program should operate by using the fewest privileges possible. In this way, the damage from an inadvertent or malicious attack is minimized.

- Economy of mechanism: The design of the protection system should be small, simple, and straightforward. Such a protection system can be carefully analyzed, exhaustively tested, perhaps verified, and relied on.

- Open design: The protection mechanism must not depend on the ignorance of potential attackers; the mechanism should be public, depending on secrecy of relatively few key items, such as a password table. An open design is also available for extensive public scrutiny, thereby providing independent confirmation of the design security.

- Complete mediation: Every access attempt must be checked. Both direct access attempts (requests) and attempts to circumvent the access checking mechanism should be considered, and the mechanism should be positioned so that it cannot be circumvented.

- Permission based: The default condition should be denial of access. A conservative designer identifies the items that should be accessible, rather than those that should not.

- Separation of privilege: Ideally, access to objects should depend on more than one condition, such as user authentication plus a cryptographic key. In this way, someone who defeats one protection system will not have complete access.

- Least common mechanism: Shared objects provide potential channels for information flow. Systems employing physical or logical separation reduce the risk from sharing.

- Ease of use: If a protection mechanism is easy to use, it is unlikely to be avoided.

Although, these design principles were suggested several decades ago, they are as accurate now as they were when originally written. The principles have been used repeatedly and successfully in the design and implementation of numerous trusted systems. More importantly, when security problems have been found in operating systems in the past, they almost always derive from failure to abide by one or more of these principles.

Security Features of Ordinary Operating Systems

A multiprogramming operating system performs several functions that relate to security. To see how, examine figure, which illustrates how an operating system interacts with users, provides services, and allocates resources.

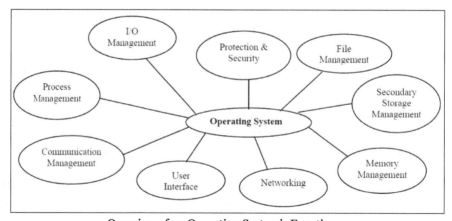

Overview of an Operating System's Functions.

We can see that the system addresses several particular functions that involve computer security:

- User authentication: The operating system must identify each user who requests access and must ascertain that the user is actually who he or she purports to be. The most common authentication mechanism is password comparison.

- Memory protection: Each user's program must run in a portion of memory protected against unauthorized accesses. The protection will certainly prevent outsiders' accesses, and it may also control a user's own access to restricted parts of the program space. Differential security, such as read, writes and executes, may be applied to parts of a user's memory space. Memory protection is usually performed by hardware mechanisms, such as paging or segmentation.

- File and I/O device access control: The operating system must protect user and system files from access by unauthorized users. Similarly, I/O device use must be protected. Data protection is usually achieved by table lookup, as with an access control matrix.

- Allocation and access control to general objects: Users need general objects, such as constructs to permit concurrency and allow synchronization. However, access to these objects must be controlled so that one user does not have a negative effect on other users. Again, table lookup is the common means by which this protection is provided.

- Enforced sharing: Resources should be made available to users as appropriate. Sharing brings about the need to guarantee integrity and consistency. Table lookup, combined with integrity controls such as monitors or transaction processors, is often used to support controlled sharing.

- Guaranteed fair service: All users expect CPU usage and other service to be provided so that no user is indefinitely starved from receiving service. Hardware clocks combine with scheduling disciplines to provide fairness. Hardware facilities and data tables combine to provide control.

- Interprocess communication and synchronization: Executing processes sometimes need to communicate with other processes or to synchronize their accesses to shared resources. Operating systems provide these services by acting as a bridge between processes, responding to process requests for asynchronous communication with other processes or synchronization. Interprocess communication is mediated by access control tables.

- Protected operating system protection data: The operating system must maintain data by which it can enforce security. Obviously, if these data are not protected against unauthorized access (read, modify, and delete), the operating system cannot provide enforcement. Various techniques, including encryption, hardware control, and isolation, support isolation of operating system protection data.

Security Features of Trusted Operating Systems

Unlike regular operating systems, trusted systems incorporate technology to address both features and assurance. The design of a trusted system is delicate, involving selection of an appropriate and consistent set of features together with an appropriate degree of assurance that the features have been assembled and implemented correctly. Figure illustrates how a trusted operating system differs from an ordinary one. Compare it with figure. Notice how objects are accompanied or surrounded by an access control mechanism, offering far more protection and separation than does a conventional operating system. In addition, memory is separated by user, and data and program libraries have controlled sharing and separation.

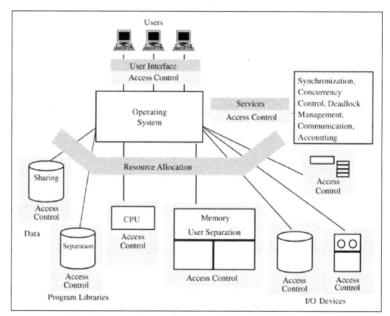

Security Functions of a Trusted Operating System.

Here, we consider in more detail the key features of a trusted operating system, including:

- User identification and authentication,
- Mandatory access control,
- Discretionary access control,
- Object reuse protection,
- Complete mediation,
- Trusted path,

- Audit,
- Audit log reduction,
- Intrusion detection.

We consider each of these features in turn.

Identification and Authentication

Identification is at the root of much of computer security. We must be able to tell who requesting access to an object is, and we must be able to verify the subject's identity. Most access control, whether mandatory or discretionary, is based on accurate identification. Identification involves two steps: finding out who the access requester is and verifying that the requester is indeed who he/she/it claims to be. That is, we want to establish an identity and then authenticate or verify that identity. Trusted operating systems require secure identification of individuals, and each individual must be uniquely identified.

Mandatory and Discretionary Access Control

Mandatory access control (MAC) means that access control policy decisions are made beyond the control of the individual owner of an object. A central authority determines what information is to be accessible by whom, and the user cannot change access rights. An example of MAC occurs in military security, where an individual data owner does not decide who has a top-secret clearance; neither can the owner change the classification of an object from top secret to secret.

By contrast, discretionary access control (DAC), as its name implies, leaves a certain amount of access control to the discretion of the object's owner or to anyone else who is authorized to control the object's access. The owner can determine who should have access rights to an object and what those rights should be. Commercial environments typically use DAC to allow anyone in a designated group, and sometimes additional named individuals, to change access. For example, a corporation might establish access controls so that the accounting group can have access to personnel files. But the corporation may also allow Ana and Jose to access those files, too, in their roles as directors of the Inspector General's office. Typically, DAC access rights can change dynamically. The owner of the accounting file may add Renee and remove Walter from the list of allowed accessors, as business needs dictate.

MAC and DAC can both be applied to the same object. MAC has precedence over DAC, meaning that of all those who are approved for MAC access, only those who also pass DAC will actually be allowed to access the object. For example, a file may be classified secret, meaning that only people cleared for secret access can potentially access the file. But of those millions of people granted secret access by the government, only people on project "deer park" or in the "environmental" group or at location "Fort Hamilton" are actually allowed access.

Object Reuse Protection

One way that a computing system maintains its efficiency is to reuse objects. The operating system controls resource allocation, and as a resource is freed for use by other users or programs, the operating system permits the next user or program to access the resource. But reusable objects must be carefully controlled, lest they create a serious vulnerability. To see why, consider what happens when a new file is created. Usually, space for the file comes from a pool of freed, previously used space on a disk or other storage device. Released space is returned to the pool "dirty," that is, still containing the data from the previous user. Because most users would write to a file before trying to read from it, the new user's data obliterate the previous owner's, so there is no inappropriate disclosure of the previous user's information. However, a malicious user may claim a large amount of disk space and then scavenge for sensitive data. This kind of attack is called object reuse. The problem is not limited to disk; it can occur with main memory, processor registers and storage, other magnetic media (such as disks and tapes), or any other reusable storage medium.

To prevent object reuse leakage, operating systems clear (that is, overwrite) all space to be reassigned before allowing the next user to have access to it. Magnetic media are particularly vulnerable to this threat. Very precise and expensive equipment can sometimes separate the most recent data from the data previously recorded, from the data before that, and so forth. In any case, the operating system must take responsibility for "cleaning" the resource before permitting access to it.

Complete Mediation

For mandatory or discretionary access control to be effective, all accesses must be controlled. It is insufficient to control access only to files if the attack will acquire access through memory or an outside port or a network or a covert channel. The design and implementation difficulty of a trusted operating system rises significantly as more paths for access must be controlled. Highly trusted operating systems perform complete mediation, meaning that all accesses are checked.

Trusted Path

One way for a malicious user to gain inappropriate access is to "spoof" users, making them think they are communicating with a legitimate security enforcement system when in fact their keystrokes and commands are being intercepted and analyzed. For example, a malicious spoofer may place a phony user ID and password system between the user and the legitimate system. As the illegal system queries the user for identification information, the spoofer captures the real user ID and password; the spoofer can use these bona fide entry data to access the system later on, probably with malicious intent. Thus, for critical operations such as setting a password or changing access permissions, users want an unmistakable communication, called a trusted path, to ensure that they are supplying protected information only to a legitimate receiver. On some trusted systems, the user invokes a trusted path by pressing a unique key sequence that, by design, is intercepted directly by the security enforcement software; on other trusted systems, security-relevant changes can be made only at system startup, before any processes other than the security enforcement code run.

Accountability and Audit

A security-relevant action may be as simple as an individual access to an object, such as a file, or it may be as major as a change to the central access control database affecting all subsequent accesses. Accountability usually entails maintaining a log of security-relevant events that have occurred, listing each event and the person responsible for the addition, deletion, or change. This audit log must obviously be protected from outsiders, and every security-relevant event must be recorded.

Audit Log Reduction

Theoretically, the general notion of an audit log is appealing because it allows responsible parties to evaluate all actions that affect all protected elements of the system. But in practice an audit log may be too difficult to handle, owing to volume and analysis. To see why, consider what information would have to be collected and analyzed. In the extreme (such as where the data involved can affect a business' viability or a nation's security), we might argue that every modification or even each character read from a file is potentially security relevant; the modification could affect the integrity of data, or the single character could divulge the only really sensitive part of an entire file. And because the path of control through a program is affected by the data the program processes, the sequence of individual instructions is also potentially security relevant. If an audit record were to be created for every access to a single character from a file and for every instruction executed, the audit log would be enormous. (In fact, it would be impossible to audit every instruction, because then the audit commands themselves would have to be audited. In turn, these commands would be implemented by instructions that would have to be audited, and so on forever).

In most trusted systems, the problem is simplified by an audit of only the opening (first access to) and closing of (last access to) files or similar objects. Similarly, objects such as individual memory locations, hardware registers, and instructions are not audited. Even with these restrictions, audit logs tend to be very large. Even a simple word processor may open fifty or more support modules (separate files) when it begins, it may create and delete a dozen or more temporary files during execution, and it may open many more drivers to handle specific tasks such as complex formatting or printing. Thus, one simple program can easily cause a hundred files to be opened and closed, and complex systems can cause thousands of files to be accessed in a relatively short time. On the other hand, some systems continuously read from or update a single file. A bank teller may process transactions against the general customer accounts file throughout the entire day; what is significant is not that the teller accessed the accounts file, but which entries in the file were accessed. Thus, audit at the level of file opening and closing is in some cases too much data and in other cases not enough to meet security needs.

A final difficulty is the "needle in a haystack" phenomenon. Even if the audit data could be limited to the right amount, typically many legitimate accesses and perhaps one attack will occur. Finding the one attack access out of a thousand legitimate accesses can be difficult. A corollary to this problem is the one of determining who or what does the analysis. Does the system administrator sit and analyze all data in the audit log? Or do the developers write a program to analyze the data? If the latter, how can we automatically recognize a pattern of unacceptable behavior? These issues are open questions being addressed not only by security specialists but also by experts in artificial intelligence and pattern recognition.

Sidebar 5-5 illustrates how the volume of audit log data can get out of hand very quickly. Some trusted systems perform audit reduction, using separate tools to reduce the volume of the audit data. In this way, if an event occurs, all the data have been recorded and can be consulted directly. However, for most analysis, the reduced audit log is enough to review.

Intrusion Detection

Closely related to audit reduction is the ability to detect security lapses, ideally while they occur. As we have seen in the State Department example, there may well be too much information in the audit log for a human to analyze, but the computer can help correlate independent data. Intrusion detection software builds patterns of normal system usage, triggering an alarm any time the usage seems abnormal. After a decade of promising research results in intrusion detection, products are now commercially available. Some trusted operating systems include a primitive degree of intrusion detection software.

Although the problems are daunting, there have been many successful implementations of trusted operating systems. In the following section, we examine some of them. In particular, we consider three properties: kernelized design (a result of least privilege and economy of mechanism), isolation (the logical extension of least common mechanism), and ring-structuring (an example of open design and complete mediation).

Kernelized Design

A kernel is the part of an operating system that performs the lowest-level functions. In standard operating system design, the kernel implements operations such as synchronization, interprocess communication, message passing, and interrupt handling. The kernel is also called a nucleusor core. The notion of designing an operating system around a kernel is described by Lampson, Sturgis and by Popek and Kline.

A security kernel is responsible for enforcing the security mechanisms of the entire operating system. The security kernel provides the security interfaces among the hardware, operating system, and other parts of the computing system. Typically, the operating system is designed so that the security kernel is contained within the operating system kernel.

There are several good design reasons why security functions may be isolated in a security kernel:

- Coverage: Every access to a protected object must pass through the security kernel. In a system designed in this way, the operating system can use the security kernel to ensure that every access is checked.

- Separation: Isolating security mechanisms both from the rest of the operating system and from the user space makes it easier to protect those mechanisms from penetration by the operating system or the users.

- Unity: All security functions are performed by a single set of code, so it is easier to trace the cause of any problems that arise with these functions.

- Modifiability: Changes to the security mechanisms are easier to make and easier to test.

- Compactness: Because it performs only security functions, the security kernel is likely to be relatively small.

- Verifiability: Being relatively small, the security kernel can be analyzed rigorously. For example, formal methods can be used to ensure that all security situations (such as states and state changes) have been covered by the design.

The similarity between these advantages and the design goals of operating systems. These characteristics also depend in many ways on modularity.

On the other hand, implementing a security kernel may degrade system performance because the kernel adds yet another layer of interface between user programs and operating system resources. Moreover, the presence of a kernel does not guarantee that it contains all security functions or that it has been implemented correctly. And in some cases a security kernel can be quite large.

How do we balance these positive and negative aspects of using a security kernel? The design and usefulness of a security kernel depend somewhat on the overall approach to the operating system's design. There are many design choices, each of which falls into one of two types: Either the kernel is designed as an addition to the operating system, or it is the basis of the entire operating system. Let us look more closely at each design choice.

Reference Monitor

The most important part of a security kernel is the reference monitor, the portion that controls accesses to objects [AND72, LAM71]. A reference monitor is not necessarily a single piece of code; rather, it is the collection of access controls for devices, files, memory, interprocess communication, and other kinds of objects. As shown in figure, a reference monitor acts like a brick wall around the operating system or trusted software.

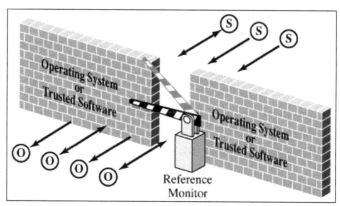

Reference Monitor.

A reference monitor must be:

- Tamperproof, that is, impossible to weaken or disable.

- Unbypassable, that is, always invoked when access to any object is required.

- Analyzable, that is, small enough to be subjected to analysis and testing, the completeness of which can be ensured.

A reference monitor can control access effectively only if it cannot be modified or circumvented by a rogue process, and it is the single point through which all access requests must pass. Furthermore, the reference monitor must function correctly if it is to fulfill its crucial role in enforcing security. Because the likelihood of correct behavior decreases as the complexity and size of a program increase, the best assurance of correct policy enforcement is to build a small, simple, understandable reference monitor.

The reference monitor is not the only security mechanism of a trusted operating system. Other parts of the security suite include audit, identification, and authentication processing, as well as the setting of enforcement parameters, such as who the allowable subjects are and which objects they are allowed to access. These other security parts interact with the reference monitor, receiving data from the reference monitor or providing it with the data it needs to operate.

The reference monitor concept has been used for many trusted operating systems and also for smaller pieces of trusted software. The validity of this concept is well supported both in research and in practice.

Trusted Computing Base

The trusted computing base, or TCB, is the name we give to everything in the trusted operating system necessary to enforce the security policy. Alternatively, we say that the TCB consists of the parts of the trusted operating system on which we depend for correct enforcement of policy. We can think of the TCB as a coherent whole in the following way. Suppose you divide a trusted operating system into the parts that are in the TCB and those that are not, and you allow the most skillful malicious programmers to write all the non-TCB parts. Since the TCB handles all the security, there is nothing the malicious non-TCB parts can do to impair the correct security policy enforcement of the TCB. This definition gives you a sense that the TCB forms the fortress-like shell that protects whatever in the system needs protection. But the analogy also clarifies the meaning of trusted in trusted operating system: Our trust in the security of the whole system depends on the TCB.

It is easy to see that it is essential for the TCB to be both correct and complete. Thus, to understand how to design a good TCB, we focus on the division between the TCB and non-TCB elements of the operating system and spend our effort on ensuring the correctness of the TCB.

TCB Functions

Just what constitutes the TCB? We can answer this question by listing system elements on which security enforcement could depend:

- Hardware, including processors, memory, registers, and I/O devices.

- Some notion of processes, so that we can separate and protect security-critical processes.

- Primitive files, such as the security access control database and identification/authentication data.

- Protected memory, so that the reference monitor can be protected against tampering.

- Some interprocess communication, so that different parts of the TCB can pass data to and activate other parts. For example, the reference monitor can invoke and pass data securely to the audit routine.

It may seem as if this list encompasses most of the operating system, but in fact the TCB is only a small subset. For example, although the TCB requires access to files of enforcement data, it does not need an entire file structure of hierarchical directories, virtual devices, indexed files, and multidevice files. Thus, it might contain a primitive file manager to handle only the small, simple files needed for the TCB. The more complex file manager to provide externally visible files could be outside the TCB. Figure shown below a typical division into TCB and non-TCB sections.

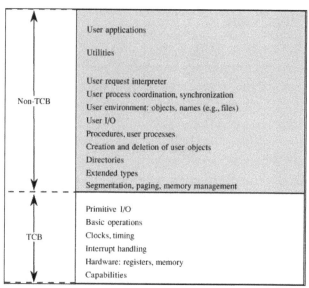

TCB and Non-TCB Code.

The TCB, which must maintain the secrecy and integrity of each domain, monitors four basic interactions:

- Process activation: In a multiprogramming environment, activation and deactivation of processes occur frequently. Changing from one process to another requires a complete change of registers, relocation maps, file access lists, process status information, and other pointers, much of which is security-sensitive information.

- Execution domain switching: Processes running in one domain often invoke processes in other domains to obtain more sensitive data or services.

- Memory protection: Because each domain includes code and data stored in memory, the TCB must monitor memory references to ensure secrecy and integrity for each domain.

- I/O operation: In some systems, software is involved with each character transferred in an I/O operation. This software connects a user program in the outermost domain to an I/O device in the innermost (hardware) domain. Thus, I/O operations can cross all domains.

TCB Design

The division of the operating system into TCB and non-TCB aspects is convenient for designers and developers because it means that all security-relevant code is located in one (logical) part. But the distinction is more than just logical. To ensure that the security enforcement cannot be affected by non-TCB code, TCB code must run in some protected state that distinguishes it. Thus, the structuring into TCB and non-TCB must be done consciously. However, once this structuring has been done, code outside the TCB can be changed at will, without affecting the TCB's ability to enforce security. This ability to change helps developers because it means that major sections of the operating system utilities, device drivers, user interface managers, and the like can be revised or replaced any time; only the TCB code must be controlled more carefully. Finally, for anyone evaluating the security of a trusted operating system, a division into TCB and non-TCB simplifies evaluation substantially because non-TCB code need not be considered.

TCB Implementation

Security-related activities are likely to be performed in different places. Security is potentially related to every memory access, every I/O operation, every file or program access, every initiation or termination of a user, and every interprocess communication. In modular operating systems, these separate activities can be handled in independent modules. Each of these separate modules, then, has both security-related and other functions.

Collecting all security functions into the TCB may destroy the modularity of an existing operating system. A unified TCB may also be too large to be analyzed easily. Nevertheless, a designer may decide to separate the security functions of an existing operating system, creating a security kernel. This form of kernel is depicted in figure.

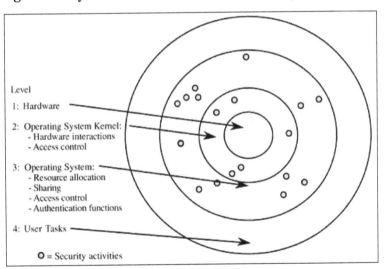

Combined Security Kernel/Operating System.

A more sensible approach is to design the security kernel first and then design the operating system around it. This technique was used by Honeywell in the design of a prototype for its secure operating system, Scomp. That system contained only twenty modules to perform the primitive security functions, and it consisted of fewer than 1,000 lines of higher-level-language source code. Once the actual security kernel of Scomp was built, its functions grew to contain approximately 10,000 lines of code.

In a security-based design, the security kernel forms an interface layer, just atop system hardware. The security kernel monitors all operating system hardware accesses and performs all protection functions. The security kernel, which relies on support from hardware, allows the operating system itself to handle most functions not related to security. In this way, the security kernel can be small and efficient. As a byproduct of this partitioning, computing systems have at least three execution domains: security kernel, operating system, and user.

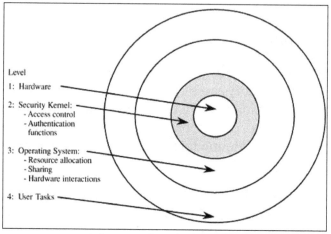

Level
1: Hardware
2: Security Kernel:
    - Access control
    - Authentication
      functions
3: Operating System:
    - Resource allocation
    - Sharing
    - Hardware interactions
4: User Tasks

Separate Security Kernel.

Separation/Isolation

Rushby and Randell list four ways to separate one process from others: physical, temporal, cryptographic, and logical separation. With physical separation, two different processes use two different hardware facilities. For example, sensitive computation may be performed on a reserved computing system; non-sensitive tasks are run on a public system. Hardware separation offers several attractive features, including support for multiple independent threads of execution, memory protection, mediation of I/O, and at least three different degrees of execution privilege. Temporal separation occurs when different processes are run at different times. For instance, some military systems run non-sensitive jobs between 8:00 a.m. and noon, with sensitive computation only from noon to 5:00 p.m. Encryption is used for cryptographic separation, so two different processes can be run at the same time because unauthorized users cannot access sensitive data in a readable form. Logical separation, also called isolation, is provided when a process such as a reference monitor separates one user's objects from those of another user. Secure computing systems have been built with each of these forms of separation.

Multiprogramming operating systems should isolate each user from all others, allowing only carefully controlled interactions between the users. Most operating systems are designed to provide a single environment for all. In other words, one copy of the operating system is available for use by many users, as shown in figure. The operating system is often separated into two distinct pieces, located at the highest and lowest addresses of memory.

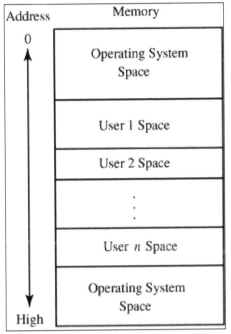

Conventional Multiuser Operating System Memory.

Virtualization

Virtualization is a powerful tool for trusted system designers because it allows users to access complex objects in a carefully controlled manner. By virtualization we mean that the operating system emulates or simulates a collection of a computer system's resources. We say that a virtual machine is a collection of real or simulated hardware facilities: a central processor that runs an instruction set, an amount of directly addressable storage, and some I/O devices. These facilities support the execution of programs.

Obviously, virtual resources must be supported by real hardware or software, but the real resources do not have to be the same as the simulated ones. There are many examples of this type of simulation. For instance, printers are often simulated on direct access devices for sharing in multiuser environments. Several small disks can be simulated with one large one. With demand paging, some non-contiguous memory can support a much larger contiguous virtual memory space. And it is common even on PCs to simulate space on slower disks with faster memory. In these ways, the operating system provides the virtual resource to the user, while the security kernel precisely controls user accesses.

Multiple Virtual Memory Spaces

The IBM MVS/ESA operating system uses virtualization to provide logical separation that gives the user the impression of physical separation. IBM MVS/ESA is a paging system such that each user's logical address space is separated from that of other users by the page mapping mechanism. Additionally, MVS/ESA includes the operating system in each user's logical address space, so a user runs on what seems to be a complete, separate machine.

Most paging systems present to a user only the user's virtual address space; the operating system is outside the user's virtual addressing space. However, the operating system is part of the logical space of each MVS/ESA user. Therefore, to the user MVS/ESA seems like a single-user system, as shown in figure.

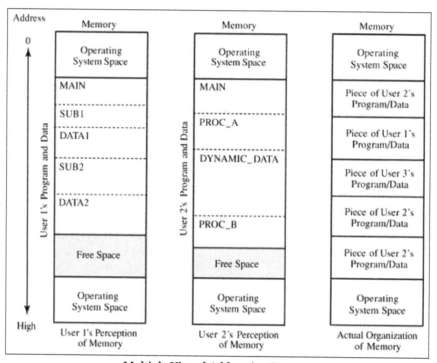

Multiple Virtual Addressing Spaces.

A primary advantage of MVS/ESA is memory management. Each user's virtual memory space can be as large as total addressable memory, in excess of 16 million bytes. And protection is a second advantage of this representation of memory. Because each user's logical address space includes the operating system, the user's perception is of running on a separate machine, which could even be true.

Virtual Machines

The IBM Processor Resources/System Manager (PR/SM) system provides a level of protection that is stronger still. A conventional operating system has hardware facilities and devices that are under the direct control of the operating system, as shown in figure. PR/SM provides an entire virtual machine to each user, so that each user not only has logical memory but also has logical I/O devices, logical files, and other logical resources. PR/SM performs this feat by strictly separating resources.

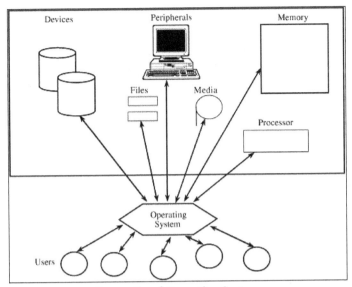

Conventional Operating System.

The PR/SM system is a natural extension of the concept of virtual memory. Virtual memory gives the user a memory space that is logically separated from real memory; a virtual memory space is usually larger than real memory, as well. A virtual machine gives the user a full set of hardware features; that is, a complete machine that may be substantially different from the real machine. These virtual hardware resources are also logically separated from those of other users. The relationship of virtual machines to real ones is shown in figure.

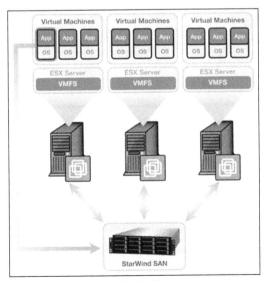

Virtual Machine.

Both MVS/ESA and PR/SM improve the isolation of each user from other users and from the hardware of the system. Of course, this added complexity increases the overhead incurred with these levels of translation and protection.

Layered Design

A kernelized operating system consists of at least four levels: hardware, kernel, operating system, and user. Each of these layers can include sublayers. For example, in (SCH83b), the kernel has five distinct layers. At the user level, it is not uncommon to have quasi system programs, such as database managers or graphical user interface shells that constitute separate layers of security themselves.

Layered Trust

The layered view of a secure operating system can be depicted as a series of concentric circles, with the most sensitive operations in the innermost layers. Then, the trustworthiness and access rights of a process can be judged by the process's proximity to the center. The more trusted processes are closer to the center. But we can also depict the trusted operating system in layers as a stack, with the security functions closest to the hardware. Such a system is shown in figure.

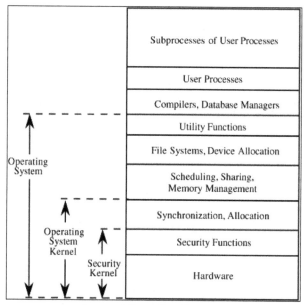

Layered Operating System.

In this design, some activities related to protection functions are performed outside the security kernel. For example, user authentication may include accessing a password table, challenging the user to supply a password, verifying the correctness of the password, and so forth. The disadvantage of performing all these operations inside the security kernel is that some of the operations (such as formatting the user terminal interaction and searching for the user in a table of known users) do not warrant high security.

Alternatively, we can implement a single logical function in several different modules; we call this a layered design. Trustworthiness and access rights are the basis of the layering. In other words, a single function may be performed by a set of modules operating in different layers, as shown in figure. The modules of each layer perform operations of a certain degree of sensitivity.

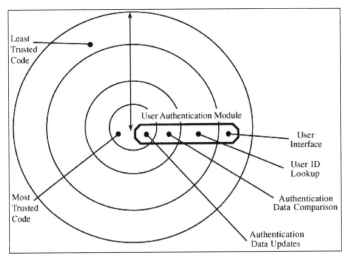

Modules Operating In Different Layers.

Neumann describes the layered structure used for the Provably Secure Operating System (PSOS). As shown in table, some lower-level layers present some or all of their functionality to higher levels, but each layer properly encapsulates those things below itself.

Table: PSOS Design Hierarchy.

Level	Function	Hidden by Level	Visible to User
16	User request interpreter		Yes
15	User environments and name spaces		Yes
14	User I/O		Yes
13	Procedure records		Yes
12	User processes and visible I/O		Yes
11	Creation and deletion of user objects		Yes
10	Directories	11	Partially
9	Extended types	11	Partially
8	Segments	11	Partially
7	Paging	8	No
6	System processes and I/O	12	No
5	Primitive I/O	6	No
4	Arithmetic and other basic operations		Yes
3	Clocks	6	No
2	Interrupts	6	No
1	Registers and addressable memory	7	Partially
0	Capabilities		Yes

A layered approach is another way to achieve encapsulation. Layering is recognized as a good operating system design. Each layer uses the more central layers as services, and each layer provides a certain level of functionality to the layers farther out. In this way, we can "peel off" each layer and still have a logically complete system with less functionality. Layering presents a good example of how to trade off and balance design characteristics.

Another justification for layering is damage control. To see why, consider Neumann's (NEU86) two examples of risk, shown in tables. In a conventional, non-hierarchically designed system, any problem hardware failure, software flaw, or unexpected condition, even in a supposedly non-security-relevant portion can cause disaster because the effect of the problem is unbounded and because the system's design means that we cannot be confident that any given function has no (indirect) security effect.

Table: Conventionally (Non-hierarchically) Designed System.

Level	Functions	Risk
All	Noncritical functions	Disaster possible
All	Less critical functions	Disaster possible
All	Most critical functions	Disaster possible

Table: Hierarchically Designed System.

Level	Functions	Risk
2	Noncritical functions	Few disasters likely from noncritical software.
1	Less critical functions	Some failures possible from less critical functions, but because of separation, affect limited.
0	Most critical functions	Disasters possible but unlikely if system simple enough to be analyzed extensively.

By contrast, as shown in table, hierarchical structuring has two benefits:

- Hierarchical structuring permits identification of the most critical parts, which can then be analyzed intensely for correctness, so the number of problems should be smaller.

- Isolation limits effects of problems to the hierarchical levels at and above the point of the problem, so the effects of many problems should be confined.

These design properties the kernel, separation, isolation, and hierarchical structure have been the basis for many trustworthy system prototypes. They have stood the test of time as best design and implementation practices.

Provable Secure Operating System

PSOS has been designed according to a set of formal techniques embodying the SRI Hierarchical Development Methodology (HDM). The influence of HDM on the security of PSOS is also discussed elsewhere. In addition, Linden gives a general discussion of the impact of structured design techniques on the security of operating systems (including capability systems).

HDM employs formally stated requirements, formal specifications defining the design of each module in a hierarchical collection of modules, and formal statements of the module interconnections. In the case of PSOS, there is a formal model describing the requirements of the basic protection mechanism and additional formal models of the requirements of various applications. HDM provides the formalism and the structure that make the formal verification of the system design and implementation possible and conceptually straightforward. This formal verification consists of formal proofs that specifications satisfy the desired requirements and subsequently that the actual programs for the system and its applications are consistent with those specifications.

The design of PSOS has been formally specified using a Specification and Assertion Language called SPECIAL. These specifications define PSOS as a collection of about 20 hierarchically-organized modules. Each module typically is responsible for objects of a particular type defined by that module. From the user point of view, the most important modules are those for capabilities, for virtual memory segments, directories, user processes, and for creating user defined abstract objects. Some modules are to be implemented in software, some in firmware, and some in hardware—as dictated by the efficiency required.

PSOS Capabilities

The concept of the capability has appeared in several other operating systems. Although capabilities are a fundamental part of the design of each of these systems, they all differ in the way they use and interpret capabilities. PSOS differs from its predecessors in its uniform use of capabilities throughout the system and in the simplicity and primitive nature of the basic capability mechanism.

Each object in PSOS can be accessed only upon presentation of an appropriate capability to a module responsible for that object. Capabilities can be neither forged nor altered. As a consequence, capabilities provide a controllable basis for implementing the operating system and its applications, as there is no other way of accessing an object other than by presenting an appropriate capability designating that object.

Each PSOS capability consists of two parts; a unique identifier (uid) and a set of access rights (represented as a Boolean array). By definition neither part is modifiable, once a capability is created.

- Unique Identifiers: PSOS generates only one original capability for each uid. Any number of copies can be made of a given capability for which a copy is to be made. Therefore, a procedure or task that creates a new capability with some uid knows that the only capabilities that can have that uid must have been copied either directly or indirectly from the original. In other words, the creator of a capability with a given uid is able to retain control over the distribution of capabilities with that uid.

- Access Rights: The set of access rights in a capability for an object is interpreted by the module responsible for that object to define what operations may be performed by using that capability. The interpretation of the access rights is constrained by a monotonicity rule, namely that the presence of a right is always more powerful than its absence. The interpretation of the access rights may differ for different objects, but the monotonicity rule must always apply.

The access rights for a segment capability (as interpreted by the segment manager) indicate whether that capability may be used to write information into the designated segment, to read that information, to call that segment as a procedure, and to delete that segment. In PSOS, a directory contains entries, each of which is a mapping from a symbolic object name to a capability. Each directory is accessed via a capability for that directory. For directories, the interpretation of access rights is done by the directory manager. The access rights for a directory capability indicate whether that capability may be used to add entries to the designated directory, to remove entries, and to use the capability contained in that entry.

A copy of a capability may be made, but the resulting capability cannot have any access rights that the original capability did not—as is seen from the following list of possible operations upon capabilities.

The PSOS Protection Mechanism

Capabilities provide the basis for a flexible protection mechanism, as follows:

Tagging of Capabilities

In PSOS, capabilities can be distinguished from other data because they are tagged throughout the system (i.e., in the processor, and in both primary and secondary memory) by means of a tag bit inaccessible to programs. Consequently, the hardware can enforce the nonforgeability and unalterability of capabilities.

Operations upon Capabilities

There are only two basic operations that involve actions upon capabilities (as opposed to actions based on capabilities, which is the normal mode of accessing objects), as follows:

c = create_capability (i.e., with a previously unused uid) having all access rights.

cl = restrict_acess(c, mask) creates a capability with the same uid as the given capability c and with access rights that are the intersection of those of the given capability c and the given maximum (mask); i.e., it creates a possibly restricted copy.

Store Permissions

The second capability operation described above appears to permit unrestricted copying of capabilities. For certain types of security policies this unrestricted copying is too liberal. For example, one may wish to give the ability to access some object to a particular user but not permit that user to pass that ability on to other users. Because simplicity of the basic capability mechanism is extremely important to achieve the goals of PSOS, any means for restricting the propagation of capabilities should not add complexity to the capability mechanism.

A few access rights (only one is currently used by PSOS itself) are reserved as store permissions. This is the only burden placed on the capability mechanism. The interpretation of the store permissions is performed by the basic storage object manager of PSOS, namely the segment manager. Each segment in the system is designated as to whether or not it is capability store limited for each store permission. If a segment is capability store limited for a particular store permission, then it can contain only capabilities that have that store permission. This restriction can be enforced by a simple check on all segment-modifying operations.

By properly choosing the segments that are capability store limited, some very useful restrictions on the propagation of capabilities can be achieved. The restriction used in PSOS is not allowing a process to pass certain capabilities to other processes or to place these capabilities in storage locations (e.g., a directory or interprocess communication channel) accessible to other processes. (Other restrictions are also possible using store permissions, such as restricting a capability to a subsystem or a particular invocation of a subsystem. More general means for restricting propagation of capabilities and for revoking the privilege granted by a capability can be implemented as subsystems of PSOS. The store permission mechanism has been selected as primitive in the system because it achieves the desired result with negligible additional complexity or cost.

Data and Procedure Abstractions

PSOS consists of a collection of data and procedure abstractions constructed in a hierarchical fashion as shown in table. Each level in the hierarchy represents a collection of abstractions introduced at that level. Abstractions at higher (numbered) levels are implemented using abstract objects introduced at lower levels in the design. It is unimportant whether an abstraction is implemented in hardware, firmware, or software. It is reasonable that abstractions introduced at lower levels be implemented largely in hardware or firmware and that abstractions introduced at higher levels be implemented largely in software. However, the demarcation between hardware and software is not established by the design, and it is quite possible that abstractions occurring throughout the system be implemented as hybrids, i.e., partially in hardware and partially in software.

Table: PSOS Abstraction Hierarchy.

Level	Abstractions
16	User request interpretation.
15	User environments and name spaces.
14	User input-output.
13	Procedure records.
12	User processes and visible input-output.
11	Creation and deletion of user objects.
10	Directories.
9	Abstract object manager.
8	Segments and windows.
7	Pages.
6	System processes and system input-output.
5	Primitive input-output.
4	Arithmetic and other basic procedures.
3	Clocks.
2	Interrupts.
1	Registers and other storage.
0	Capabilities.

It is convenient to group the levels of table into generic categories as shown in table. The generic categories collect abstractions satisfying similar goals. At the base of the hierarchy is the capability mechanism, from which all other abstractions in the system are constructed. Above the basic capability mechanisms are all the physical resources of the system, e.g., primary and secondary storage, processors and input/output devices. From the physical resources are constructed the virtual resources. These virtual resources present a more convenient interface to the programmer than the physical resources, permit multiplexing of the physical resources in a manner largely invisible to the user, and allow the system to allocate the physical resources so as to maximize their efficient use. Next in the PSOS hierarchy come the abstract object manager, providing the mechanism by which higher-level abstractions may be created. It is possible to construct higher-level abstractions based solely on the capability mechanism; however, the abstract object manager provides services that make construction of such abstractions easier. The top two categories in the generic hierarchy include community abstractions and user-created abstractions. The community abstractions are intended to be used by a large group of users, e.g., by all the users at a particular site. Such abstractions may be simple utility routines such as a compiler, or may actually create and control access to new virtual resources such as directories. The user abstractions are those intended for use by a limited group of individuals.

Table: PSOS Generic Hierarchy.

Level	Abstractions	PSOS Levels
F	User abstractions	14-16
E	Community abstractions	10-13
D	Abstract object manager	9
C	Virtual resources	6-8
B	Physical resources	1-5
A	Capabilities	0

Of the properties stated previously, there are two important ones that make PSOS capability particularly useful in the construction of abstract objects.

- The capability serves as a unique name for an abstract object.

- The capability is unforgeable.

This means that a capability can be used as a name (guaranteed to be unique) by which an abstract object can be referenced, and access to the object can be controlled by limiting the distribution of the capability.

In addition, there are several important pragmatic reasons why PSOS capabilities are useful as a naming and protection mechanism for supporting abstract objects.

- The capability mechanism has a very simple implementation. This allows capabilities to be built into the system at the lowest level of abstraction, thus making capabilities available for the most primitive objects.

- Capabilities are uniform in size, making them easy to manage.

- The inclusion of access rights in capabilities permits efficient fine-grained control of access to objects.

- Capabilities can be written into storage (including secondary storage) and retrieved from storage in the same manner as other data, and therefore have many of the properties of other data.

Capabilities serve as names or tokens for all objects of PSOS. It is because the basic capability mechanism is so simple in concept and in implementation that construction of the most primitive objects (e.g., input/output channels, processors, and primary memory) as well as the most complex system objects (e.g., directories and user processes) and user application objects (e.g., a data management system) is possible using capabilities. This promotes a high degree of uniformity throughout the system and eliminates the need for many special-purpose facilities.

Objects that have many properties and operations in common and are managed by a single program are said to have a common type; that program is called a type manager. The type manager implements operations on an abstract object in terms of operations on the more primitive objects used to represent the abstract object. The type manager must be able to determine which objects is part of the representation used to implement an abstract object denoted by a given capability. In other words, a type manager must be able to map the unique identifier of a given capability into capabilities for its representation objects. The capability mechanism of PSOS does not predispose a type manager to any particular implementation of this mapping. Different type managers will require diverse mapping algorithms, depending upon the number of abstract objects and representation objects they must manage, the desired efficiency of operations on the abstract object, the desired simplicity of the mapping algorithm, and numerous other factors. For example, the segment type manager uses a mapping algorithm that is in almost all cases extremely fast; however, the algorithm is quite complex, requiring implementation in both hardware and software. Extreme speed is essential to the operations of the segment type manager because the segment operations are useful very frequently (at least once on every instruction). The directory type manager uses a less speedy algorithm because fast access is less essential.

Although, the capability mechanism of PSOS does not prescribe a particular mapping algorithm, the system does provide some assistance in managing abstract objects. The abstract object manager provides a set of operations by which type managers can associate capabilities for abstract object with the capabilities for their representation objects. The type manager can then retrieve the representation capabilities by presenting to the abstract object manager the abstract object capability. This is done in such a way that only the type manager program itself can obtain the representation capabilities, and then only upon presentation of the abstract object capability. The abstract object manager performs the mapping from abstract object capabilities to representation object capabilities, some of the bookkeeping functions necessary to implement abstract objects, and some storage allocation. Although, the abstract object manager is intended to be useful and appropriate for a wide variety of type managers and does make the programming of a type manager much easier, it is only a service and is not essential to the construction of type managers.

The capability mechanism itself could have been constructed with many of the facilities of the abstract object manager included. This would have resulted in a capability mechanism that would be more elaborate and— for some applications—more efficient and easier to use. This is the approach taken by other capability systems cited above. On the other hand, such a capability mechanism would have required a more complex implementation. More significantly, the capability mechanism could then not have been placed at the lowest level of abstraction in the system design, and some of the physical and virtual resources of the system could not have been implemented using capabilities—requiring a different means for reference. Although having several different naming schemes is possible (and common in most systems), it destroys the uniformity, conceptual simplicity, elegance, ease of use, and possibly the efficiency of the system. It is for this reason that PSOS has a very simple, but fully general, capability mechanism, and that programs enhancing the use of the capability mechanism can be introduced as extensions at higher levels of the design.

There is no clearly delineated system boundary in PSOS. One would normally draw the system boundary at the interface to the community abstractions. However, all the programs that implement the community abstractions (such as directories or user processes) could be provided by users as user programs. The community programs have no special privilege other than claiming resources at initialization by taking possession of certain capabilities. For example, the user-process type manager takes possession of the capabilities for certain system processes, which it then multiplexes to create many user processes. If the system's user-process type manager did not claim all the available system processes, then it would be possible for a user to provide a different user-process type manager with the same or different facilities. Similarly, the abstract object manager has no special privilege at all. A user might program his own abstract object manager if he so desired.

The abstractions at or below any level in the design of table form a consistent and useful system. Clearly, the lower the level chosen as the "top level" of the system, the more primitive that system will be. If all of the physical resources (levels 1 through 5) are present, then the full PSOS could be reconstructed on the restricted system, but more likely, one would construct a somewhat different system. Thus, the PSOS design represents a family of systems. One can choose the level that provides the best set of resources to fulfill the needs of the desired system without having to include unnecessary facilities. Then one can augment this level with the new type managers to create abstract objects appropriate to the desired applications. Writing such "system" type managers requires no additional skill or privilege other than that required to write ordinary user programs. The distinction between a "system" program and a "user" program is thus indeed blurred.

PSOS Relationship to Kernels

Several recent operating systems have been constructed using a "kernel" architecture. Such systems include the Kernelized Secure Operating System (KSOS) and two precursor systems developed at MITRE and UCLA. The term kernel is used loosely in the literature, but for the purpose of this discussion a kernel is that part of the operating system that is both necessary and sufficient to satisfy certain requirements of the system. For example, if the essential requirement of a system is that it enforces a certain security policy, then that part of the system that enforces the security policy constitutes the kernel. By this definition, a kernel is meaningful only with respect to some requirement or some set of requirements. The kernel must contain all those parts of the system that pertain to meeting the requirements, i.e., there is no part of the system outside the kernel that can cause the system not to meet its requirements. Also, the kernel can contain only those parts of the system that are necessary to meet the requirements, i.e., the kernel should not contain anything that does not pertain to the meeting of the requirements. The reasoning behind kernel-based architectures is that since a kernel contains only that part of the system essential to meeting requirements, it can be small, compared to the system as a whole, and therefore has a better chance of being correct. One of the main advantages of the kernel approach is the clear statement of purpose of the system. Since a kernel is meaningful only with respect to some explicit requirements, these requirements serve as the statement of purpose of the system. The other main advantage is the enhanced probability of correct operation. Since, the programs that are critical to the correct operation of the system were isolated in the kernel, a great deal of attention can be paid to getting this code right, and less attention can be paid to other system code that may be important but is not critical. The relatively small size of the kernel significantly improves the chances of applying formal verification techniques to the programs in the kernel in a cost-effective manner, where applying these techniques to the entire system would be unwieldy.

There are, as one might expect, some disadvantages to the use of kernels. Kernels cannot be casually modified because, by definition, all the code in the kernel is essential to meeting the requirements of the system, and any modification is likely to cause the system to deviate from that which is required. One must take extreme care to be sure that a change in the kernel will not compromise its correct operation.

In order to be able to construct a small kernel, the requirements limit the applications for which the kernel is useful. For, example, if the requirement of a kernel is to enforce a particular security policy, then only applications requiring that policy can be reasonably implemented using that kernel. It is not possible to implement another security policy that is inconsistent with the given security policy.

Yet another of the major problems with the kernel approach is the difficulty of designing a system in such a way that those programs essential to meeting the requirements are isolated from the nonessential programs. Finally, experience with the systems mentioned above indicates that kernels are still quite large. Clearly the size of a kernel depends upon the requirements it is supposed to meet, but reasonable requirements tend to require a large part of the system to be part of the kernel. Large kernels do not enhance one's confidence in the correct operation of the system.

Consider, for example, the kernels of KSOS and of the MITRE system. The requirement of these kernels is that they enforce a multilevel security policy. Upon close examination of these systems, it is seen that what is labeled the "kernel" is not really the kernel at all, but is only part of the kernel. These systems have so-called trusted processes, namely programs that are internally able to violate the requirements, but whose external interface is consistent with the requirements. These trusted processes include programs for file system backup and retrieval, I/O spooling, and network interfaces. These programs are not labeled as part of the kernel because their function is in some sense peripheral to the main task of the system. However, their correct operation is as essential to meeting the requirements as any kernel program. If the system is to be proven correct, the programs that are used by the trusted processes must be formally verified. Inclusion of the code for the trusted processes into the kernel makes the resulting kernel much larger. This illustrates a difficulty in designing a small kernel.

It is a matter of judgment as to whether the advantages of the kernel approach outweigh the disadvantages. For the situation in which one has clearly defined, specific-overriding requirements for which a small kernel can be constructed, then the kernel approach is ideal.

PSOS is well suited to situations in which one wants to support many applications with different or conflicting requirements. Because PSOS is highly extensible and easily supports different type managers with strong control over access to objects and type managers, it makes possible the support of many different sets of requirements on one PSOS implementation. For example, several subsystems have been designed for PSOS that enforce different security constraints. A particular task could be constrained to have access to only two of these subsystems, but several tasks may be executing different subsystems simultaneously. In a sense, each of these subsystems can be viewed as a "kernel" for the tasks having access to them, but PSOS can support any number of such subsystems. Of course, one still has the problem of assuring the correctness of these subsystems and those parts of PSOS which the subsystems use. However, assuring the correctness of these subsystems on PSOS should be significantly easier than assuring the correctness of a stand-alone kernel, because each subsystem will be much smaller and simpler than it would be if it had to be implemented as a stand-alone system. The UCLA system is an interesting case in that its requirements for security are very broad and general. The UCLA kernel attempts to be like PSOS in its ability to support a wide range of security policies simultaneously. However, the resulting requirement does not permit as wide a range of policies to be implemented, and the system design is not as uniform or elegant as the PSOS design.

Requirements of Secure Operating Systems

Most of the current operating systems provide discretionary access control, that is, someone who owns a resource can make a decision as to who is allowed to use (access) the resource. Moreover, because the lack of built-in mechanisms for the enforcement of security policies in such systems, the access control is normally a one-shot approach: either all or none privileges are granted, rarely supporting the "principle of least privilege" (without limiting the privileges a program can inherit based on the trustworthiness).

The basic philosophy of discretionary controls assumes that the users and the programs they run are the good guys, and it is up to the operating system to trust them and protect each user from outsiders and other users. Such perception could be extremely difficult to hold true and no longer be considered as secure enough for computer systems of "information era" with broad connectivity through the Internet and heavily commercialization of e-commerce services. Systems with stronger security and protection will require evolving from the approach of discretionary control towards the concept of mandatory (non-discretionary) control where information is confined within a "security perimeter" with strict rules enforced by the system about who is allowed access to certain resources, and not allow any information to move from a more secure environment to a less secure environment.

Some of basic criteria or requirements of a secure operating system are discussed below:

Mandatory security: A built-in mechanism or logic within the operating system (often called system security module or system security administrator) that implements and tightly controls the definition and assignment of security attributes and their actions (security policies) for every operation or function provided by the system. Generally, a mandatory security will require:

- A policy independent security labeling and decision making logics. The operating system implements the mechanism, whereas the users or applications are able to define security policies.

- Enforcement of access control for all operations. All system operations must have permission checks based on security labeling of the source and target objects. Such enforcement requires controlling the propagation of access rights, enforcing fine-grained access rights and supporting the revocation of previously granted access rights, etc.

- The main security controls include permission or access authorization, authentication usage, cryptographic usage, and subsystem specific usage, etc.

Trusted path: A mechanism by which a trustworthiness relationship is established among users and application software so that:

- A user or application may directly interact with trusted software, which can only be activated by either user or trusted software.

- Mutually authenticated channel is needed to prevent impersonation of either party.

- The mechanism must be extensible to support subsequent addition of trusted applications.

Support of diverse security policies: Traditional MAC mechanisms (such as the multi-level security – MLS) are usually based its security decisions strictly on security clearances for subjects and security labels for objects , and are normally too restricted to serve as a general security solution. A secure architecture requires flexibility for support of a wide variety of security policies:

- Separation of security policy logic from the mechanism of policy enforcement, so that a system can support diverse security policies.

- Support for policy definition and policy changes with well-defined policy interfaces and formats.

- Provider of default security behavior of the system so that to maintain tight system security without requiring detailed system configuration.

Assurance: A process or methodology to verify the design and implementation of the system that should actually behave as it claims to be and meet the security requirements:

- The process generally involves two elements, (i) statement of the security properties a system is claimed to satisfy; and (ii) some kind of argument or evidence that the system does satisfy those properties.

- The structure of such systems normally requires a small security kernel or module so that the system behavior would relatively easy be verified.

- One of the concerns for a secure operating system is the so-called covert channels, which are the means to circumvent the security barrier enforced by the system in prevention of passing information from one security domain to a less secure domain. For example, one possible covert channel is a "timing channel", where a Trojan horse program alternately loops and waits, in cycles of, say one minute per bit, and a program outside the perimeter that constantly tests the loading of the system may sense the information the Trojan horse intended to send. There is no general way to prevent all covert channels. It is more practical to introduce enough noise or reduce the bandwidth of such channels in the system so that they won't be useful to an intruder.

The efforts for the development of secure operating systems can be dated to the earlier days of operating system development.

With the rapid growth of Internet connectivity and e-commerce, recent development of secure operating systems spreads from traditional focus of defense or military related systems to more general commercial systems.

References

- Os-security, operating-system: tutorialspoint.com, Retrieved 31 March, 2019

- Operating-system-security-os-security, definition: techopedia.com, Retrieved 14 July, 2019

- Michael larabel (12 march 2014). "replicant developers find backdoor in android samsung galaxy devices". Phoronix. Archived from the original on 30 march 2014. Retrieved 25 april 2014

- Choosing-secure-operating-system: spamlaws.com, Retrieved 17 May, 2019

- "Sun common criteria certification". Archive.org. 13 october 2004. Archived from the original on 13 october 2004. Retrieved 9 april 2018

- Operating-system-security-secure-operating-systems: giac.org, Retrieved 19 April, 2019

Deadlock

Deadlock is referred to as a condition where a computer process waits for a resource which is being used by another process. Deadlock handling has three main methods which are deadlock detection, deadlock prevention and deadlock avoidance. This chapter closely examines the varied aspects of deadlock to provide an extensive understanding of the subject.

Every process needs some resources to complete its execution. However, the resource is granted in a sequential order.

- The process requests for some resource.

- OS grant the resource if it is available otherwise let the process waits.

- The process uses it and release on the completion.

A Deadlock is a situation where each of the computer process waits for a resource which is being assigned to some another process. In this situation, none of the process gets executed since the resource it needs, is held by some other process which is also waiting for some other resource to be released.

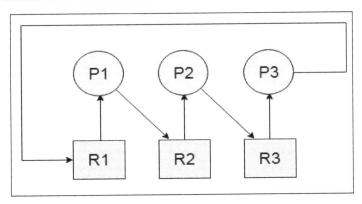

Let us assume that there are three processes P1, P2 and P3. There are three different resources R1, R2 and R3. R1 is assigned to P1, R2 is assigned to P2 and R3 is assigned to P3.

After some time, P1 demands for R1 which is being used by P2. P1 halts its execution since it can't complete without R2. P2 also demands for R3 which is being used by P3. P2 also stops its execution because it can't continue without R3. P3 also demands for R1 which is being used by P1, therefore, P3 also stops its execution.

In this scenario, a cycle is being formed among the three processes. None of the process is progressing and they are all waiting. The computer becomes unresponsive since all the processes got blocked.

Difference between Starvation and Deadlock

Sr.	Deadlock	Starvation
1	Deadlock is a situation where no process got blocked and no process proceeds.	Starvation is a situation where the low priority process got blocked and the high priority processes proceed.
2	Deadlock is an infinite waiting.	Starvation is a long waiting but not infinite.
3	Every Deadlock is always a starvation.	Every starvation need not be deadlock.
4	The requested resource is blocked by the other process.	The requested resource is continuously be used by the higher priority processes.
5	Deadlock happens when Mutual exclusion, hold and wait, No preemption and circular wait occurs simultaneously.	It occurs due to the uncontrolled priority and resource management.

Conditions for Deadlock

There are following four necessary conditions for the occurrence of deadlock:

- Mutual Exclusion,
- Hold and Wait,
- No pre-emption,
- Circular wait.

Mutual Exclusion

By this condition,

- There must exist at least one resource in the system which can be used by only one process at a time.
- If there exists no such resource, then deadlock will never occur.
- Printer is an example of a resource that can be used by only one process at a time.

Hold and Wait

By this condition:

- There must exist a process which holds some resource and waits for another resource held by some other process.

No Preemption

By this condition:

- Once the resource has been allocated to the process, it cannot be preempted.

- It means resource cannot be snatched forcefully from one process and given to the other process.

- The process must release the resource voluntarily by itself.

Circular Wait

By this condition:

- All the processes must wait for the resource in a cyclic manner where the last process waits for the resource held by the first process.

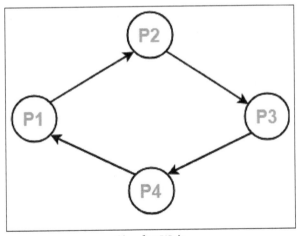

Circular Wait.

Here:

- Process P1 waits for a resource held by process P2.

- Process P2 waits for a resource held by process P3.

- Process P3 waits for a resource held by process P4.

- Process P4 waits for a resource held by process P1.

Deadlock Handling

Deadlock Ignorance

Deadlock Ignorance is the most widely used approach among all the mechanism. This is being used by many operating systems mainly for end user uses. In this approach, the Operating system assumes that deadlock never occurs. It simply ignores deadlock. This approach is best suitable for a single end user system where User uses the system only for browsing and all other normal stuff.

There is always a tradeoff between Correctness and performance. The operating systems like Windows and Linux mainly focus upon performance. However, the performance of the system decreases if it uses deadlock handling mechanism all the time if deadlock happens 1 out of 100 times then it is completely unnecessary to use the deadlock handling mechanism all the time.

In these types of systems, the user has to simply restart the computer in the case of deadlock. Windows and Linux are mainly using this approach.

Deadlock Prevention

If we simulate deadlock with a table which is standing on its four legs then we can also simulate four legs with the four conditions which when occurs simultaneously, cause the deadlock.

However, if we break one of the legs of the table then the table will fall definitely. The same happens with deadlock, if we can be able to violate one of the four necessary conditions and don't let them occur together then we can prevent the deadlock. Let's see how we can prevent each of the conditions.

Mutual Exclusion

Mutual section from the resource point of view is the fact that a resource can never be used by more than one process simultaneously which is fair enough but that is the main reason behind the deadlock. If a resource could have been used by more than one process at the same time then the process would have never been waiting for any resource.

However, if we can be able to violate resources behaving in the mutually exclusive manner then the deadlock can be prevented.

Spooling

For a device like printer, spooling can work. There is a memory associated with the printer which stores jobs from each of the process into it. Later, Printer collects all the jobs and print each one of them according to FCFS. By using this mechanism, the process doesn't have to wait for the printer and it can continue whatever it was doing. Later, it collects the output when it is produced.

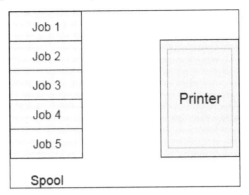

Although, Spooling can be an effective approach to violate mutual exclusion but it suffers from two kinds of problems:

- This cannot be applied to every resource.

- After some point of time, there may arise a race condition between the processes to get space in that spool.

We cannot force a resource to be used by more than one process at the same time since it will not be fair enough and some serious problems may arise in the performance. Therefore, we cannot violate mutual exclusion for a process practically.

Hold and Wait

Hold and wait condition lies when a process holds a resource and waiting for some other resource to complete its task. Deadlock occurs because there can be more than one process which are holding one resource and waiting for other in the cyclic order.

However, we have to find out some mechanism by which a process either doesn't hold any resource or doesn't wait. That means, a process must be assigned all the necessary resources before the execution starts. A process must not wait for any resource once the execution has been started.

(Hold and wait) = !hold or !wait (negation of hold and wait is, either you don't hold or you don't wait)

This can be implemented practically if a process declares all the resources initially. However, this sounds very practical but can't be done in the computer system because a process can't determine necessary resources initially.

Process is the set of instructions which are executed by the CPU. Each of the instruction may demand multiple resources at the multiple times. The need cannot be fixed by the OS.

The problem with the approach is:

- Practically not possible.

- Possibility of getting starved will be increases due to the fact that some process may hold a resource for a very long time.

No Preemption

Deadlock arises due to the fact that a process can't be stopped once it starts. However, if we take the resource away from the process which is causing deadlock then we can prevent deadlock.

This is not a good approach at all since if we take a resource away which is being used by the process then all the work which it has done till now can become inconsistent.

Consider a printer is being used by any process. If we take the printer away from that process and assign it to some other process then all the data which has been printed can become inconsistent and ineffective and also the fact that the process can't start printing again from where it has left which causes performance inefficiency.

Circular Wait

To violate circular wait, we can assign a priority number to each of the resource. A process can't request for a lesser priority resource. This ensures that not a single process can request a resource which is being utilized by some other process and no cycle will be formed.

Condition	Approach	Is Practically Possible?
Mutual Exclusion	Spooling	No
Hold and Wait	Request for all the resources initially	No
No preemtion	Snatch all the resources	No
Circular Wait	Assign Priority to each resources and order resources numerically	Yes

Among all the methods, violating Circular wait is the only approach that can be implemented practically.

Deadlock Prevention Algorithms

Deadlock prevention algorithms are used in concurrent programming when multiple processes must acquire more than one shared resource. If two or more concurrent processes obtain multiple resources indiscriminately, a situation can occur where each process has a resource needed by another process. As a result, none of the processes can obtain all the resources it needs, so all processes are blocked from further execution. This situation is called a deadlock. A deadlock prevention algorithm organizes resource usage by each process to ensure that at least one process is always able to get all the resources it needs.

Distributed Deadlock

Distributed deadlocks can occur in distributed systems when distributed transactions or concurrency control is being used. Distributed deadlocks can be detected either by constructing a global wait-for graph, from local wait-for graphs at a deadlock detector or by a distributed algorithm like edge chasing.

Phantom deadlocks are deadlocks that are detected in a distributed system due to system internal delays but no longer actually exist at the time of detection.

There are many different ways to increase parallelism where recursive locks would otherwise cause deadlocks. But there is a price. And that price is either performance/overhead, allow data corruption, or both.

Some of examples include: lock hierarchies, lock reference-counting and preemption (either using versioning or allowing data corruption when preemption occurs); Wait-For-Graph (WFG) algorithms, which track all cycles that cause deadlocks (including temporary deadlocks); and heuristics algorithms which don't necessarily increase parallelism in 100% of the places that deadlocks are possible, but instead compromise by solving them in enough places that performance/overhead vs parallelism is acceptable.

Consider a "when two trains approach each other at a crossing" situation. Just-in-time prevention works like having a person standing at the crossing (the crossing guard) with a switch that will let only one train onto "super tracks" which runs above and over the other waiting train(s).

- For non-recursive locks, a lock may be entered only once (where a single thread entering twice without unlocking will cause a deadlock, or throw an exception to enforce circular wait prevention).

- For recursive locks, only one thread is allowed to pass through a lock. If any other threads enter the lock, they must wait until the initial thread that passed through completes n number of times it has entered.

So the issue with the first one is that it does no deadlock prevention at all. The second does not do distributed deadlock prevention. But the second one is redefined to prevent a deadlock scenario the first one does not address.

Recursively, only one thread is allowed to pass through a lock. If other threads enter the lock, they must wait until the initial thread that passed through completes n number of times. But if the number of threads that enter locking equal the number that are locked, assign one thread as the super-thread, and only allow it to run (tracking the number of times it enters/exits locking) until it completes.

After a super-thread is finished, the condition changes back to using the logic from the recursive lock, and the exiting super-thread.

- Sets itself as not being a super-thread.

- Notifies the locker that other locked, waiting threads need to re-check this condition.

If a deadlock scenario exists, set a new super-thread and follow that logic. Otherwise, resume regular locking.

Issues not Addressed Above

A lot of confusion revolves around the halting problem. But this logic does not solve the halting problem because the conditions in which locking occurs are known, giving a specific solution (instead of the otherwise required general solution that the halting problem requires). Still, this locker prevents all deadlocked only considering locks using this logic. But if it is used with other locking mechanisms, a lock that is started never unlocks (exception thrown jumping out without unlocking, looping indefinitely within a lock, or coding error forgetting to call unlock), deadlocking is very possible. To increase the condition to include these would require solving the halting issue, since one would be dealing with conditions that one knows nothing about and is unable to change.

Another issue is it does not address the temporary deadlocking issue (not really a deadlock, but a performance killer), where two or more threads lock on each other while another unrelated thread is running. These temporary deadlocks could have a thread running exclusively within them, increasing parallelism. But because of how the distributed deadlock detection works for all locks, and not subsets therein, the unrelated running thread must complete before performing the super-thread logic to remove the temporary deadlock.

One can see the temporary live-lock scenario in the above. If another unrelated running thread begins before the first unrelated thread exits, duration of temporary deadlocking will occur. If this happens continuously (extremely rare), the temporary deadlock can be extended until right before the program exits, when the other unrelated threads are guaranteed to finish (because of the guarantee that one thread will always run to completion).

Further Expansion

This can be further expanded to involve additional logic to increase parallelism where temporary deadlocks might otherwise occur. But for each step of adding more logic, we add more overhead.

A couple of examples include: expanding distributed super-thread locking mechanism to consider each subset of existing locks; Wait-For-Graph (WFG) algorithms, which track all cycles that cause deadlocks (including temporary deadlocks); and heuristics algorithms which don't necessarily increase parallelism in 100% of the places that temporary deadlocks are possible, but instead compromise by solving them in enough places that performance/overhead vs parallelism is acceptable (e.g. for each processor available, work towards finding deadlock cycles less than the number of processors + 1 deep).

Deadlock Avoidance

In deadlock avoidance, the request for any resource will be granted if the resulting state of the system doesn't cause deadlock in the system. The state of the system will continuously be checked for safe and unsafe states.

In order to avoid deadlocks, the process must tell OS, the maximum number of resources a process can request to complete its execution.

The simplest and most useful approach states that the process should declare the maximum number of resources of each type it may ever need. The Deadlock avoidance algorithm examines the resource allocations so that there can never be a circular wait condition.

Safe and Unsafe States

The resource allocation state of a system can be defined by the instances of available and allocated resources, and the maximum instance of the resources demanded by the processes.

A state of a system recorded at some random time is shown below:

Resources Assigned

Process	Type 1	Type 2	Type 3	Type 4
A	3	0	2	2
B	0	0	1	1
C	1	1	1	0
D	2	1	4	0

Above tables and vector E, P and A describes the resource allocation state of a system. There are 4 processes and 4 types of the resources in a system. Table shows the instances of each resource assigned to each process.

Resources Still Needed

Process	Type 1	Type 2	Type 3	Type 4
A	1	1	0	0
B	0	1	1	2
C	1	2	1	0
D	2	1	1	2

$E = (7\ 6\ 8\ 4)$

$P = (6\ 2\ 8\ 3)$

$A = (1\ 4\ 0\ 1)$

Table shows the instances of the resources, each process still needs. Vector E is the representation of total instances of each resource in the system. Vector P represents the instances of resources that have been assigned to processes. Vector A represents the number of resources that are not in use.

A state of the system is called safe if the system can allocate all the resources requested by all the processes without entering into deadlock. If the system cannot fulfill the request of all processes then the state of the system is called unsafe.

The key of Deadlock avoidance approach is when the request is made for resources then the request must only be approved in the case if the resulting state is also a safe state.

Banker's Algorithm

Banker's algorithm is a deadlock avoidance algorithm. It is named so because this algorithm is used in banking systems to determine whether a loan can be granted or not.

Consider there are n account holders in a bank and the sum of the money in all of their accounts is S. Everytime a loan has to be granted by the bank, it subtracts the loan amount from the total money the bank has. Then it checks if that difference is greater than S. It is done because, only then, the bank would have enough money even if all the n account holders draw all their money at once.

Banker's algorithm works in a similar way in computers.

Whenever a new process is created, it must specify the maximum instances of each resource type that it needs, exactly.

Let us assume that there are n processes and m resource types. Some data structures that are used to implement the banker's algorithm are:

1. `Available`: It is an array of length m. It represents the number of available resources of each type. If `Available[j]` = k, then there are k instances available, of resource type `R(j)`.

2. `Max`: It is an n x m matrix which represents the maximum number of instances of each resource that a process can request. If `Max[i][j]` = k, then the process `P(i)` can request atmost k instances of resource type `R(j)`.

3. `Allocation`: It is an n x m matrix which represents the number of resources of each type currently allocated to each process. If Allocation`[i][j]` = k, then process `P(i)` is currently allocated k instances of resource type `R(j)`.

4. `Need`: It is an n x m matrix which indicates the remaining resource needs of each process. If `Need[i][j]` = k, then process `P(i)` may need k more instances of resource type `R(j)` to complete its task.

   `Need[i][j] = Max[i][j] - Allocation [i][j]`

Resource Request Algorithm

This describes the behavior of the system when a process makes a resource request in the form of a request matrix. The steps are:

1. If number of requested instances of each resource is less than the need (which was declared previously by the process), go to step 2.

2. If number of requested instances of each resource type is less than the available resources of each type, go to step 3. If not, the process has to wait because sufficient resources are not available yet.

3. Now, assume that the resources have been allocated. Accordingly do,

   ```
   Available = Available - Requesti

   Allocation(i) = Allocation(i) + Request(i)

   Need(i) = Need(i) - Request(i)
   ```

This step is done because the system needs to assume that resources have been allocated. So, there will be less resources available after allocation. The number of allocated instances will increase. The need of the resources by the process will reduce. That's what is represented by the above three operations.

After completing the above three steps, check if the system is in safe state by applying the safety algorithm. If it is in safe state, proceed to allocate the requested resources. Else, the process has to wait longer.

Safety Algorithm

1. Let Work and Finish be vectors of length m and n, respectively. Initially,

   ```
   Work = Available
   ```

```
Finish[i] =false for i = 0, 1, ... , n - 1.
```

This means, initially, no process has finished and the number of available resources is represented by the Available array.

2. Find an index i such that both

    ```
    Finish[i] ==false
    ```

    ```
    Needi <= Work
    ```

    If there is no such i present, then proceed to step 4.

    It means, we need to find an unfinished process whose need can be satisfied by the available resources. If no such process exists, just go to step 4.

3. Perform the following:

    ```
    Work = Work + Allocation;
    ```

    ```
    Finish[i] = true;
    ```

    Go to step 2.

    When an unfinished process is found, then the resources are allocated and the process is marked finished. And then, the loop is repeated to check the same for all other processes.

4. If `Finish[i] == true` for all `i`, then the system is in a safe state.

    That means if all processes are finished, then the system is in safe state.

Deadlock Detection

Deadlock detection is the process of actually determining that a deadlock exists and identifying the processes and resources involved in the deadlock.

The basic idea is to check allocation against resource availability for all possible allocation sequences to determine if the system is in deadlocked state a. Of course, the deadlock detection algorithm is only half of this strategy. Once a deadlock is detected, there needs to be a way to recover several alternatives exists:

1. Temporarily prevent resources from deadlocked processes.

2. Back off a process to some check point allowing preemption of a needed resource and restarting the process at the checkpoint later.

3. Successively kill processes until the system is deadlock free.

These methods are expensive in the sense that each iteration calls the detection algorithm until the system proves to be deadlock free. The complexity of algorithm is $O(N^2)$ where N is the number of proceeds. Another potential problem is starvation; same process killed repeatedly.

Deadlock Detection with One Resource of Each Type

Let us begin with the simplest case: only one resource of each type exists. Such a system might have one scanner, one CD recorder, one plotter, and one tape drive, but no more than one of each class of resource. In other words, we are excluding systems with two printers for the moment.

For such a system, we can construct a resource graph of the sort illustrated in figure. If this graph contains one or more cycles, a deadlock exists. Any process that is part of a cycle is deadlocked. If no cycles exist, the system is not deadlocked.

As an example of a more complex system than the ones we have looked at so far, consider a system with seven processes, A though G, and six resources, R through W. The state of which resources are currently owned and which ones are currently being requested is as follows:

1. Process A holds R and wants S.

2. Process B holds nothing but wants T.

3. Process C holds nothing but wants S.

4. Process D holds U and wants S and T.

5. Process E holds T and wants V.

6. Process F holds W and wants S.

7. Process G holds V and wants U.

"Is this system deadlocked, and if so, which processes are involved?"

To answer this question, we can construct the resource graph. This graph contains one cycle, which can be seen by visual inspection. The cycle is shown in figure below. From this cycle, we can see that processes D, E, and G are all deadlocked. Processes A, C, and F are not deadlocked because S can be allocated to any one of them, which then finishes and returns it. Then the other two can take it in turn and also complete.

Although, it is relatively simple to pick out the deadlocked processes by eye from a simple graph, for use in actual systems we need a formal algorithm for detecting deadlocks. Many algorithms for detecting cycles in directed graphs are known. Below we will give a simple one that inspects a graph and terminates either when it has found a cycle or when it has shown that none exist. It uses one data structure, L, a list of nodes. During the algorithm, arcs will be marked to indicate that they have already been inspected, to prevent repeated inspections.

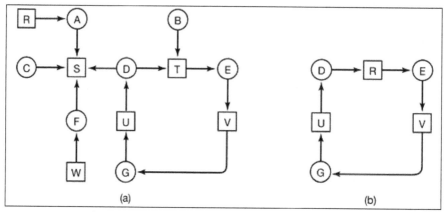

(a) A resource graph. (b) A cycle extracted from (a).

The algorithm operates by carrying out the following steps as specified:

1. For each node, N in the graph, perform the following 5 steps with N as the starting node.

2. Initialize L to the empty list, and designate all the arcs as unmarked.

3. Add the current node to the end of L and check to see if the node now appears in L two times. If it does, the graph contains a cycle (listed in L) and the algorithm terminates.

4. From the given node, see if there are any unmarked outgoing arcs. If so, go to step 5; if not, go to step 6.

5. Pick an unmarked outgoing arc at random and mark it. Then follow it to the new current node and go to step 3.

6. We have now reached a dead end. Remove it and go back to the previous node, that is, the one that was current just before this one, make that one the current node, and go to step 3. If this node is the initial node, the graph does not contain any cycles and the algorithm terminates.

What this algorithm does is take each node, in turn, as the root of what it hopes will be a tree, and does a depth-first search on it. If it ever comes back to a node it has already encountered, then it has found a cycle. If it exhausts all the arcs from any given node, it backtracks to the previous node. If it backtracks to the root and cannot go further, the sub graph reachable from the current node does not contain any cycles. If this property holds for all nodes, the entire graph is cycle free, so the system is not deadlocked.

To see how the algorithm works in practice, let us use it on the graph of figure. The order of processing the nodes is arbitrary, so let us just inspect them from left to right, top to bottom, first running the algorithm starting at R then successively, A, B, C, S, D, T, E, F, and so forth. If we hit a cycle, the algorithm stops.

We start at R and initialize L to the empty list. Then we add R to the list and move to the only possibility, A, and add it to L, giving L = [R, A]. From A we go to S, giving L = [R, A, S]. S has no outgoing arcs, so it is a dead end, forcing us to backtrack to A. Since A has no unmarked outgoing arcs, we backtrack to R, completing our inspection of R.

Now we restart the algorithm starting at A, resetting L to the empty list. This search, too, quickly stops, so we start again at B. From B we continue to follow outgoing arcs until we get to D, at which time L = [B, T, E, V, G, U, D]. Now we must make a (random) choice. If we pick S we come to a dead end and backtrack to D. The second time we pick T and update L to be [B, T, E, V, G, U, D, T], at which point we discover the cycle and stop the algorithm.

This algorithm is far from optimal.

Deadlock Detection With Multiple Resources of Each Type

When multiple copies of some of the resources exist, a different approach is needed to detect deadlocks. We will now present a matrix-based algorithm for detecting deadlock among n processes. P_1 through P_n. Let the number of resource classes be m, with E_1 resources of class 1, E_2 resources of class 2, and generally, E_i resources of class i ($1 < i < m$). E is the existing resource vector. It gives the total number of instances of each resource in existence. For example, if class 1 is tape drives, then $E_1 = 2$ means the system has two tape drives.

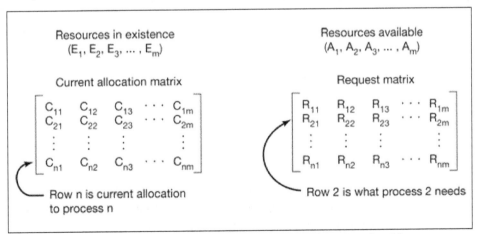

The four data structures needed by the deadlock detection algorithm.

At any instant, some of the resources are assigned and are not available. Let A be the available resource vector, with A_i giving the number of instances of resource i that are currently available (i.e., unassigned). If both of our two tape drives are assigned, A_1 will be 0.

Now we need two arrays, C, the current allocation matrix, and R, the request matrix. The i-th row of C tells how many instances of each resource class P_i currently holds. Thus C_{ij} is the number of instances of resource j that are held by process i. Similarly, R_{ij} is the number of instances of resource j that P_i wants. These four data structures are shown in figure.

An important invariant holds for these four data structures. In particular, every resource is either allocated or is available. This observation means that,

$$\sum_{i=1}^{n} C_{ij} + A_j = E_j$$

In other words, if we add up all the instances of the resource j that have been allocated and to this add all the instances that are available, the result is the number of instances of that resource class that exist.

The deadlock detection algorithm is based on comparing vectors. Let us define the relation A ≤ B on two vectors A and B to mean that each element of A is less than or equal to the corresponding element of B. Mathematically, A ≤ B holds if and only if $A_i \le B_i$ for $1 < i < m$.

Each process is initially said to be unmarked. As the algorithm progresses, processes will be marked, indicating that they are able to complete and are thus not deadlocked. When the algorithm terminates, any unmarked processes are known to be deadlocked.

The deadlock detection algorithm can now be given, as follows:

1. Look for an unmarked process, P_i, for which the i-th row of R is less than or equal to A.

2. If such a process is found, add the i-th row of C to A, mark the process, and go back to step 1.

3. If no such process exists, the algorithm terminates.

When the algorithm finishes, all the unmarked processes, if any, are deadlocked.

What the algorithm is doing in step 1 is looking for a process that can be run to completion. Such a process is characterized as having resource demands that can be met by the currently available resources. The selected process is then run until it finishes, at which time it returns the resources it is holding to the pool of available resources. It is then marked as completed. If all the processes are ultimately able to run, none of them are deadlocked. If some of them can never run, they are deadlocked. Although the algorithm is nondeterministic (because it may run the processes in any feasible order), the result is always the same.

As an example of how the deadlock detection algorithm works, consider figure. Here we have three processes and four resource classes, which we have arbitrarily labeled tape drives, plotters, scanner, and CD-ROM drive. Process 1 has one scanner. Process 2 has two tape drives and a CD-ROM drive. Process 3 has a plotter and two scanners. Each process needs additional resources, as shown by the R matrix.

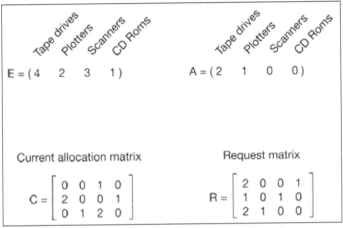

An example for the deadlock detection algorithm.

To run the deadlock detection algorithm, we look for a process whose resource request can be satisfied. The first one cannot be satisfied because there is no CD-ROM drive available. The second cannot be satisfied either, because there is no scanner free. Fortunately, the third one can be satisfied, so process 3 runs and eventually returns all its resources, giving

$$A = (2\ 2\ 2\ 0)$$

At this point process 2 can run and return its resources, giving

$$A = (4\ 2\ 2\ 1)$$

Now the remaining process can run. There is no deadlock in the system.

Now consider a minor variation of the situation of figure. Suppose that process 2 needs a CD-ROM drive as well as the two tape drives and the plotter. None of the requests can be satisfied, so the entire system is deadlocked.

Now that we know how to detect deadlocks, the question of when to look for them comes up. One possibility is to check every time a resource request is made. This is certain to detect them as early as possible, but it is potentially expensive in terms of CPU time. An alternative strategy is to check every k minutes or perhaps only when the CPU utilization has dropped below some threshold. The reason for considering the

CPU utilization is that if enough processes are deadlocked, there will be few runnable processes, and the CPU will often be idle.

Deadlock Detection in Distributed Systems

In the centralized approach of deadlock detection, two techniques are used namely: Completely centralized algorithm and Ho Ramamurthy algorithm (One phase and Two-phase).

- Completely Centralized Algorithm: In a network of n sites, one site is chosen as a control site. This site is responsible for deadlock detection. It has control over all resources of the system. If a site requires a resource it requests the control site, the control site allocates and de-allocates resources and maintains a wait for graph. And at regular interval of time, it checks the wait for graph to detect a cycle. If cycle exits then it will declare system as deadlock otherwise the system will continue working. The major drawbacks of this technique are as follows:

    ° A site has to send request even for using its own resource.

    ° There is a possibility of phantom deadlock.

- HO Ramamurthy (Two-Phase Algorithm): In this technique a resource status table is maintained by the central or control site, if a cycle is detected then the system is not declared deadlock at first, the cycle is checked again as the system is distributed some or the other resource is vacant or freed by sites at every instant of time. Now, after checking if a cycle is detected again then, the system is declared as deadlock. This technique reduces the possibility of phantom deadlock but on the other hand time consumption is more.

- HO Ramamurthy (One Phase Algorithm): In this technique a resource status table and a process table is maintained by the central or control site if the cycle is detected in both processes and resource tables then, the system is declared as deadlock. This technique reduces time consumption but space complexity increases.

Recovery from Deadlock

Suppose that our deadlock detection algorithm has succeeded and detected a deadlock. What next? Some way is needed to recover and get the system going again.

Recovery Through Preemption

In some cases it may be possible to temporarily take a resource away from its current owner and give it to another process. In many cases, manual intervention may be required, especially in batch processing operating systems running on mainframes.

For example, to take a laser printer away from its owner, the operator can collect all the sheets already printed and put them in a pile. Then the process can be suspended (marked as not runnable). At this point the printer can be assigned to another process. When that process finishes, the pile of printed sheets can be put back in the printer's output tray and the original process restarted.

The ability to take a resource away from a process, have another process use it, and then give it back without the process noticing it is highly dependent on the nature of the resource. Recovering this way is frequently difficult or impossible. Choosing the process to suspend depends largely on which ones have resources that can easily be taken back.

Recovery Through Rollback

If the system designers and machine operators know that deadlocks are likely, they can arrange to have processes checkpointed periodically. Checkpointing a process means that its state is written to a file so that it can be restarted later. The checkpoint contains not only the memory image, but also the resource state, that is, which resources are currently assigned to the process. To be most effective, new checkpoints should not overwrite old ones but should be written to new files, so as the process executes, a whole sequence of checkpoint files are accumulated.

When a deadlock is detected, it is easy to see which resources are needed. To do the recovery, a process that owns a needed resource is rolled back to a point in time before it acquired some other resource by starting one of its earlier checkpoints. All the work done since the checkpoint is lost (e.g., output printed since the checkpoint must be discarded, since it will be printed again). In effect, the process is reset to an earlier moment when it did not have the resource, which is now assigned to one of the deadlocked processes. If the restarted process tries to acquire the resource again, it will have to wait until it becomes available.

Recovery Through Killing Processes

The crudest, but simplest way to break a deadlock is to kill one or more processes. One possibility is to kill a process in the cycle. With a little luck, the other processes will be able to continue. If this does not help, it can be repeated until the cycle is broken.

Alternatively, a process not in the cycle can be chosen as the victim in order to release its resources. In this approach, the process to be killed is carefully chosen because it is holding resources that some process in the cycle needs. For example, one process might hold a printer and want a plotter, with another process holding a plotter and wanting a printer. These two are deadlocked. A third process may hold another identical printer and another identical plotter and be happily running. Killing the third process will release these resources and break the deadlock involving the first two.

Where possible, it is best to kill a process that can be rerun from the beginning with no ill effects. For example, a compilation can always be rerun because all it does is read a source file and produce an object file. If it is killed part way through, the first run has no influence on the second run.

On the other hand, a process that updates a database cannot always be run a second time safely. If the process adds 1 to some record in the database, running it once, killing it, and then running it again will add 2 to the record, which is incorrect.

References

- Os-deadlocks-introduction: javatpoint.com, Retrieved 26 July, 2019

- Deadlock-in-os-conditions-for-deadlock: gatevidyalay.com, Retrieved 8 January, 2019

- Os-strategies-for-handling-deadlock: javatpoint.com, Retrieved 13 May, 2019

- Bankers-algorithm, operating-system: studytonight.com, Retrieved 25 February, 2019

- Recovery-from-deadlock, tanenbaum, mirrors: odiemus.cz, Retrieved 16 January, 2019

- Deadlock-detection-in-distributed-systems-2: geeksforgeeks.org, Retrieved 29 March, 2019

Permissions

All chapters in this book are published with permission under the Creative Commons Attribution Share Alike License or equivalent. Every chapter published in this book has been scrutinized by our experts. Their significance has been extensively debated. The topics covered herein carry significant information for a comprehensive understanding. They may even be implemented as practical applications or may be referred to as a beginning point for further studies.

We would like to thank the editorial team for lending their expertise to make the book truly unique. They have played a crucial role in the development of this book. Without their invaluable contributions this book wouldn't have been possible. They have made vital efforts to compile up to date information on the varied aspects of this subject to make this book a valuable addition to the collection of many professionals and students.

This book was conceptualized with the vision of imparting up-to-date and integrated information in this field. To ensure the same, a matchless editorial board was set up. Every individual on the board went through rigorous rounds of assessment to prove their worth. After which they invested a large part of their time researching and compiling the most relevant data for our readers.

The editorial board has been involved in producing this book since its inception. They have spent rigorous hours researching and exploring the diverse topics which have resulted in the successful publishing of this book. They have passed on their knowledge of decades through this book. To expedite this challenging task, the publisher supported the team at every step. A small team of assistant editors was also appointed to further simplify the editing procedure and attain best results for the readers.

Apart from the editorial board, the designing team has also invested a significant amount of their time in understanding the subject and creating the most relevant covers. They scrutinized every image to scout for the most suitable representation of the subject and create an appropriate cover for the book.

The publishing team has been an ardent support to the editorial, designing and production team. Their endless efforts to recruit the best for this project, has resulted in the accomplishment of this book. They are a veteran in the field of academics and their pool of knowledge is as vast as their experience in printing. Their expertise and guidance has proved useful at every step. Their uncompromising quality standards have made this book an exceptional effort. Their encouragement from time to time has been an inspiration for everyone.

The publisher and the editorial board hope that this book will prove to be a valuable piece of knowledge for students, practitioners and scholars across the globe.

Index

CPSIA information can be obtained
at www.ICGtesting.com
Printed in the USA
LVHW061520100222
710781LV00007B/371